Sharon,

Find your own rainbow...
it is just beyond the
storm!

My best,
Bob

10-30-16

Beyond The Rainbow Promise

Shattered Dreams. Shifting Realities.
Broken Hearts. An inspiring journey
through the storms of life.

ROBERT M. OTTMAN

WESTBOW
PRESS
A DIVISION OF THOMAS NELSON
& ZONDERVAN

WestBow Press books may be ordered through booksellers or by contacting:

WestBow Press
A Division of Thomas Nelson & Zondervan
1663 Liberty Drive
Bloomington, IN 47403
www.westbowpress.com
1 (866) 928-1240

ISBN: 978-1-5127-5678-4 (sc)
ISBN: 978-1-5127-5679-1 (hc)
ISBN: 978-1-5127-5677-7 (e)

Library of Congress Control Number: 2016915142

Print information available on the last page.

WestBow Press rev. date: 10/3/2016

INTRODUCTION

Contemplation ....

Choices

Waiting, lurking
Seeking just the right moment to strike
With no warning, it pounces
Wreaking havoc
Changing my understanding of life
Creating turmoil
Forcing an exploration of self
Reshaping the "me"
Adversity comes on like a tsunami
Questioning my strength
Giving me options I did not ask for
Finding ways to overcome
Or quietly retreat
My choice
Hovering just beyond reach
Lurking in my soul
Adversity waits for my answer

By: Robert Mapes

The Story ....

Into every life comes adversity and strife. At times, these trials can seem to run a course of their own, plowing right through the simple life we lead like a summer's storm, leaving havoc and chaos in their wake. Who do you turn to when you find yourself in this kind of place? What happens to your soul when adversity shows up and swallows your life whole?

This is a story about a horrific kind of adversity and strife, the very kind that threatens life as we know it, and the very kind that can change the meaning of life itself!

It is the story of a remarkable woman and her fight against metastatic cancer. It is the story of a man who loses his footing along the way, and their incredible journey together to beat back a formidable foe. It is the story of a giving God who loves us in spite of ourselves. It is a story that defines who we become.

This is my story. It is the story of my wife Natalie, and her fight against metastatic breast cancer. It is all that I learned as we journeyed and battled together against an unseen foe, an evil monster. It is a story about a move to a new land amidst the storm, a new job, the mighty hammer of fate, and a child that finds himself at risk. It is a story about the challenging times of my life, what I learned along the way about God and myself.

Hopefully, my story will speak to your heart, and will help you understand your own world, your life and the role God can play in it. Perhaps my story will help you find your way through adversity, should the mighty hammer of fate deliver a visceral blow to your world, creating a storm you think you'll never survive.

Since I think it is important that we protect the privacy of people and institutions, I've fictionalized my story by changing the names of characters and institutions to respect those rights and privileges. I also changed the locations throughout my story to bring an additional level of protection. In addition, I consolidated some events and shortened timelines in order to ensure the book maintained an enjoyable reading pace.

Yes, I made my way through the storms of adversity. It was not easy. It was painful, and yet, it is an incredible journey. I am here to tell you that you too can live through the storm that has become your life, whatever storm you are facing, and come out the other side, and then be courageous enough, to one day, tell your story!

Inspiration..

Be strong and courageous. Do not be afraid or terrified because of them, for the Lord your God goes with you; he will never leave nor forsake you.

Deuteronomy 31:6

Reflection ....

It is in my adversity that I get a personal glimpse, deep into my soul, and for the first time, a chance to see who I really am and what I am made of.

CONTENTS

"Tears shed for yesterdays lost, hinder our chance for today's hope and tomorrow's joy."

BOOK 1

Adversity

The Storm

The storm looms large
On the horizon
Appearing to be bigger than life
Is it even something
That I can endure
That I want to endure
Can I find my way through
Could I become so consumed?
That I miss the chance
To become a better me
To face life's storm head on
To survive and learn
With my spirit intact
It seems an impossible task
So all alone I feel
As the storm looms large
On the horizon

By: Robert Mapes

The Story ....

Cold and gray. The late December, New Hampshire gloom presses down on my world. The rhythmic beating of my heart pounds in my head, reminding me that the world as I know it... is at risk. The low hanging clouds do little to warm the day or my soul. The damp, New Hampshire cold, cuts to the bone and does not lift my troubled spirits. As I enter the garage to warm up the car, the cold grabs hold of me, and I feel an unexpected shiver rack my body. It creates a horrible trembling I can't explain. I work to control my shaking body, and with every breath I take, try to keep my emotions in check. I need to be the strong one. I prompt myself to 'stay strong'!

While others excitedly prepare for the New Year, I am in a panic mode this December 31st. I feel my life is slipping out of my control. It is hard to imagine that friends are considering parties and New Year's resolutions while Natalie and I are considering recovery and results. I remind myself that it is just going to be a simple biopsy. There is nothing to be concerned about said the doctors.

How I wish I believed it, but as a pretty good read of people, I could tell from the look on the doctor's face at the last meeting, that this is not just a simple biopsy. There is something worrisome going on, and it troubles me. Maybe I am reading too much into this. I have this nagging feeling in the pit of my stomach that something is not quite right with the world.

As the car warms up, I take a moment to pray to the Lord and ask Him to strengthen me and prepare me, prepare us, for whatever might lay ahead. I take a deep breath; hold it in, as it is time to gather up Natalie and head to the hospital. It is time to find answers to the questions hovering in our world, and confront the uncertainties staring us straight on. Happy New Year, so I hope anyway.

Natalie and I sit quietly in the outpatient surgery waiting room, afraid to say too much to each other for fear of losing control and becoming a weeping mess. I wonder if others gathered in this same place are as scared as we are - if they too are afraid of the monsters that might be lurking, ready to throw life into a cascading world of chaos.

The minutes tick away slowly, and after what seems to be an eternity, a nurse calls Natalie's name. We look at each other, fighting to hold back the tears, and darn if Natalie doesn't smile that comforting smile of hers. I realize that this is going to be a defining moment for us, and for our future. The next few hours will forecast what will become of the simple and wonderful life we were living. We hug tightly, grounding each other in love, before Natalie is led away by the nurse, to a world of uncertainty.

The doctor explained the biopsy as being a simple procedure, and would take about 45 minutes. Dr. Wilson, the surgeon, would make a small incision in the area of the mass, now the size of a small lemon, under Natalie's left arm, and remove a tissue sample. This sample would get sent to pathology for immediate assessment. At 36, the hope is that this rapidly growing mass, once the size of a small pea will be benign and that it will be the cat scratch fever some doctors thought it might be. That is my hope and prayer anyway!

Slowly, the waiting room empties out, and the outside world begins to darken as daylight disappears, along with the day and what remains of the year. As the last person left in the waiting room, I find myself very alone. I don't want or need to be alone with my thoughts and fears running rampant. I tell myself, don't panic! Still, I can feel my face going flush. It doesn't make sense that I would be left all alone in the waiting room. Deep down in the dark recesses of my soul, I sense that something is definitely wrong here. What is happening? Where is Natalie? It has been an hour, so what is taking so long?

I try my best to collect my roiling emotions and thoughts and set out to the nursing station to see if someone, anyone, can help me figure out what is going on. I find a nurse and ask if she has any status on Natalie. She looks at me sadly and says, "Hasn't the surgeon been to talk to you?" I share with her that I hadn't heard a thing from anyone and ask if she could at least let me know if Natalie was okay. The nurse indicates that Natalie is out of surgery and resting comfortably in recovery. I ask, "Are there any results from the biopsy?" The nurse says to talk to Dr. Wilson about the results. Come on here people! Can't you see I am struggling to hang on!

The nurse sets off to find Dr. Wilson and returns in short order, letting me know that he is in his office waiting for me. PANIC! The nurse escorts me to his office, carrying on a meaningless conversation that becomes noise in my head. Dr. Wilson greets me and asks me to have a seat, using everything in his power to avoid making eye contact with me. I sense that this is not going to be a good conversation.

With little care for his message, Dr. Wilson says, "The biopsy was positive for breast cancer." After hearing the word cancer, an odd feeling overcomes me. I feel myself enter into some alternative universe, a place where I can run and hide from my grim reality. Try as I might hide here, Dr. Wilson pushes forward, almost uncaringly, and tells me that he knew immediately it was cancer and that when he biopsied some of Natalie's lymph nodes, they tested positive for cancer. I feel stoic, just staring forward. How can this be happening?

I am here but don't want to be. I don't want any of this. I am not interested in hearing anything else… enough. I know that is both cowardly and selfish. I know I need to get some basics covered, so I pull myself together and go for it. "Dr. Wilson, can you tell me how bad it is?" He quickly responds. "Given that it is in the lymph nodes, it is at least a Stage 2 Cancer." Stage… what in the world is a stage? I am confused by this cancer speak. I am overwhelmed. Sensing my confusion, Dr. Wilson explains that additional testing is necessary to truly assess the staging, which defines the spread of the disease.

"Does Natalie know the results yet?" I find myself mumbling. Dr. Wilson hears me just the same. "No, not yet." My internal wheels are spinning, how do you begin to tell the one you love that they have cancer? Haven't a clue, since this is new for me. I am scared, fearful of what this means. I feel myself choking up. Tears call to me from the heart, I catch a quick breath, my body shakes briefly… tears win out. They fall easily, rolling down my cheeks. I need to get to Natalie. I pull myself together best I can and say, "Well then Dr. Wilson, I guess we need to tell Natalie."

Good news, Natalie is alone in the recovery room. I think this might make delivering such traumatic news a bit easier, no prying eyes to watch the sad scenario play out. As we all enter the recovery room, I can sense Natalie's anxiousness. It is evident in her eyes. She knows. I barely have a chance to greet her before Dr. Wilson launches into his news, laying out the facts without compassion.

I grab Natalie's hand; she holds on tightly. I can tell she is scared. Heck, I'm scared. Dr. Wilson is very scientific as he continues walking us through the procedure, and what he has found. After he says, "Most likely stage 2 breast cancer," Natalie doesn't hear him. How could she? The nurse reaches out to hold Natalie's other hand. Dr. Wilson continues with the facts.

Natalie does not sob or fall apart, but a quiet stream of tears run down her beautiful, white porcelain cheeks. Though life delivered her a crushing blow, her beauty, her love of God and life still radiated strength. I lean in to hold her, and she hugs me in return, her body slightly trembling.

Dr. Wilson walks us through the tests he will order as a next step, including a CT scan, an MRI, a bone scan and a mammogram. These tests will be used to determine the spread of the disease and the best treatment options. Before we leave the hospital on this fateful December 31st, we have an appointment for January 2nd for the tests and one with an oncologist, Dr. Davidsen, on Friday, January 3rd. It would appear that we are getting fast-tracked, increasing my worry factor to a 100, on a scale of 1 to 5!

Eventually, we get to collect our things and make our way home. With her left arm in a sling, Natalie and I walk hand-in-hand solemnly through the deserted hospital hallways. Neither of us can speak, we're both keeping our emotions in check. We make it to the car, and as I open the car door for my lovely bride, we fall into each other, and I quietly whisper, "I'm sorry" to her over and over. Tears slowly slip from her eyes. She whispers in my ear, her breath warm on my neck, "I don't want to die. It can't be my time; it can't be." As we separate, she smiles that reassuring smile of hers and struggles to get in the car with her one good arm. I help her best I can, and tell her, "It will be ok, I promise, we'll beat this monster together."

The CT scan, bone scan, and MRI are a non-event from an evasive perspective, but the mammogram proves to be an entirely different story. The mammography techs and eventually the radiologist, have difficulty finding the primary cancer site in Natalie's breast. You would think that cancer that grows to be the size of a lemon under her left arm would easily be evident in her breast, but that is not the case. After about 45 minutes of painful mammography testing, a small tumor is found deep in Natalie's left breast, close to the muscle wall. While the medical practitioners are pleased that they found something, I am not. For a brief moment, I thought that maybe, they had this thing all wrong.

It is an exhausting week of surgery, tests and rattled emotions. Of course, we are trying to balance Natalie's recovery, the new world of breast cancer and the demands of three young children, Ryan - 9, Jake - 7, and William - 4. We aren't sure how to handle this shift in our world with them. It will certainly affect them. What do you tell them? Should you tell them? We decide to, knowing the world will soon know, but will focus on the basics, delivered in a rather casual way. No need for alarm!

I don't want to have this conversation. Period. With all the confidence I can dredge up, I tell the boys that their Mom is very sick and that we have the very best doctors taking care of her. But, the treatments she would receive will make her very sick. Sounds crazy as I say it! Maybe it is crazy? The good news for their Mom - she would be better by the end. I stay positive, but it is tough, as all I'm feeling is negative. The good news for me is that they didn't play the inquisitive card and ask questions.

We arrive at the facility for our first doctor's appointment, and our entry into the world of cancer care. We are surprised by all of the activity in the Cancer Clinic. People are coming and going, and I get the sense that many are in the fight for their lives. Obviously, cancer knows no bounds, afflicts the young and the old alike. An evil monster threatening life whenever and however, it could.

After a lengthy registration process, they call Natalie's name, and a gracious, and compassionate nurse brings us back to Dr. Davidsen's office. Dr. Davidsen, a young woman with a kind and caring spirit, greets us warmly and immediately makes me feel a bit better about our circumstance.

Dr. Davidsen reviews Natalie's family history and is surprised that there hasn't been breast cancer somewhere in the family. Dr. Davidsen tells us she has the test results and will review them with us. She grabs the tests and takes us to a wall of brightly lit monitors. Her plan is quickly evident; she will display the tests and show us the results first-hand.

Dr. Davidsen briefly explains the purpose of each test and what they will tell us. She slides all of the tests onto the monitors and patiently walks us through each one, pointing out the good as well as the bad. Good! Surely the good Doc is playing with me. I thought that anything to do with cancer had to be bad, really bad!

First in the lineup is the mammogram, the one test that took the longest to complete. Dr. Davidsen explains the difficulties the staff had in finding the primary cancer site. She directs our attention to the monitor holding the mammogram and points to this tiny, little minuscule shadowy looking area and says, "This appears to be the primary site." I say incredulously, "You're kidding, right? The cancer is so tiny. How could it have created such havoc?"

She smiles, saying, "It is small; under a centimeter in length. It is tight up against the muscle wall, making it tough to find. But the size doesn't matter. This is considered the primary site." As I look at this gray image, I am struck by the size and the havoc it has been able to create within the human body. I wonder how this evil monster could be in a position to destroy so much.

Next in the lineup is the MRI, which shows a compression fracture on L4 of Natalie's spine, the destruction is the result of the cancer. At least an explanation for the lower back pain she has been experiencing. The doctor explains that this fracture is significant, and it appears that pressure and weight from the upper torso are compromising the integrity of the vertebra. I can easily see what she is talking about, as the vertebra seems crushed to my untrained eye. Difficult to imagine cancer could destroy bone that way.

Dr. Davidsen goes on to explain that this is a serious issue as any slippage in the spine could mean paralysis. Ok, reality check time! She looks to Natalie and says, "No quick movements, no bending down, and no picking up children. None at all! There could be catastrophic outcomes!" It is too much to absorb all at once; my brain is spinning just trying to keep up.

We move on to the view of the chest cavity, starting with the bone structure, where there is a gaping hole in the sternum that even I can't miss! The evil monster has been busy at work. It is sad that I do not need Dr. Davidsen to point this out. Even though I feel numbed by this latest bit of news, the doctor moves onto the CT scan and pinpoints a couple of little spots on the lungs that are also cancerous.

Are we finished yet? I am not sure how much more of this I can take in. Natalie is unusually quiet, trying to take it all in herself. Me, I am mindless, wandering in a new world where the rules make little sense. I think I have had enough! I'm not sure how much more news I can process.

"Now for some good news," says Dr. Davidsen. She points to the test on the monitor and indicates that the liver shows no signs of cancer. Good news, who would've thought? We quickly learn from Dr. Davidsen that it doesn't really matter where the cancer is, what often matters is where the cancer is not! Dr. Davidsen goes on to explain that breast cancer will often find its way to the liver and the fact that the liver is clean, is a good thing.

Next, Dr. Davidsen draws our attention to a monitor holding the image of Natalie's brain. Like the image of the liver, she indicates that there is no sign of cancer, more good news. Based on what I hear from the doctor, we need to hope and pray cancer does not spread to the brain! Dr. Davidsen reaches up and starts grabbing all of the tests. A sigh of relief escapes my lips, not sure I could handle much more! With tests results in hand, Dr. Davidsen leads us back to her office.

Once behind closed doors, we come to understand the severity of our situation. Dr. Davidsen tells us that Natalie's kind of breast cancer is hormone-driven and that her cancer is the most aggressive type of breast cancer. If I wasn't feeling defeated before, I certainly am now. Can this get any worse? My thoughts race to the birth of our children and Christmases past. I think about all of the wonderful celebrations and family milestones. Will our future memories be at risk? I quickly push these thoughts away.

Swinging back to the present moment, Dr. Davidsen expresses the need to discuss treatment options and survival rates. What is this about survival rates? Dr. Davidsen presses forward and states rather scientifically, "Without treatment, Natalie has three months to live... maybe six, best case." I can feel myself begin falling inwardly, wanting to run and hide from this horrific reality.

The doctor's office gets quiet, but I need it to collect my thoughts and feelings, which are running rampant, almost uncontrollably. My heart is hammering loudly in my chest. How can this be? Somehow I pull myself together and ask the question that has plagued me for days. "If Natalie gets treatment, will she live?"

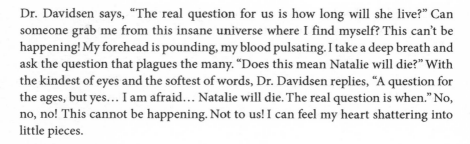

Dr. Davidsen says, "The real question for us is how long will she live?" Can someone grab me from this insane universe where I find myself? This can't be happening! My forehead is pounding, my blood pulsating. I take a deep breath and ask the question that plagues the many. "Does this mean Natalie will die?" With the kindest of eyes and the softest of words, Dr. Davidsen replies, "A question for the ages, but yes… I am afraid… Natalie will die. The real question is when." No, no, no! This cannot be happening. Not to us! I can feel my heart shattering into little pieces.

She then launches into a bunch of statistics and associated longevity timeframes, nothing of which registers with me. I am stuck on the word *when*. As Dr. Davidsen continues, I pull my spirit back into the moment and the conversation at hand. I feel helpless. I want to fix it all, make it right, and get it all to go away. I want to wake up, hoping this is nothing but a bad dream. I realize here in this moment, what a simple, uncomplicated life we were living and enjoying.

She continues, not missing a beat, and explains that we could expect Natalie to live up to two years given the nature and extent of her breast cancer. This approach would require some very aggressive treatments. Two years, that is more like a death sentence. Two years isn't much time, is it? We should have a lifetime together. As two years settles down around me like a noose, I realize that life offers no one any guarantees. I never thought something this horrid would end up in my world. Never! Two years, someone has this all wrong. This can't apply to Natalie. It just can't.

Our best hope, Dr. Davidsen explains, is to be accepted into a cutting-edge clinical trial. Depending on the disease and treatment responses, not everyone is a good candidate. Natalie will have to meet certain criteria before being accepted. Oh no! My thoughts spin out of control. We're not trying to get into college here! What if she is not a good candidate? What then? My soul shudders at the possibility.

Death sentence. That's what this is, no way around it! That is the reality! Natalie's reality; our shared reality. I question the 'why' of it all. What have we done in our lifetime that we deserve such a deplorable circumstance? Surely Dr. Davidsen has this thing all wrong. There is no way. I can't even begin to think about what this means! Death. I have never even thought about death, and here it is, daring me to believe otherwise! I think I want out of my life, and I want out now!

What a painful, horrible, no good day.

Inspiration ....

My heart is in anguish within me; the terrors of death assail me. Fear and trembling have beset me; horror has overwhelmed me. I said, "Oh, that I had the wings of a dove! I would fly away and be at rest."

Psalm 55: 4-6

Reflection ....

Too fast! Too fast! The mighty hand of fate reaches down from behind the land of promises and dreams and tosses me willy-nilly into the hamster cage of life. Without warning, I find myself on the hamster wheel, spinning wildly, seemingly out of control -my control. Little care has the hand of fate for what I am dealing with or feeling. How is it I find myself here?

On some level, I knew life would not go exactly as I had planned. It never does. I get that. Nothing ever led me to believe that my life would tumble into a realm ruled by chaos and fear! Cancer! Death! Limited options for survival! Within minutes, I am forcibly moved from a world full of joy and certainties of life to a world filled with fear and uncertainties. Life issued a warped speed ahead command. Things are on the fast track, leaving little time for me to adjust my perspectives. It has only been a matter of days, and here we are confronting death.

Wished I received an advance heads-up when things were about to go south in such a big way. Better yet, how about getting an opt-out, a chance to walk away from it all, leaving my life, as I knew it, intact. Right now, I kind of like the opt-out option.

Or, maybe there will be a grace period so I can at least process all the stuff that is happening. I need to get my heart, soul and spirit aligned. Is there a ref out there that can blow the whistle on the game of life, and grant me a time out? Just a simple time out, is that too much to ask? Does it have to happen so fast?

Life on the hamster wheel caused by a cancer diagnosis creates dissonance in my land. There is a new harsh reality for me, not of my choosing. Here there will be no opt-out, no grace period, or the sound of a ref's whistle. The reality of cancer fills my life. It's the fight for life! I'm not equipped to handle this kind of adversity now looming large on the horizon. I am only a week into this journey, and already it sucks!

As I wander around the hamster cage, I wonder if we are subject to some predetermined plan. Are we all part of something called fate, some randomness no one controls? It makes me question my life. It makes me question my faith and God's plan for my life. I question why I, or anyone for that matter, would need to experience such beastly events. It seems that fate is in charge, a rather randomness of the world and that God is absent. Surely God would not purposely set me up for what lay ahead, would He?

Is it possible that this bit of adversity, this painful reality coming straight at me, challenging everything I know, is, by His design, being laid deliberately before me? To strengthen and shape me to be the man He wants me to be? Lord, there has got to be a better way! If not, I am not so sure I am your man!

No matter the 'why', I am here just the same. This circumstance has taken ownership of my life. I want an easy way out, a shortcut. Does that make me weak to want to avoid this kind of horror? Do we all want to take the easy way out when adversity strikes? I could easily cave into this horrible circumstance, wave my white flag and let fate control my life and the surrounding events. Why not? Sure, it would be easier to play the victim. Yeah! Be the victim, I like it. Why not? I never asked for this, so why not play the victim card.

All of this contemplation of purpose and reason won't make any of this go away. It won't make it be anything other than what it is. So, maybe there is a better question for me. Perhaps the question is not so much about the why, and the role of fate, or me figuring a way around this dreadful circumstance.

Maybe the question for me is about the how? Will how I react and manage this challenge, this grisly circumstance that has come my way, be how I will be measured in this game of life? Will the how define me? Will I be judged by what I do with this heartbreaking and unexpected circumstance, this thing called cancer? Is this circumstance part of a bigger plan? Will I then be defined by what I do with all that I learn about myself as I journey forward through the trial set before me?

Truthfully, I am fearful of such an intimate experience with fate. How deep into myself will I have to travel? What if I don't like what I see along the way? Will I find myself in a place where I am too fearful to face my tomorrows? A place where fear takes control of my life? How do I manage my way forward and not become the victim, and lose myself in the chaos?

I turn to my heavenly Father, and pray for His help, that He would strengthen me for the tasks ahead, and intervene and make Natalie well. I pray this prayer often.

I am a patient servant, but it seems over this past week, that my prayers are going unanswered, and life is circling on the cusp of turmoil, just touching the edges of chaos.

So how do I travel through this adversity? Is it a belief that things will get better for us and me? Believing that we will beat the evil monster at his evil game? That this time, the monster will not take a life? Nor will the monster control mine? Is it about me being courageous in spite of overwhelming odds? Believing I shall prevail?

So many questions! Tough ones with no easy answers! I'll just keep reminding myself that I am courageous. That I shall prevail. That answers will unveil themselves to me. And soon I hope.

Lord, are you out there? Have you heard my plea? Just a simple answer Lord, all I ask. It just might make this doable. Lord, are you out there?

BOOK 2

Hope

<u>Hope</u>

Life's perception is changing
The direction changes like the shadows
Shifting in ways I don't understand
New constraints at every corner
Expectations that prove to be unreal
A monster seems to own my soul
It has a lock on my existence
Control is beyond my reach
I am tempted to throw down the chains
To run away from it all
The mountainous walls crumble about me
There is a darkness inside me that won't fade
I feel lost in the tumultuous wilderness
Is the battle over before it has even begun
Why have I let the evil monster
Have such a hold on me, and my life
Will the monster determine the life I lead
Is there a chance that the light
Coming from the spirit of hope
Burning brightly on the horizon near
Will strengthen me for the challenging days ahead
And the darkness that is sure to follow

By: Robert Mapes

The journey home is a rather somber affair. I am not sure what to say. After what seems like an eternity, I decide to break the dark silence that has surrounded us. "How are you holding up, kiddo?" As only Natalie can, she smiles that easy smile

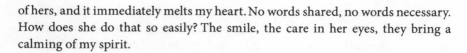

of hers, and it immediately melts my heart. No words shared, no words necessary. How does she do that so easily? The smile, the care in her eyes, they bring a calming of my spirit.

After a few moments, she says, "I don't see that we have many options at this point, we are already at mission critical." She's right! Her life hangs in the balance. Three to six months! Dr. Davidsen's words bounce around my brain. We then discuss our options. We realize that no matter what, we have to move very quickly. There is no question; we want to beat the evil monster into submission.

The plan is to do exactly as Dr. Davidsen recommended, immediately start an aggressive regimen of chemo and radiation therapies while exploring alternative treatment programs. Dr. Davidsen had indicated that any alternative or experimental treatments would want to see some positive results before they would consider a patient like Natalie. So, let's get the party started, let's show some results!

The spine is a big concern, and two things are going to happen quickly. First, Natalie is going to be fitted for a back brace to protect her spine from any possible structural damage. Next, radiation will begin immediately with chemo following closely behind it on January 17th. A big focus of the radiation will be the spine.

I still wonder if it is possible that they have this thing all wrong? That maybe everything up to now has been some big mistake, a huge false positive? Or is this me just wanting something different because I am afraid? I admit it, I am terrified. I can't put my arms around this, all of this. It is just happening too fast! Decisions need to be made quickly, and they deal with life and death.

It is reassuring to get home, to see the lights all ablaze, to know the boys are well cared for, and that my parents, Todd and Alice, are providing the care they need. They are the glue keeping our family together, as we struggle to figure things out. They have been with us since December 31st, which is now only a mere three days ago. Seems like a lifetime. How can so much happen in such a short period of time? Wow… only three days!

The boys and my parents greet us at the door. My parents can read everything they need from the sadness imprinted on our faces. I try really hard to be upbeat and positive, especially as the boys gather around me. It is tough to smile and be happy, but smile I do, even though I keep hearing Dr. Davidsen's words rattling around in my brain… it is a question of when.

Somehow, we manage to have dinner together, as a family. I don't much feel like eating, my stomach is one big knot! I realize that keeping a normal schedule, like dinner together, will be a good thing for all. It might even help me keep my wits about me. It is kind of comforting tonight, to be together. I guess I needed that.

As soon as dinner is over, the phone seemingly jumps off the hook. Everyone in the world wants to know what we found out at the doctor's appointment. Of course, no one wants to hear what I really have to say, any more than I want to say it. Stage 4 is a showstopper in each conversation, the phone line becoming eerily quiet. Surprisingly, everyone knew what Stage 4 meant, and understood that Natalie's life hung in the balance. All I needed was one little, mournful, sound to escape from the caller, and I was done for. Everyone works to stay strong and 'in the moment'. Natalie is just so overwhelmed that she goes to lie down, leaving me to deal with the masses.

About four calls in; my Dad reaches out and takes the phone from me, and runs with it from there. What a guy, he knew it was just too much, too soon. He does his best to inform everyone and to give the facts. To reduce the stress, he asks some family members to call other family members and friends to call friends, keeping disruption to a minimum. He knew three young ones were watching and assimilating everything. The boys, like it or not, were reaching their own conclusions based on their observations.

The following Monday, Natalie sees a specialist who fits her with some kind of funky metal back brace. It is so hard to see her in this awkward, metal monstrosity. Big and cumbersome, it is a collection of aluminum, awkwardly pieced together, in what seems no logical way. Absolutely necessary, ugly just the same.

We are now one week in and so much has happened. I quickly realize that this catastrophic circumstance requires fast decision-making and action. The problem is that my emotions and understanding are not traveling at the same rate of speed as the catastrophe. They are stuck at December 31st, hovering and maintaining, trying to protect me, denying my reality. Try as I might, I can't make sense of any of this. How did we come to find ourselves in this place? What had we done wrong in this game of life?

I continue working best I can. I still have a family to provide for. The world, though, is just swirling around me like an incoming storm. I am that little old rowboat stuck in the brewing storm; doing my best to clutch on to any ray of hope I can, fearful that I am going to get sucked into the black abyss of the raging storm that is my life. Everything feels dark and gloomy, the light of hope having been extinguished by the swirling storm!

My parents will stay with us up through Natalie's first chemo treatment. After that, they will return to their own home, some 7 hours away, in Maine. I am thankful for their gift of care and time. This allows me to work either mornings or afternoons, based on the demands of the day. Fortunately, I work for a really supportive and caring company. My fellow team members do what they can to help me out while key corporate leaders know what I am up against and support me in every way possible. I am indeed a blessed man!

Natalie and I make the 45-minute jaunt to the Concord New Hampshire Medical Center where the radiation treatments will happen. It is a pensive commute. Natalie is in her body armor, as I call it. The winter sun is trying to burn through the gray skies, and warm our hearts. The gray of winter hangs heavy on my soul, and the battle ahead of me sends ripples of fear through my body. Fear of the unknown I tell myself. Nothing to worry about here, right?

We meet with the radiologist, Dr. Williams, and he walks us through the radiation treatment plan, what it will look like and what it will do. The good news... it will immediately begin to kill the cancer cells in Natalie's spine, sternum and lungs. Dr. Williams goes on to say he will actually mark Natalie's body with some permanent dye, markers he calls them. These markers will allow the therapists to line up the equipment precisely each time Natalie comes in for treatment. Dr. Williams goes on to explain that treatment would be every weekday for six consecutive weeks, starting next Monday. All of a sudden, six weeks sounds like a very, very long time! And the battle is just beginning!

Immediately, thoughts begin bouncing around my brain. How am I going to get Natalie to treatment every day for 6 weeks, work for a living, take care of three boys and a very sick wife, and do all of this each and every day without fail? Are you kidding me here? There is no way; there just is no way! And ...what of school, shopping, cooking, cleaning, running kids to and fro, there just is no way! I close my eyes briefly and try to settle my spirits so I can be in the moment, right where I need to be.

For whatever manly reason, I feel that I need to be the one to carry the burden, especially when it comes to caring for Natalie and the boys. Reality jumps in, and I come to realize that I cannot do all of this, be the number one in charge of everybody's everything. Then, out of the blue, our wonderful church family steps forward and volunteers to get Natalie to and from her radiation treatments. God will, and does, send angels!

My sense is that chemo is going to be tough for Natalie. It is hard to believe that purposely injecting deadly toxins into her body is the way to go. It just seems, on so many levels, to be wrong. Friday comes all too quickly, and although Natalie is only five days into the radiation treatments, it is time to begin… the… dreaded… chemo.

The weather is still cold and depressing, a typical January kind of day, and everything hangs heavy on my soul. We meet again with Dr. Davidsen, and she begins the appointment by checking Natalie out from head to toe, poking and prodding. She is looking for any physical sign that would indicate the breast cancer is setting up shop somewhere else. Good news today, things with the monster appear to be stable. Whew!

While I celebrate this great news, I wonder about the nonphysical aspects of the disease. Who will help manage the emotional and spiritual aspects of this frightful journey? Poor Natalie, it seems she just keeps getting hammered, and it breaks my heart. I feel helpless, and I am afraid of the future, and what outcomes might be. Fear is tearing me apart piece by piece. Not sure what to do with it, and I knowingly give it more and more control over my life. Sadly, I am not equipped to fight it.

Dr. Davidsen does a refresher on what chemo will be like, the physical demands and all of the horrible physical side effects. Given the frequency and dosage of chemotherapy drugs Natalie will receive, she will have a *Hickman Line* inserted. What? Seriously? Who is this Hickman and what does he have to do with any of this? How can I just be hearing this?

I am not sure where Hickman came from, I must have been asleep somewhere along the way, but it seems he is here to stay. I guess too much is happening too fast; can't absorb it all. I feel like I am in a batting cage with baseballs being hurled my way. The only problem is… I don't have a bat. Cancer is consuming my life and trying to destroy the life of the one I love! This is getting complicated, and the abyss of the unknown is growing!

Dr. Davidsen agrees to do a refresher on a Hickman Line and jumps right on it. She explains that it is a tube of sorts that would be surgically inserted into a large vein in Natalie's chest. This line would have two access points. One would be used to deliver chemo and other medicines and one would be used for blood draws and for giving Natalie blood. Natalie getting blood! No one has said anything about that. Then bammo! Dr. Davidsen blows my world wide open. Me, the guy who dreads anything dealing with blood, will be the guy responsible for keeping this Hickman thingy clean and sterile.

I sit back in my seat and close my eyes. I have to; I can't take all of this in. I want to scream, enough already! But I won't. I am still working to come to terms with the notion of cancer, and now we are talking about catheters, wounds, and cleaning of sites, and ports, and needles. How can I do all of this? I am working for a living, maintaining a household and doing most of the care for three young boys. Wow! Wow! Wow!

I give myself a few seconds and then force myself back into the present. I explain my concerns about load balance with Dr. Davidsen, and she gently nods her head in understanding. She gets it, and says that she will arrange for a visiting nurse to help, but I must learn how to do it, and must ultimately take the task on! I am kind of hoping that never happens. Not sure I'll ever be ready for it!

Before I know it... I am in that same... dreadful... waiting room. It is hard to believe we are already confronting another surgery. It seems like it has been a year already! The panic I felt that dreadful day is still present, and raw. Familiarity with the waiting room does little to ease my weary soul. Dr. Wilson explained that the procedure was rather simple, and should take about 45 minutes. Haven't I heard this before? Doesn't matter, for the painful waiting process starts yet again!

As I pace the waiting room, wander the halls, and sit quietly, trying to calm my troubled spirit, I realize that there will be absolutely no certainties in the journey against the monster and that the unexpected will become our expected. I know that there is no way life can come with certainties and knowns. I get that. Like most people, I want a somewhat predictable life. My harsh new reality is that life will not play out as I thought!

I check the time, and it has only been 30 minutes since they took Natalie back, seems longer somehow. I guess it is the anticipation. I continue to pace, trying to work off my nervous energy. I can sense I am creating lots of nervousness for those around me. I work to calm my spirit and get myself into a seat. The last thing I want to do is create havoc for others; they had their own battles to deal with. I wonder if they feel alone in their battle, like me.

I decide it is a great time for another prayer! I ask my Heavenly Father to be with those gathered around me, that He calm their hearts and spirits, and bring them good outcomes and tranquility. I ask that He be with the healers and that He guide their hands, their gift to mankind. I ask that He be with Natalie and that He bring her back to me safely! I ask that He bring me calm of spirit that I might be prepared to deal with whatever lies ahead!

Time continues to pass slowly. It is painful. Minutes seem like hours. Before I know it, the 45-minute mark arrives, with no sign of Dr. Wilson or Natalie. Painfully, time pushes up against the two-hour mark, and I start to freak out, my entire psyche going to a really bad place. I feel like I am going to jump right out of my skin, and that will not be a pretty site for anyone!

Finally… Dr. Wilson arrives and asks me to join him in the hallway. I do not like this. It is too familiar! The good news, he says Natalie is resting comfortably. I say a quiet Amen to myself as he launches into the procedure and how it went down. I am kind of zoning out, but he grabs my attention when he said the word difficulty. Immediately I am back in the present. This cannot be a good thing. Apparently, Natalie had broken her clavicle somewhere along the way, and this made it difficult for Dr. Wilson to insert the Hickman Line, hence the long surgery.

Dr. Wilson gives me the all clear to go to Natalie in the recovery room. I peek my head in, and I can see the apprehension in her bright blue eyes. But she gives me that carefree smile of hers, and it somehow quiets my spirit, reassuring me. So, here she is, reassuring me! Shouldn't it be the other way around? Natalie has always had this way about her, never one to complain, always the soul that makes others feel at peace. Even at this moment, she is a calming force.

To bring a bit of levity to the moment, I say to Natalie, "Okay, so let me get this all straight! The guy who nearly passed out in the ER, and turned three shades of green when Ryan needed a few stitches, is now the one who will be taking care of your Hickman Line… and flushing these things called ports? I'm this guy? You sure about this Natalie? You just might, just maybe, want to rethink this whole thing?" She smiles and grabs my hand. All I need!

The first chemo treatment is here, three weeks after the biopsy, and I am dreading it. I worry about the dark spirits, and the horrors they foretell about the dreaded nauseous and vomiting. In theory, we have the new wonder drug, Zofran, in our court, which is reported to help reduce the sometimes-cruel side effects. Natalie receives two small syringes filled with chemo, before a much larger syringe filled with a chemo called *big red*, delivers the final blow.

Amazingly, Natalie is feeling pretty good on the ride home. We are actually encouraged. I am encouraged! Yeah me! I assumed the chemo effects were going to be bad immediately, and when they aren't, it is almost pleasant. Maybe a mindset change is in order? So much has happened that I am considering this moment to be pleasant. Wow! Amazed that I would even consider being in this place. Just maybe, I can do this thing and come out the other side. And maybe, the evil monster within will be beaten back!

The boys run to greet Natalie! It is heartwarming. They all gathered around her, hugging her as tightly as they can. With the brace in place, there is no bending for Natalie; it doesn't matter to the boys. They grab whatever part they can, and embrace her tightly. I wonder if they know just how bad this thing is, in spite of the positive spin we are trying to put on it.

My parents are still with us, and as I look up to see them watching, the little bit of hope I might have found quickly dissipates. I suddenly realize that this is Natalie's first chemo treatment, and it is also the milestone that would free my parents to return to their home and their own lives. As that thought settles in, I realize I will be alone in the muck and mire that has become my life. Ugh, my spirit quickly sinks! Me, alone! Going to be tough.

Reality slides right in with a crushing and visceral blow! Our welcome to the world of cancer treatment and chemo arrives with more vomiting than one could think possible. Anything and everything comes out as quickly as it goes in. It is so sudden and intense. It is just relentless… ceaseless… endless. It's hard for me to watch, I feel so helpless. There is so little that I can do to make it go away!

The violent vomiting drains Natalie all too easily, and she passes out on the bathroom floor. Luckily, I am in close proximity, just not close enough that I can grab her and prevent her free fall. PANIC! All I can think of is the spine, and the danger I knew sudden movement could place her in. Heinous evil monster! Havoc! I rush to her, not sure what state I will find her in.

The boys quickly gather, panic in their wide eyes. I clear the room and get them out into the hall. I get Natalie into a decent position as she comes back from the darkness that consumed her. I do the best I can to make her comfortable in a cramped bathroom. I am worried about her. I did not expect something like this to happen.

As she becomes clear of mind, she gingerly tries to get up. I see her movement as a good thing. I steady her on her feet, grab her good arm and we work our way slowly to the bedroom. I help her get undressed and into bed where maybe, just maybe, things will calm down. The boys watch all this with great interest, and I can see they are struggling with their rapidly changing world. The look of fear, evident in their eyes, hurts my heart. They know, I think to myself, they know. They know this is bad!

Little serenity comes to us this night. Sleep… it is becoming a treasured gift as the battle against the monster continues. I am on high alert while poor Natalie continues feeling nauseous and sick, the vomiting continuing, unending. Not much left to vomit I should think.

Monday is going to show up, and I am not entirely sure what my plan for care is going to be. I have to work, kids to get to and from school, and there is poor Natalie, who obviously will need some care. I have to have something in place, so I reach out to my sister-in-law Christina, hoping she might be able to help me out a bit during the week. Being the gracious and giving sister she is to me, she agrees to jump on in and help out.

The weekend drags on, and Sunday finds me in a bit of a funk. I wander aimlessly about the house; stuff is tossed and piled up everywhere. I am not sure where to start to clear the clutter. So I begin by gathering up clothes from around the house. I corral the boys, while Natalie rests, and off to the cellar, we go to get a start on a mountain of laundry.

The basement is cold and damp, just like my spirit. Lack of sleep has fogged my conscious thinking; lethargy has settled in and is trying to own the day. I plop William on the dryer so I can keep a watchful eye on him. I manage to coerce Ryan and Jake into helping me sort the laundry into some kind of order. Their pure innocence touches my heart. They jump right in and do their best to help me sort it out. I get this vibe that they know we need to work together to get this thing done.

I feel alone in the dark, dank cellar. I am worried about the how. How will I keep this family going, meet the demands of my changing world, and a job? There is just no way I can pull this off without things falling by the wayside. An idea pops into my consciousness unexpectedly. I wonder if I could create a network of family, like Christina, and friends from the community, and church, that can pitch in and help manage family life during the week. Keep household tasks on track and provide Natalie with the general kind of care she will need? I like the idea and think it might work.

I thought to be courageous meant I would have to fight the fight alone. If I asked for help, I was in some way being cowardly. I guess my judgment was overshadowed by the magnitude of it all. The reality is I can't do it all. I come to understand that courage is as much about asking for, and accepting help, as it is about being the one to do it all. Yes, accepting help. Why was I so reluctant to go there? Is this a guy thing, or is it a control thing?

The Caring Network becomes a reality. God sent a group of nine caring and loving souls to help hold the family together. These nine women would each take a morning or afternoon throughout the week, and would help get laundry done, manage the house best they could, take care of Natalie and the boys. Christina would be on point for an entire day, rounding out the schedule. For the first time in weeks, I feel like I have a handle on this care thing. Well, sort of anyway!

Friday rolls around again, and it is time for our weekly appointment with Dr. Davidsen. Natalie shares what the week has been like, the monstrosity of last Friday, and the weekend! Right off the block, there is a blood draw, and I quickly realize that blood levels will be regularly monitored. Blood levels will help determine if and when chemo will be administered.

We are then cleared for round two of chemo. There is some good news for us this day! Big red is not going to be in the mix; so only 2 chemo agents will be infused. Natalie is given an advance dosage of Zofran. I wonder if this dosage will mitigate the cruel side effects of last week's chemo. One can hope, right?

It is late by the time we get to the chemo room. We are all gathered when Dr. Davidsen gets a call from the pathologist at the Boston Cancer and Research Institute. Dr. Davidsen mentioned that she had reached out to inquire about their experimental two-step program, and see if Natalie could qualify as a candidate.

Here is my non-medical take on how things would work. Step One: Beat Natalie's internal system down to its lowest point using aggressive doses of chemo, then transplant Natalie's own T- Cells back into her body where they will rebuild her internal system. Step Two: Beat the internal system down even further, to it's very lowest, using the most aggressive doses of chemo, and then transplant Natalie's own bone marrow, back into her body. The ultimate goal during the beat downs is to eradicate any living, fast dividing cancer cells, making it impossible for the evil monster to gain any kind of stronghold in the future!

As mortality rates and longevity tables float through my consciousness, I come to realize that Natalie has to get into this treatment program. There is no question about it. It just has to happen. I see her life hanging in the balance, and the balance will be skewed in the monster's favor if we cannot make this thing happen. The monster clearly does not need an advantage!

Dr. Davidsen finishes up her call and heads our way. She sums up the conversation with the pathologist... Natalie is not a good candidate for the program. There must be a tumor that is at least one centimeter in length. This tumor would become the marker and would be used to track the success of the treatments. The one measurable tumor in Natalie's breast, the one evil monster lurking silently, is not quite one centimeter in length.

It is a critical blow to the spirit. The world quickly closes in on me. How can this even be happening? I don't understand. Surely, there is some kind of mistake here? While all of this is swirling and bouncing around me, I look down at Natalie and watch her silent tears tumble from her eyes. This cannot be happening. A life hangs in the balance, Natalie's life.

Dr. Davidsen brings me out of my darkness, explaining that she made a pitch to the pathologist for Natalie to be accepted just the same, and that the tumor was indeed large enough to be tracked and measured over time. The good news, the Cancer Center agreed to go back and review Natalie's case and reassess her candidacy for the program. Natalie slowly gets out of the infusion chair and falls into me, hugging me tightly.

I am learning how to clean and sterilize the Hickman Line. Who would have thought? Certainly not me! I now own this process, and with the help of the Visiting Nurses Association, I am learning how to do the sterilization process around the insertion point. Each and every day, I become more confident in my ability to do this thing. Natalie watches me like a hawk just the same!

The battle takes hold in the lives of the innocent when Ryan grabs me after dinner. He says he has a question he needs to ask me. Odd that he wants me by himself. I look into his young boy eyes and can sense there is something big going on in his little ole third grade head.

We get off the beaten path there in the house, and I get down so I can be face-to-face with him. And then it is out there. "Dad, is Mom going to... die?" I am caught off-guard. How can he be thinking this? Our talks with the boys have been about getting Mom well. Die has never entered any conversation. Before panic settles in on my spirit, I ask him, "Why do you think your Mom is going to die?" With a pained expression on his face, Ryan simply says, "All the kids at school are asking me? They are saying Mom has cancer and could die."

There it is, mortality all too easily finding its way to the innocence of my young son. To think we had been trying to protect him from it. I know I have to respond, failure to do so would send a message of a different sort. My gut tells me honesty is always the best policy. I explain to Ryan that his Mom does have cancer, and that she is very sick, and that her treatments will help make her well. He looks at me intently, eyes like saucers. I can't imagine what is rolling around in his little boy brain. I give him a big hug. He falls into me easily, and hugs me closely. I'd say the kid is scared. I know the feeling.

With no warning, a large, solid, pencil length growth emerges on the inside of Natalie's left arm over the weekend! PANIC! It is so sudden! Natalie and I really don't have an understanding of how cancer works quite yet, and see this as a very troubling development. Is the cancer already moving and taking up new residence? Ugh! No, it just can't. It can't!

We rush off to the doctor's early Monday morning, not sure what we are up against, certainly fearing the worst! The fear settles in the pit of my stomach and sets my heart to race! I am overwhelmed by it all. Dr. Davidsen sees us right away, and the news is good, she says, "The hardening has nothing to do with the cancer." Whew! A huge sigh escapes through my parched lips and a smile slowly comes across Natalie's face.

It seems though, that this large, solid pencil length growth is merely a blood clot! A bit of joy finds its way to my heart. But it is quickly beaten back as Dr. Davidsen goes on to explain that a blood clot is a serious matter, and is likely a by-product of the cancer treatment. She then adds, "I'll need to keep Natalie in the hospital until the blood clot is dissipated. During this time we will have to play around with the necessary drugs to ensure we won't bump into this again."

I shake my head in defeat, did not see this one coming. Time motors on just the same, and it has been a tiring three days, lots of back and forth to the hospital. The boys have not seen Natalie. We have been trying to protect them from that part of the world. But with no discharge in our line of sight, it seems inevitable that they are going to end up at the hospital at some point. I figure I might as well get it over with, and take the boys to the hospital. A little surprise for one and all might be just what is needed.

The boys are clueless, but they figure it out once we get to the hospital. Their eyes light up like a Christmas tree. Excited… you bet. I convince them to move quietly through the halls so we can really surprise Natalie. Surprise! It is awesome! They all crawl in bed with her, trying to get as close as they can. It is a heartwarming, Hallmark kind of moment. It calms my spirit just a bit. Nurses gather, smiling at the beautiful scene before them!

Natalie is hospitalized for seven… very long days. She is discharged just in time for our weekly appointment with Dr. Davidsen, and another round of chemo. The doctor says she has something she needed to share with us. My insides begin jumping around, assuming the worst. Dr. Davidsen then reveals some good news. The pathologist from the Cancer Center called back as promised, and after a review of Natalie's disease, the research team felt she was a good candidate for the treatment program. Natalie and I easily fall into each other, while Dr. Davidsen begins with the high fives.

Our excitement carries across the wires like nothing I have ever seen. We call the home front to share the news, and from there, word hits the streets of New Hampshire so quickly that neighbors gather to celebrate with us when we arrive home. I make many exciting phone calls to family members and friends, and I find myself being genuinely hopeful for the very first time since the New Year rolled on in! Is this me beginning to accept this for what it is? Maybe!

The visiting nurse came for the mid-week blood draw. Our excitement from last week comes to a screeching halt when Dr. Davidsen calls and explains that Natalie needs to be admitted to the hospital for a few days. Her recent blood work was not favorable. Off to the hospital we go, again. My sister Marybeth agrees to watch the boys. Upon admission, a quick temperature check shows Natalie has a fever. It seems Natalie was destined to be in the hospital. I feel like the monster has a lock on our lives!

Winter's grasp on the world and my spirit begins melting away with the snow. Long gone are the dark, depressing nights and the monotonous grays that shroud my world. With each passing day, the sun grows warmer and more powerful; as do my hopes that the evil monster will not be the victor. I am more confident that we will be victorious and believe that our lives will one day return to normal.

As much as I try to hang onto hope, there seems to be something lurking out there just waiting to test that hope. The unexpected death of a neighbor, who lost her fight to hang onto hope, and bring an end to the monsters that tormented her, throws me off course. A needless loss of life… it is haunting. Natalie fights bravely

for hers, and this loss of life, so close to home, scares me. It is way too close! Our children play together. What pain they must be dealing with. I try to imagine their loss, wishing I could make for a different outcome.

And then a horrible thought flashes before me. It shakes me to my core! I work to push it away, push it back; I demand it to leave my consciousness. It holds on tight, and a hallow voice whispers, "This too… is your fate!" As my heart races, I turn to the Lord and pray, for the children in both our families and for me, that I am strengthened to handle whatever it is He is planning on sending my way! That He stands by Natalie's side, and that He let our outcome be different!

Each subsequent chemo treatment seems to escalate Natalie's nausea and vomiting. I watch painfully from the sidelines as Natalie struggles to eat… to keep anything down. I hope this repetitive approach to chemo is wreaking as much havoc on the evil monster. Large ulcers have shown up in her mouth, and as painful as they are, they are nothing compared to the horrible convulsions that shake her body and rattle her mind. It is painful to watch, and I am completely helpless. I want to change it, make it better somehow. I am at a loss. I question if we made the right decision when we decided to fight this beast.

I arrive home from work one day to find Natalie in bed, her body in a frenzied state, contorting like an acrobat, while three little boys cuddle their Mom, trying their best to comfort her, their love and concern never more evident. So what does a guy do, he jumps right in bed, suit and all, and tries to comfort one and all. Eventually, the seizures pass and a settling of her spirit allows Natalie to return to our world. She does slowly, and is a bit confused as she does, but finds the strength to smile at the boys just the same. I can see the relief in their anxious eyes. I send them on their way to watch cartoons and lay down beside my courageous bride. It is tough cuddling her shrinking body.

In a unique alignment of events, the research facility contacts Dr. Davidsen to set up an appointment to meet with us, a necessary step in securing a coveted place in the experimental program. Dr. Davidsen lets us know that it is time to evaluate the effectiveness of both the radiation and chemo. She recaps, telling us these tests will have to show positive results for Natalie to get into the program. It is time to end the monster's hold, and bring an end to its tyranny in our lives!

We begin a new round of testing, which makes for another emotional week, hoping and praying! While the level of pain in Natalie's back and sternum has subsided, we are still worried that the monster has taken up a stronghold in other parts of her body. Friday finally arrives, and I am on pins and needles waiting for the test results.

Dr. Davidsen puts all of the tests up on the monitors and walks us through each one. The cancer in the sternum is almost entirely gone. The cancer in the back… significantly reduced. The spots on the lungs … G.O.N.E.! The good doctor continues with the good news by pointing out that there are no new sites, and that the liver and the brain continue to be clean. It may not have been 1980, but we all begin celebrating just like Kool & The Gang would have hoped, and I am certain we made them proud, even Dr. Davidsen gets in on the fun!

We return to Dr. Davidsen's office with a bit of pep in our step, feeling a sense of victory against the monster. She is quick to caution us that although these were favorable results, the cancer could be in stealth mode waiting for new opportunities to attack! While I appreciate her words of caution, absolutely nothing is going to dampen my spirits today.

Wham! Bam! Slam! Dr. Davidsen quickly brings me back to our more pressing realities and tells us that Natalie's white blood cell counts were critically low and that perhaps Natalie should be admitted to the hospital as a precautionary measure. With so much to celebrate and with so many to celebrate with, the thought of hospitalization is disheartening. I think Dr. Davidsen gets that read from us and decides on a different tack. She suggests we go home, promising her that any fever or unusual weakness or dizziness be a call to action on our end. It is a good plan!

It is a beautiful spring day when we arrive home. We are both flying high and share the news with the boys, friends, and just about anyone who asks! The warm afternoon sun, the blooming springtime flowers, all join together in a cacophony of joy that is almost indescribable. Maybe we will beat the odds and beat cancer into oblivion! Just maybe!

Inspiration..

Therefore do not worry about tomorrow, for tomorrow will worry about itself. Each day has enough trouble of its own.

Matthew 6:34

Reflection ....

Hope has left my life. Packed up the bags, and flat out moved on. This loss of hope creates a bleak and tormented outlook. I am negative. I think I have every right to be! This situation is challenging, beyond my ability to cope. Do my negative feelings prevent me from hoping? Does the apparent silent voice of my Heavenly Father play a role in my loss of hope?

As I look at my world, things scientifically make sense. It is what it is. There is no denying the science, it speaks for itself, and the facts stand on their own. I guess knowing that my love is attached to the science makes it difficult for me to harness and manage my emotions. There isn't time to reflect, or contemplate, or even try to figure out the right way forward.

This leaves me in a world of uncertainties. A world filled with more unknowns than knowns. Routine, a certain order of things, the very ones I took for granted, are long gone. I admit that I liked my routines. These new uncertainties enter unannounced and unwelcome, and they create turmoil for me, true hopelessness. I find myself distant at times, and often in a dark, scary place in my mind. While I realize I am not alone in these feelings, I feel as if I am.

I work hard to protect my heart from the sharp, painful realities of life that seemingly pierce it. The silent retreat seems to work. But every time I retreat, I allow my emotions to have control. Maybe I am trying to avoid my suffering. Every little thing has become a torturous everything. My inner struggle rages, tumultuous. I have never found myself in such dark places before, and I am not sure how to find my way through such darkness.

Over time, I find myself alone on an island. While on my island, I think about hope, and what it might mean to my journey, to our journey. Hope! I know hope holds an unbelievable amount of power for the human spirit, I do. I am not sure how hope relates to my journey and me. Am I selfishly tied to my circumstance, and all of my fears, and do I too easily let them stomp over what hope I could have?

So... here I am. Cancer and the fight for life, how can I hope when death hangs in the balance? How can I hope when the one I love shakes from the terror of chemo, convulsions rocking her already shrinking body? How can I hope as I watch three tormented souls struggle with the meaning of life? How can I hope when I am helpless?

Whatever hope is and does; it seems to be outside of my grasp now. I see my life as all consuming, leaving little room for the notion of hope. Little room for me to even consider hope! I've become an emotional hostage. So, an internal battle rages within me. Am I choosing to turn away from hope? Is it because I am just so overwhelmed that I can't see how hope can play out in my life? Interestingly, as I step away from hope, I also find myself turning away from the Lord. I am not sure how He fits into any of this, or how He fits into my life now?

Here we are… it is ugly, and truth be told, I am mad and angry about it. There, said it. It feels good to say it! I am mad and angry. Might even be mad and angry with God. There… said that too. Well, there is not a 'might be' about it. I am furious with God. How could He do this, how could He? We are good people, always His servants, so how could He let this happen?

Just allowing myself to be angry, and to acknowledge my anger toward God is freeing. Amazingly, lightning bolts do not shoot down from the heavens. The earth does not open up and swallow me whole. I wonder how faith fits into the hope picture. Is my faith tightly connected to hope?

I realize that hope is always within our grasp, and is a powerful tool to the human spirit. What I failed to understand is that the loss of hope would make for a very troubled spirit. So, instead of hoping, I by default, find myself wandering in the quagmires of my day-to-day life, and the mucky mess that has become my life. As I aimlessly wander, I find myself lacking conviction in the power of hope, prayer, and a waning relationship with God.

It takes me a while, but over time, I realize that I cannot stay in this place where hope is lacking. There are too many dark spirits and depressing thoughts coming from the dark shadows. These thoughts frighten me, they scare me, and I know I am not good to anyone, particularly myself if I stay in this place.

As time passes… I try reaching out to hope. Interestingly, as I reach out, my spirit lifts, and I feel encouraged, even inspired. Hope seems to give me confidence, which leads to greater hope. I gain a sense that I can endure whatever lies ahead and that I can do this thing laid down before me. That I can hold my family and myself together as we manage the seas of life in our little wooden raft! I find my relationship with God improving, at least to the point where I can pray, and seek His love and understanding. Don't get me wrong, I am still pretty angry, but am encouraged that I am at least talking with my Heavenly Father.

I know it is up to me, I see that now. I have to be the one to reach out to hope. I just might want to hang on tight. I know a life hangs in the balance, and it just might be mine!

BOOK 3

Courage

Contemplation..

<u>Purpose</u>

Is the purpose, Lord
To courageously face each circumstance
Growing and learning
Becoming a better me?
Is the purpose, Lord
To celebrate life's adversities
Embracing the challenge
Building our inner self?
Is the purpose, Lord
To face my unknowns
With courage in my heart
Enlightening my soul?
Is the purpose, Lord
To graciously accept
Whatever comes my way?
Without question or doubt?
Is this the purpose, Lord
To overcome my fear
Against outcomes that are uncertain
Building a spirit today?

By: Robert Mapes

The Story ....

The journey to Boston this fine April day is invigorating. The sky is a bright blue and the sounds of Boston Harbor are calling our names. I feel a sense of tranquility. Natalie and I love the sea and receive great solace from being close to the rolling waves and shifting tides. These waves and shifts are the kinds I can easily deal with. We decide to make our journey to the Cancer Center an adventure of sorts. We explore Boston a bit, have lunch at Faneuil Hall, and delight in being a regular couple. We take a little stroll along the coast hand in hand. It is refreshing to be amongst the land of the living.

This is our first visit to the Cancer Center, and it is a bit intimidating! You'd think I'd be used to the world of cancer by now. I am not! Just the same, everyone is gracious and kind, and from the first greeting through all of the loops and hoops, never do we feel that we are a burden. After what seems like hours of paperwork, we find ourselves propelled to the part of the center where breast cancer research takes place and meet with some of the practitioners.

Our first stop, the lead research nurse, who walks us through the program, and the grim realities of success rates and life expectancies. They are not pretty, but that is why we are here. The program will begin with Natalie receiving chemo 24 hours a day for 3 consecutive days using an infusion pump. The pump will contain the chemo, and manage the flow. The pump will be connected directly to a port in Natalie's Hickman Line. Given the rigor and aggressive nature of the chemo, Natalie will receive a daily injection of a drug called G-CSF. The drug will stimulate the production of white blood cells, which are important for fighting infection.

The research nurse goes on to explain that the drug has to be administered subcutaneously and that yours truly is going to be on point to do this… daily. Don't they realize I am not their guy for this? I am still struggling with my other medical duties, and now I get to add this to the mix. The nurse, sensing my panic, explains I would be trained first, and will have to administer a shot of saline to Natalie before we would get the all clear to begin. Shoot, at this rate, I'll be an RN before I know it!

Then Dr. Weston walks us through the experience, the good, the bad and the ugly. She discusses the timing of the 2-step process in the overall treatment game plan, a refresher on the kind of chemo that will be used, and how the t-cells and bone marrow will be reintroduced into Natalie's body. Overwhelming!

Dr. Weston walks us through the bone marrow biopsy and bone marrow harvesting process. Given we are only in April, we will need to complete several more rounds of chemo, under Dr. Davidsen's watchful eye before we can begin the program. Best-case scenario, Dr. Weston believes we are looking at a possible July or August admission timeframe. In the meantime, we need to stay the course with the chemo and get a bone marrow biopsy done.

At the end of our time in Boston, I realize how much everyone cared for us and that they really understand everything we are up against. Every doctor, nurse and caregiver treated us with compassion and showed Natalie that they planned to be with her as the battle continued. The program is scary just the same. While Natalie sees all of this as a means to an end, I see it as destructive and harmful. Her body can barely take the weekly infusions without catastrophic fallout, how will her body ever be able to handle all of this aggressive chemo? Might not have a choice here!

On the way home, Natalie tells me she is glad she is the one fighting the fight and not one of the boys. It could as easily been one of them! As always, my calm and compassionate wife put it right on out there, and said seeing so many children with cancer at the center, gave her a better perspective about her own battle to survive.

I am amazed at the parents who have children fighting the fight against the monster known as cancer. These kids and their parents are the real heroes in this game of life. Looks like I might be able to learn a thing or two from these courageous spirits. I just might need to remember the love of another, who sacrificed His life for me.

Natalie continues with the chemo, and with each subsequent treatment, the effects seem to move from the hurtful category into downright harmful! Eating and keeping anything down is becoming harder and harder, and Jello and Gatorade have become Natalie's mainstays. Things come to a head one warm May night, when convulsions move into hyper drive and fever comes on like a winter's storm. It is the wee hours of the morning, and I am concerned enough that I call Dr. Davidsen's emergency service. No surprise when I get the callback, and it is off to the ER we go.

I make a quick call to my sister Marybeth, wake her up in the wee hours, and hope she can run on over and watch the boys. Marybeth hustles on over, and Natalie and I rush to the ER. As I drive to the hospital, I am hoping Dr. Havers is on. She had admitted Natalie before, knew the drill, and could fast track the admission. As luck would have it, she is on, and I smile to myself when I see her.

It is about time for the sun to dawn on a new day when I get home. A good thing, I want to be there before the boys wake up so I can explain what is going on. I do my best to downplay this latest development. There is little reaction when I update them. Sadly, they have almost become accustomed to Natalie being in the hospital, or away.

It is mid-May in New Hampshire, and the world around me is alive! It is filled with wonderful colors and smells. All welcome after the dark days of winter. The chemo continues and so do the horrible side effects. Natalie's body is being beaten up from the inside out, and the outside in, her delicate frame now showing signs of wear. Her body, now thin and frail, a mere image of the beautiful woman she was. The dark circles under her eyes tell the tale of the battle, and her once sparkling eyes are dimmer, the vibrancy waning. She is short of breath often, and she seems to struggle to move from room to room. It pains me to see this unfold before my helpless eyes.

Blood transfusions have become the norm, and in many instances require a hospital stay. Such is my life, and somehow I am adapting, not willingly, but adapting none-the-less. The sad part is that the boys have adapted too, and where they would once upon a time panic when I showed up without their Mom, now they just casually observe her missing, and go on about their business. This weighs heavily on me.

As May begins to round itself out, chemo side effects escalate, this time out it is fever, convulsions, and dry heaves on steroids. Marybeth is Johnny-on-the-spot and moves quickly my way once again in the wee hours of the night. It is as if the hospital was expecting us. We pass easily through the ER to a hospital room where the miracle of medicine brings comfort, calm and placidity to a tortured soul. I sneak out of the room and return to home before dawn's first light. There will be little rest for me this night.

Friday rolls around again all too quickly. Day and night seem to have lost meaning, and seemingly blend together. I am a bit anxious about our appointment today. Dr. Davidsen said she should have the results of the bone marrow biopsy. She is in great spirits today, so I am encouraged coming right out of the box. She, too, is excited about something, and she quickly shares the results of the bone marrow biopsy… CLEAN, CLEAN, CLEAN! A cause for celebration, and cause for a silent prayer of thanks to my Savior and Lord!

Dr. Davidsen talks candidly with us about the treatment journey so far, and where we are in relation to the original treatment plan. We talk openly about Natalie's tattered body, and her ability to continue to handle the chemotherapy. We are now almost through the fifth cycle. A cycle for Natalie means 3… consecutive… weeks… of chemo with one week off… and then the next round begins. Intensive! The treatment program requires at least seven cycles of chemo. Ugh! I shudder to think about the days ahead. Dr. Davidsen says that we need to go one more cycle,

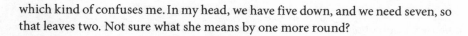

which kind of confuses me. In my head, we have five down, and we need seven, so that leaves two. Not sure what she means by one more round?

She goes on to tell us that in discussing Natalie's disease and treatment to date with the Cancer Center, in addition to her body's response to the treatments, both good and bad, that they would count the 72-hour pump cycle as treatment number 7. This meant Natalie would only need one more cycle of chemo during the month of June, making us ready for the next phase of the treatment to take place in July. I'm not sure how I feel about this. I am both excited and scared at the same time.

We have been so worried about the battle that little thought has gone into worrying about costs. While we have been blessed with good insurance coverage, so many expenses are not covered or require some payment on our part. Treatment is expensive! And... the experimental program might not be covered. My- sister-in-law Christina steps forward and creates a fundraising team to help secure the funds we may need for treatment.

Knowing Christina as I do, this will not be just some small-scale operation, more like an all-hands-on-deck charity operation, and many will have a chance to be involved. Christina easily rallies the troops and helps secure items for a large-scale silent auction that will include hundreds of contributors and attendees. The big event is scheduled for August. It helps us all believe that the evil monster can be beaten, and everyone can play a role in the battle plan.

Our arrival at the Cancer Center for the 72 hours of chemo, is both somber and sobering. As we enter, we are met by a variety of patients awaiting treatment, many of them children, many of them clearly in a dire state, the pain and agony of their own battles etched into their sweet, innocent faces, bald headed with hallow, sunken eyes... a bit of a reality check. Natalie feels a special connection to these bald headed wonders, although it saddens her to see them.

It is quite some time before we get into the treatment room and Natalie gets hooked up to the pump. I am not sure what to expect. The treatment pump is a square kind of contraption, with the chemo drugs contained in a clear acrylic bottom, and the pump completing the square on the top. The pump is programmed to deliver the chemo at regular intervals, and the nurse connects it to Natalie's chemo port, and with the push of a button... game on.

I cannot imagine what the next 72 hours will be like. I know they just might be the longest 72 hours of my life. The daily commutes into Boston, each morning from New Hampshire, alarm me a bit. Natalie will need to be closely monitored by the Cancer Center. Chemo plays havoc on Natalie's body with excruciating nausea. I cannot picture what these commutes into Boston will be like, given the chemo pump!

As we walk through the parking garage, arm in arm, I feel like a regular couple just strolling along. It is nice, incredibly nice to feel like a normal couple, if only for a moment. I wonder what people think as we walk on by? Are they thinking I feel so bad for them? Or are they thinking what a cute couple? I hope it is the latter.

I open the car door for my beautiful wife and help her get situated. Her blue eyes sparkle and dance in the little bit of light in the garage. They glisten like the boys. Her skin still has that Ivory Girl purity. I guess a few weeks reprieve gave her a chance to recover a bit. The only thing missing is her beautiful brown curls, the ones that dance about her.

The pump, though, is already keeping a regular cadence, taking me back to earlier horrors. I go around to my side of the car and start it up. Just as the car starts, the pump does its thing. It is pretty quiet. The sound is certainly discernible with a hint of a small motor of sorts kicking into some kind of action. Except I know what the action is, and more importantly, I know what it will eventually do to Natalie's already worn and tired body.

I turn to look at Natalie, my gaze does not waver, and with every beat of my heart, I pray for good outcomes, and that I can be her white knight, the one that swiftly rides in and saves her from harm. She turns to look at me, and our eyes meet, and seeing those baby blues and that reassuring smile, is a light unto my soul. It is only momentary, though. Something is gnawing deep within me, and it has for some time now. I am not sure where it comes from, or why it surfaces here in this moment, seemingly out of nowhere. But for some reason, I find myself saying, "It should have been me! This should be me; this shouldn't be you! Why did this have to be you?"

She holds my gaze and asks me to come around and open her door. I think immediately that here comes the vomiting. Let the games begin. I jump out of the car and run around to her door to help her out! She reaches up and grabs my shoulders, looks me square in the eyes from her seat, says, "It had to be me!"

To which I say, "No, it should have been me, little boys need a mother!" I fight to hold my tears in check. Natalie continues with a tight grasp of my shoulders, looks into my eyes lovingly and says softly, "It has to be me! Did you not see those little children back there fighting for their own chance at life? It could have been one of our boys, our children. Don't you see it had to be me?"

"I know, I know," I somehow manage to mumble. "But… it should have been me!" She holds my gaze and very tenderly says, "It had to be me… don't you see… little boys become young men… and young men will need a Dad… much more than they'll ever need a Mom… don't you see it had to be me?" She gingerly steps out of the car and takes me into her warm embrace, and holds me, as I cry like a little boy!

I am not so convinced it had to be her, what I do know is that it took courage to say those words to me. To stare at her own mortality and then to hold me… unbelievable. We are all called to be heroes at certain times, in our own ways, and in our own lives, and we can either step up to the challenge, or we can back away. Natalie chose to deal with the challenge in her life, courageously. I think about another courageous being, and of the love He has for me, and the tremendous sacrifice He made for all of mankind. Hard to imagine what that was like!

The ride home starts out quietly. It isn't long before the wagon comes unhitched, with nausea, vomiting, and convulsions reigning supreme. I hate to say it, but it was more of the 'same old, same old.' While I had hoped for a different outcome, that is not going to be the case this time around either. It is a long journey home!

I spend lots of time on the phone with the nurse and doctor trying to help get things under control. This round is intense. Wicked I'd say! We have an appointment in Boston again tomorrow, and the word from Boston is that we are just going to have to push through. Why is life like that sometimes? I have to keep reminding myself that this is about the battle against the cancer, not the incremental pain points. Difficult to do! It is hard to focus on the goal while your ladylove is suffering. Best I can do is comfort her, which doesn't seem like very much.

Morning finally rolls around, and it is time for my first ever injection of G-CSF. Using a syringe, I draw the necessary dosage from the vial, remove any air bubbles, clean the injection site and administer the drug. My hand shakes a bit, and I ask Natalie to look away. I think it might take some of the pressure off. Deep breathe and hold! Whew… nail it the first time out.

Off we go to Boston with a pail in hand and a continued belief that we are entering the final phase of the battle, where we will win over the monster. It seems like weeks since we traveled to Boston last, in reality, it has only been 24 hours. There is so much going on physically and emotionally that it doesn't seem possible that we may be closing in on the end of the journey.

The jaunt into Boston is long and tough. Once in Boston, there is a quick blood draw, a physical exam and a review of the results. The blood test shows deterioration already in both white and red blood cell counts. Blood levels will continue to be monitored closely and will be evaluated tomorrow when we return to Boston, yet again. The good news, if there is any, is that we are now 24 hours into our own private version of war. Only 48 more hours to go!

Here on day two, the pump seems to have taken on a life of its own. Maybe it is because the pump sounds louder in my head than it actually is. Natalie is so sick on the way home that she quietly retreats, hoping for a break from the vomiting. The quiet inside the car makes the pump sound even louder and each time it kicks in, a sense of panic grabs hold of me and squeezes tightly around my chest. I fear a serious round of convulsions while commuting home, and I am not sure what I will do!

Somehow, we make the one and one-half hour commute home, and Natalie rushes off to bed. The boys are doing their own thing when we arrive. Sadly, it seems that they have come to accept that this is their life and how things are going to be. Mom and Dad completely consumed by doctor visits, Mom being so sick she is unable to be with and do much with them, and Dad distracted and worried all the time.

Dark hallows of dread beckon to me, I can't sleep a wink, and visions of sugarplums do anything but dance! I lay in bed waiting for the call of pain, the sound of the pump, the signal that vomiting would surely begin. She hasn't eaten in days, how can she have anything to vomit? How can she have any energy to be sick? I snuggle in best I can, and hold her while she vomits, her body quivering. The sound of the pump brings tears to my eyes; I know what the chemo is doing to her tired soul. I remind myself that I must endure this moment in time. That I must stay vigilant. But I am feeling anything but vigilant tonight. The harmony that comes from sleep will never find its way to me. It is going to be a painful countdown until morning's first light!

My soul is tortured, and I find myself contemplating the role quality of life plays in all of this mess. Pumps, chemo, convulsions and midnight runs. There is such an intense focus on the battle that it takes complete control of our family. We have so little time together, to be a family, and there are no easy answers on what we can do about it! I imagine the quality of life question is something that many struggle with.

Day three of this tortuous round is here, and as I administer the G-CSF, I try to create a positive mindset. I try to convince myself that we are nearing the finish line and, that maybe, we will make it through the last 24 hours and come out the other side in one piece and at peace! Maybe then, things will settle down a bit, and we can re-enter the land of the normal, and start worrying about what kid needs to be where and when and not which medicine to administer and how. I long for a return to those kinds of days. Once we get through all of this, you won't hear me complaining about the demands of parenting and family life and how exhausting it all is. I'll celebrate them.

A sense of déjà vu sets in as we head off to Boston! Any positive self-talk I had quickly evaporates. The commute is painful. The nauseous feeling settles in, making this trek unbearable! Once in Boston, there is the blood draw and physical check, and we find the bloods have continued to deteriorate. I want Natalie to be admitted, I am over my head, and don't have the skills, tools or medicines to help her. It is painful to watch, and I hate this helpless state. I broach the subject with Dr. Weston, and I am told to stay the course, that she would re-evaluate again tomorrow. Not what I want to hear! I don't think they realize how agonizing this is for me; this helpless sense I have.

Food intake is not an option here in day three for Natalie. Her body continues to shrink before my eyes. Just how tiny she has become. Her hallowed eyes telling the tale, the sunken cheeks confirming my fears, that this chemo stuff would take its toll on her physically. Thoughts bounce around my brain, and center on the gravity of the disease and the treatment, and I question which is worse. Right here, right now, I don't have a good answer!

Finally… nighttime descends, and the demons of the night quietly intercede and make their presence known. There isn't much that can calm my heart or my troubled spirits. I am at a complete loss about what to do. How can one person be so sick, and there not be one solitary thing I can do to help make things better? It just isn't right. I am angry… angry that this is happening and angry that I can do nothing about it.

The pump eerily sounds in our darkened bedroom, signaling that more toxins are being delivered. My hearts races a bit each time I hear the sound, fearful at what it will mean. I hold my breath, hoping this dose will pass, and not create a new horror. I wait quietly. Natalie does not stir. Whew! Dodged that bullet! It is only a matter of moments before the next dose.

I am suffocating under the weight of it; the pump calls out with pain! As it sounds, I hear the push of the chemo. I hold my breath again. Natalie stirs suddenly, and… dry heaves target the weak and worn. I jump out of bed, dash to her side, and hold the pink bin for her. I sit close to her; wrap an arm around her, hoping it will help calm her body and soul. Eventually, the spell passes. I lean down to kiss her forehead, it is clammy and damp. I fight my tears back. It is going to be a long night!

The pump continues to sound the call of the forlorn, and with each push of toxins, the sound grows louder and louder in my mind. I cannot sleep, I toss and turn, my own body worked into its own clammy state. My psyche is on hyper drive, horrible thoughts floating in and out randomly. I am a tortured soul! I angrily turn to the Lord, and in my desperate state, I ask that He fix things, do the things I expect Him to do. As my sleepless night continues, I come to realize that God is not going to do things exactly as I want Him to, or as I try to direct Him to. I want to be in control, can't He see that?

I am exhausted and filled with a growing sense of dread. Just the same, I come to understand that I am never going to be in control, and that I need to turn this all over to the One that truly is in control. In the wee hours of the morning, I roll away from Natalie, tears roll gently, and I do just that. I turn it all over to my Lord and Savior, Jesus. "Into Your hands my Lord, I place the one I love, and may thy will be done, Amen!"

With that Amen, I feel a kind of tranquility come to me, and oddly, the anger and turmoil I have been hanging on to begins to subside. I am not sure if it is my struggle here in this moment, or if it is my accumulated frustration, but it feels good to turn it over and let it go. With that newfound sense of peace, I slowly fall into an in-between state of sorts, where I am neither asleep nor awake. I am not sure how long I stay in this state, but the pump sounds, and the game continues.

It was a tough night, and I am afraid the commute today will be just as tough. I am not sure I can get us to Boston safely in my sleep-deprived state. I help Natalie get dressed, and as beat as she is, she is determined to look her best. Knowing this is the end of the 72 hours seems to give her a newfound sense of energy. Maybe a bit of a celebration is called for. We made it, and I was not so sure we would. It has been the longest 72 hours of my life! Natalie is weak though and counts on me to steady her tired and worn body. I catch a bit of her encouraged spirit, and find myself determined to make it back and forth to Boston in one piece.

The results from the daily blood draw are not favorable, no surprise there. The chemo has surely beaten her down. Inside and out! Dr. Weston is concerned enough that she decides it is time to admit Natalie. Hallelujah! Time to bring Natalie comfort and serenity. Time to rest her tormented body. I have wanted this for days now. While I am relieved that Natalie will be hospitalized, she is going to be in Boston! Wow! Here we go!

Natalie is moved into a room quickly, and the nurses begin their work to bring her comfort. I am torn! Do I stay in Boston with Natalie, or go home and be with the boys? No easy answer! Natalie notices my quiet mood and senses my internal struggle; maybe she can read it on my face. She smiles that easy smile of hers, and says, "I am going to be ok now. You need to go and be with the boys. Do something fun! I'm thinking pizza." I am uneasy. Not sure I want to… should I really leave? "Bob, I am planning on going to a quiet, restful place, please… go be with the boys." I go to her, kiss her forehead, happy that it is not as clammy and warm. She grabs my hand, and squeezes it and says, "I love you, Bob." I squeeze her hand back. "I love you, Natalie. I'll see you tomorrow!"

It is late afternoon, and the boys are all outside playing with the neighbors as I pull in the driveway. It is great to see them enjoying a warm summer day. They come running to the car! They immediately notice Natalie missing, and I watch the joy on their faces slip away. "Hey, guys! Guess what? Mom is doing great, and get this, the doctors have some new medicines they want to give her that will get her home to us quickly. But she needs to be in this hospital for a few days." I stretch the truth a bit, but I sense the boys' need for words of comfort. It is what it is, sadly so!

"Hey guys, can I interest anyone in a quick road trip to the park?" Smiles greet me, and I feel alive in the moment. Car doors fly open, and we are ready to make a jaunt to one of their favorite parks. While I cannot return to the innocence of my childhood, there is absolutely nothing preventing me from being a child here in this moment. I join the boys for some of the fun at the park, and we all hit the swings, slide and climbing tower, me right alongside the boys, my boys. It is so great to see them smile! Better than that, it feels good to smile. I continue to play like a crazy man, tag and all. They love it. For a moment, I am able to forget about the monster. It feels weird, though, like a part of us is missing. A part of us is missing. A horrible thought jumps into consciousness, and I push it away, far away. I will not think about it! I will not! It has no place in my world!

Inspiration ....

Have I not commanded you? Be strong and courageous. Do not be terrified; do not be discouraged, for the Lord your God will be with you wherever you go.

Joshua 1:9

Reflection ....

I am struggling to hang on... my environment changing by the minute... life and death hang in the balance. It is scary stuff, and it is tricky for me to manage my perspectives and outlook. As soon as I get my heart around where I am, things change. As things change, so does my spirit, not always in the best way.

Natalie is positive! Here she is, in the heat of the battle, bombs bursting in air, her body being ravaged, and yet she easily smiles, no matter her circumstance. She has every reason to complain, to make things miserable for others, yet... she... does... not. Not a sound! Not a single peep!

Natalie is in this to win, and understands that wallowing around in a pool of self-pity is not going to change things, or make for different outcomes. So, she stays strong, not creating a dark world for those around her. Her perspective inspires me, but I do wonder how she can maintain it, without fail, when things so often go sideways. Her powerful, unwavering faith, keeps her spirit strong, knowing that together with God, she can beat the odds.

I think she knows that fear is her biggest obstacle and that the power of her fear is fueled by the power she chooses to give it. She seems to understand that there are choices to be made along the way. She knows she can be either fearful or courageous. Natalie chooses courageous! She takes hold of her fear and turns it into courage.

Me on the other hand, I tend to live in the land of the forlorn. Not sure why that is? If Natalie can courageously look into the eyes of her circumstance, why can't I? Is it a practical matter for me? Do I keep muddling along? Or do I choose to become more aware of my roadblocks and myself? If I do this, can I be more courageous? I want to be courageous, I do. I want to be ready for whatever lies ahead.

I wish there were an easy answer out there for me, one that would just pop into my brain. Of course, when it comes to self-reflection and self-awareness, there are never easy answers for me. I am going to have to turn inwardly, a scary thought, and go to a place where I can inspect self. Not an easy thing for me, especially here in the heat of the battle.

It doesn't come to me all at once. It comes in pieces and parts over time; just randomly, and my thoughts fuse around two key roadblocks to me being courageous, two demons. They are the demon of 'the unexpected' and the demon of 'what if?' I know, right? How do these prevent someone like me from being courageous?

Let's start with the unexpected. It seems that unexpected events, situations, and conditions change the natural order of things, my order. It appears that they catch me off guard. Things appear to be going along best they can, and I think I've got things under control, and then BAMMO! All of a sudden, I'm a shattered spirit, broken against the rocks of life because something unexpected has entered my realm. I flat out don't like it. It threatens the order of things. Am I fearful of the unexpected? Do I give it control, so much so, that I cannot put a courageous foot forward? Absolutely! I give the unexpected control.

If the demon of the unexpected isn't interfering with my courage, it seems that the other demon, what if, all too easily steps in. As the chemo pump pulsated, delivering another catastrophic blow to a ravaged soul, I wondered what if all this pain was in vain? What if the chemo isn't working? What if Natalie does not make it through the 72 hours of terror? What if missing so much work costs me my job? What if? Left untethered, these random what if thoughts race endlessly, all too easily owning my spirit, preventing me from being courageous. Do I give the demon what if control? You know it!

In this time of personal hardship, of adversity, of circumstance, allowing these demons to work in my realm creates a painful darkness for me. Dark spirits circle, and own me! I wonder if this current circumstance has been placed before me willfully? Is it an initiation of sorts? Am I being tested and strengthened for some new kind of circumstance, something that has yet to cross the radar of my life? Am I being prepared for something worse down the road? The thought sends a shiver down my spine! Is my ability to control my demons, and my ability to walk forward courageously, going to be important for some future battle?

It seems that my courage is tied to my ability to manage my personal demons. In understanding what these demons are, it is easier to understand how they might work to control and manipulate the human spirit, my spirit. If I am going to conquer my demons, then I must walk in courage. I need to be a brave spirit and meet my circumstance, whatever it is, and head on! Is all of this then, really about my personal perspectives? Is courage for me, all about what I do with the circumstances I am handed in this game of life, and my ability to walk it forward beating the demons back?

Yes, the circumstances that have become my life suck. No question about it, they do. I do want to be courageous, and I have come to realize that I can walk forward in courage when circumstances arise or shift. I must manage my spirit when the demons show up. I own the attitude, and I get to decide what that attitude will be. Will it be one of courage? My answer… to walk forward in courage!

I know that the blackest of nights will give way to the brightest of days. I know now that my courage is tied to my ability to manage my demons. I get to decide if my circumstance is a harbinger of the dawn or the mournful call of the night.

Will it be as easy? There's only one way to find out.

BOOK 4

Uncertainty

Shadows

I stand, unconscious of life about me
I look deep into my heart
I see an image, dark and threatening
I beckon it forward, calling it into a view
Is it a thought, a memory?
I catch a glimpse as it dashes wildly about me
Is it pieces and parts of a dream
The dull and shapeless visage hides
Afraid to show itself
It makes a soft sound, a whisper
Letting me know it is real
But I cannot quite grasp it
I want to reach in, to lay my hands upon it
It shifts haltingly in the shadows of my consciousness
Is it the mighty hammer of fate?
It dances illusively along the recesses of my mind
Suddenly a deep desperation hits my soul
Pounding relentlessly against a life of certainty
Tears spring painfully from my eyes
And immediately I know
That I am in a battle against an unparalleled storm
It grows tenacious and more energetic
Life as I knew it was at risk
My world is tumultuous, hammering my very being
It is made up of wild feelings
Broken promises and shattered hopes
The battle for life does not wait
It has already begun

By: Robert Mapes

The Story ....

It is an early morning, and the house is quiet, eerily so. Sunlight floods the family room; sunrays seemingly dance and lift my spirit. Since Natalie's discharge from the Cancer Center, things have been a bit on the low-key side, and I like this return to some kind of normal. Having Natalie at home, alert and aware has been a delight to all. It is recovery time; strength will be needed before the big guns arrive on the battle scene. Me, I have been in the business of crazy for so long now that I find myself unsettled. How is that for crazy? The quiet ends today. It is time to head back to Boston and load up the battleship for an all out offensive.

Natalie's treatments have been extremely expensive; such is the fight for life. Expenses are adding up quickly. I am worried about our ability to survive financially. All this deductible, co-pay and coinsurance stuff. I had no idea and suspect that most people don't until they find themselves in this same place. Costs can run away pretty quickly! Where is that Aflac Duck when you need him?

Christina is busy at work on the fundraiser, and I appreciative all of her hard work and the work of the team she has put together. I feel bad that I can't squeeze in one more thing, and actively participate in the fundraising. I am just too busy fighting the fight.

The groaning of the tires on the highway is almost hypnotic. I have to work to keep myself in the moment as we journey into Boston. The few weeks reprieve we've had should have made me ready for the jaunt. I thought I'd be well rested by now. Must be tied to my lack of sleep from last night. Couldn't sleep... I am worried about the upcoming treatments.

It is a warm summer day in Boston, and the glowing sunshine feels good on my skin. We play like a real couple, and find our way to Faneuil Hall for lunch, choosing to sit outside at a small café. Looking at her, you would never know how much she has endured, or that she is even in the fight for life. The past two weeks have been kind to her. Her smile delights the world around her. It is nice to be a regular couple enjoying lunch on a fine Boston day.

Reality hits home as we pass through the automatic doors of the Cancer Center. The antiseptic smell hits me head on, and a bad vibe settles around me. I try to shake it, but to no avail. We find our way to Dr. Weston's office, where the nurse does a blood draw and rather casually mentions that Natalie will need to have a heart ultrasound today. Whoa! Where did that come from? This is the first I hear of this. I look to Natalie; she seems as confused as I am. Are we not asking the right questions along the way? Is it that we don't know the right questions? What is going on?

I reach for the old panic button but decide I might be better served by dialing my reaction back a bit. I recognize my demon friend the unexpected, and realize that I need to walk forward courageously. In spite of my inner turmoil, I ask the looming question of the nurse. "Why do we need to do a test of Natalie's heart?" The answer shared so matter-of-factly. "Natalie has been receiving aggressive chemo and these agents have the potential to create heart damage. We need to assess Natalie's heart for possible damage."

What? Heart damage? Surely I would have remembered something like this. We would never have embarked, unknowingly, into a world where a heart could be damaged, would we? No way! This is a news flash! OK, get a grip here! It seems there will be no way around this one. I look to Natalie, and I can see the panic in her eyes. Tears dance eloquently down her delicate cheekbone, falling softly to her blouse. I hold my demon at bay. Not today demon, you are not welcome here.

We follow the nurse rather aimlessly; we are off to meet the next great challenge head on. The tech administers the test, and it seems to take forever, like two days. I feel life hanging in the balance. In a moment of grace, with the promise of our golden silence, the tech tells us her interpretation of the test. While it is obvious that Natalie's heart has been damaged, it is under the maximum threshold. Halleluiah! Thank the good Lord, and thanks to that thoughtful tech. I don't think she realizes how much she just did for a couple of panicked fools. Or maybe she does.

By the time we wind our way through the cold and septic corridors and get to Dr. Weston's office, the test results are officially available. She excitedly gives us the official word; we are good to go with the next step in the treatments. It is a joyous moment! I cannot believe, though, that I am celebrating what I know will be the continuation of more chemo horrors. Although fearful, I know I must keep my demons at bay, and focus on the battle before me. The evil monster cannot prevail. Not this time!

We walk away with a date as we journey toward victory. Treatment will begin on July 5th. This means that Natalie will have to be at the treatment facility on July 4th for check in! So we will be celebrating July 4th in true revolutionary style, with a battle under way against a very different kind of tyrant! Like our forefathers, we plan to be the victor against a tyrant.

Our six-month journey into the world of cancer begins this warm July day, by saying goodbye, to the three little loves of our life. Natalie down on her knees, hugging each loving spirit, hanging on for dear life. A thought catches in my throat. I swallow it back, and get down on my knees and go in for a group hug. Everyone holds onto the other as if a lifeline. William, with a tight hold around Natalie's neck, has his face buried, trying to capture her essence. Slowly, we come unglued, both physically and emotionally. Tears slide naturally from Natalie's eyes. Without a word, she turns from the boys, the pain evident in her every move. She quietly heads to the car.

Our commute into Boston is a quiet, somber affair. We are both deep in thought, me wondering if we made the right choice, not that we really had one. The thoroughfares are free and clear, it seems as everyone is already celebrating this great Independence Day. What is it about the holidays and us?

Check-in at the facility is just as easy as the commute, and we are done quickly. Novel concept! There is still some bright sunlight, Natalie is feeling good, and knowing what is headed our way, I feel the need for an adventure. We head out of the facility, looking for a quick bite to eat. Natalie's hand feels good in mine as we walk the streets. Without warning, Natalie's foot becomes entangled in the sidewalk, and as we move forward… her foot stays behind. Her balance is thrown off, creating a free fall… and Bammo! Everything moves in slow motion. I try to grab her before her fall, but I am not quick enough. She is down!

I drop down to help her up. She is weaker than I realize. Her head has cracked the hard concrete, blood oozing out an open wound, pouring down her face. The guy, who becomes queasy at the sight of blood, tries to figure out how to control the bleeding. As panic begins to settle in, a Good Samaritan comes out of nowhere, offering us assistance. This angel quickly loads us into his car and gives us a quick lift back to the Cancer Center. Not the adventure I had in mind.

Luckily, Dr. Weston is on call and sees Natalie immediately. She cannot believe our bad luck. Dr. Weston is concerned about head trauma since it was a free fall. She gives Natalie a good work over before putting stitches in her head. Things go sideways when Dr. Weston suggests that chemo might not be an option tomorrow, Natalie's open wound could be a deal breaker. Me, I am beating myself up for letting this happen on my watch. I feel like I have let the world down.

My dismay, visible in my face, calls out to Natalie. She catches my eye, gently takes my hand in hers, and smiles warmly. "You've been by my side every step of the way, helped me through all of this. There was not a single thing you could have done

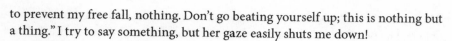

to prevent my free fall, nothing. Don't go beating yourself up; this is nothing but a thing." I try to say something, but her gaze easily shuts me down!

It is reassuring to know that mankind can be thoughtful and that there are good Samaritans in the world that will drop everything when they see someone in distress. Our Good Samaritan saw the disaster unfold, and did not miss a beat in reaching out and helping. An important lesson revisited today. If only we could rally all of mankind around this simple story from the Bible, what a wonderful world this would be. To care, honestly and lovingly, for one another. Good-bye, hate and ridicule, hello, love and kindness. Could it be that easy?

With a crack in her head, Natalie is surprisingly approved to begin treatment. She is quickly moved to a room so the chemo can begin. I am there when the poisonous drip starts, and while I am happy to be in this place, I am not so sure I am ready for the fallout! Aggressive chemo… I can only imagine what it is going to look like at the end of the 48 hours!

I have arranged to work periodically out of our Boston Office. Since it is just a quick mass transit ride away, I head off to work after visiting with Natalie, who is hanging on in spite of the horrific toxins plaguing her body. Maybe I have been worried about nothing? The nurses assure me that they have this thing! I know they do. They are all so kind and caring, and it brings me a sense of serenity. I am still trying to balance all of the stuff in my life, work being one of them, which is always a struggle, even on a good day. I had thought my life before cancer was all consuming. How little I knew.

The company CFO, Edward, happens to be in the office and asks to meet with me. He is a great guy, very caring, and always asks about Natalie, the boys and how things are going. I can't ask for more than that, to work with and for people that care so much for their team. And it was with this kind of compassion that he talks to me about some strategic changes the company is making.

Edward explains that the company is going to undergo a huge consolidation of their smaller, locally operated servicing facilities into larger, regional operations. That said, the smaller facility I am responsible for in Plymouth, New Hampshire, would be consolidated. The company's future operating state included five larger, metropolitan based operations. Edward goes on to explain to me how valued I am to the company, and that they want to keep me as part of the team… but it will definitely mean a move for the family and me. Did not see this one coming, and the potential impact on my life is just numbing!

While I am being knocked off my rocker at work, Natalie is being knocked out of hers. The poisonous drip continues, a reminder of the dire nature of the battle. Round the clock chemo is hard to imagine, and I shudder to think what these poisons will do to her ravaged body. I remember that I need to focus on the goal... destroy any cancer cells that survived the last go around, eradicating them from our world.

My debilitating work day ends, and I take the Boston T Commuter Rail to the Cancer Center. I plan to spend time with Natalie, maybe even the night. Natalie is sort of awake when I arrive, and smiles easily when she sees me. It gives me an immediate boost! Barely above a whisper, she says, "Hey Hon, so far so good. Not much vomiting. But I am so tired. Not sure what day we are in." I smile at her and gingerly kiss her forehead.

Her forehead is warm, hot almost; my lips tingle at the touch. The chemo seems to be creating an intense heat within her. She is flush and red. I reach out to touch her soft face, and I can feel heat coming from her body. Not a fever kind of heat, just a heat that is screaming... Please, don't do this to me.

Natalie seems to float to another time and place, so I saddle on in for the long haul. Nausea sets in, despite all of the wonder drugs. Natalie retreats to her special place, just trying to get from one minute to the next. Eventually, she comes back into the moment and tries to have a conversation with me. It is tough, though. Her thoughts are disjointed and disconnected. I can't help but wonder if the chemo is affecting her mind. It seems to me that each round of chemo steals pieces of her.

I decide to spend the night in the recliner in Natalie's room. Torture device is more like it. Talk about uncomfortable! Night slowly becomes day just the same and I decide to work just a few hours in the morning, allowing me to spend most of the day with Natalie. I am anxious about this company consolidation and how it is going to impact my world, our world! I feel as if all of this stuff is just going to eat me alive from the inside.

The sound of pumps, machines, and alarms greets me when I return to the cancer center from work. Natalie is sound asleep, and as I peek in, I see her looking oddly peaceful, a bit of an angel draped in the white sheets gathered around her. I want to wake her, but think better of it, and quietly find my way to the recliner. I plop myself down and saddle up for the long haul.

I try to numb my mind, push all of the turmoil off to the back recesses, and calm my spirit. The nurse comes in to check on Natalie and breaks my reverie. She tells me that Natalie is well medicated and stable, a good thing considering the toxins entering her body. I am thankful there is no power vomiting taking place, at least at the moment, or any of those dreadful convulsions. I settle on in for a bit and stay with her until the wee hours of the morning. I somehow lose the sense of time.

Eventually, the walls start to close in on me; the hospital smells overwhelming and controlling. Forgetting the hour, I decide that I need to get out of the recliner, and head to the boarding house, my home away from home. Home, until we get the all- clear to return to New Hampshire. As I walk along the Boston Streets, I find myself enjoying the quiet summer's eve. Although it is a tad bit balmy, it is nice to be outside and in the land of the living. I look to the heavens and find a beautiful starlit night. I sense God's presence, and pray for Natalie's strength and good health, that together we win the battle, and celebrate victory together with Jesus. This moment grounds me and confirms that there is a greater power in our lives and that God is in control, not me. A tough reality check, I want to be the one in control!

I rest fitfully, and rejoin the land of the living as the sun breaks the horizon, and peaks into my small room. I'll spend the day with Natalie; we are closing in on the 48-hour mark! It is bright, a rather warm summer morning. As I work my way from the boarding house, I stop and buy cards for each of the boys. I want to send them something; it is so hard to be away! I feel I am missing so much of their lives, I know it, and it pains me. It is all about choices, tough as they are at times.

Natalie is kind of, sort of, awake when I arrive. She tells me the day, so far, has been a good one by our new standards. What a difference it makes having the right team of caregivers. It is hard for me to imagine what is really happening. As the chemo goes in, it begins the hunt for fast dividing cancer cells. A good thing! At the same time though, it is also destroying all other healthy fast dividing cells. Scary notion! Makes me wonder if all of this will be in vain? I realize the slippery slope I am approaching and immediately escort this demon out of my realm.

Tonight is going to be a big night! It is the night of the Natalie Mapes Cancer Benefit Fund Raiser, taking place back in Plymouth. All kinds of people have come forward with donations and gifts, many of which are homemade and very personal and special. How I wish that we could be in attendance. Timing did not work in our favor.

Throughout the course of these grueling 48 hours, food trays come and go, all of them untouched. Even when Natalie comes out of her somewhat catatonic state, the last thing on her mind is food, fearing what goes down will all too quickly come back up! I bring her Gatorade and keep it on hand in the room. I can't help noticing how quickly she is shrinking, a mere image of the woman she was just months ago.

I call my Dad after the fundraiser and hear all about the event. The boys were resplendent in their matching jackets and ties, and so well behaved. They did their Mom proud. My Dad told me that they raised over $40K, and I am immediately blown away. The goodness of mankind, and the willingness to care for others, it restores my belief that we can beat the evil monster at his own game!

The Benefit Fund news is so encouraging that I quietly share it with Natalie; she smiles easily, especially when I speak of the boys. Her face is flush and I can see her fighting to stay in the present. She slides back into her catatonic state, leaving me alone with my thoughts. I feel overwhelmed. I want to be a whole family again. I don't want to be in Boston, not by a long shot. I miss the boys, my life, my everything. I find my way to a quiet stairwell, and lean up against the wall, my head falling back. The medicinal smells are overpowering, even here. A surge of emotions hits me square upside the head, and I found myself having my own pity party, alone and overwhelmed, in the stairwell!

Suddenly, the door to the stairwell creaks a bit. Dang, wouldn't you know it; someone is going to find me falling apart in the stairwell. I look up with sad eyes, to find a fellow soldier in this game of life, his own tears running like a river. I am not sure what to do or what to say. Some kind of force propels me forward, and I say, "It will all be okay, I promise, it will all be okay. Know you are not alone, not by a long shot." We do an awkward man hug, and as he pulls away, he says a simple, "Thank you."

As he leaves the stairwell to face his own uncertainties, I realize that I am not the only one journeying this road, and no matter what comes from all of this, I have to do something with what I am learning about myself, and about this game of life. Maybe I can help others!

Night drags into day, and I lose track of time. I feel trapped, both by my circumstance and the hospital environment. The recliner, a chair designed in some alternative universe as a torture tool, adds to my miserable state. Just the same, we make it, finally, to the 48-hour mark. It is with quiet fanfare that the infusion begins, T-cells, now the key to Natalie's survival. It seems as if many gather for the big event. Natalie is lucid, best she can be, and she knows the deal. She smiles, and it warms up the entire room, and my heart, all at once. I say a private hallelujah, thank God for getting us this far, and ask for His healing hand and a restoration of Natalie's health.

I ask the staff how long it will be before we know if things are working as planned. They explain that it really depends on the patient and that we should see the presence of baby stem cells in her blood sometime in the next 48 hours. It seems the worst of this round is over, and now Natalie is in recovery mode. The staff encourages me to go to work for a bit, to join the outside world. They promise to call me if anything seems to be going down the wrong path.

It is early afternoon as I begin my return to Natalie's side. I jump off the T and run into a store and grab some Gatorade and premade Jello, thinking a little gift might bring her joy. For good measure, I pick up a Kit Kat bar, one of our favorite chocolate kinds of treats. It is a little something we have always done for each other, just a simple gesture of love. No time like the present for that! Natalie is somewhat alert when I get to her and is happy to see me. I surprise her; she smiles easily, kisses my hand tenderly, and eagerly goes for the Kit Kat Bar. I think this is a good sign.

As minutes become hours, and hours become days, the miracle of the human body unfolds before us. Natalie's body, as predicted, begins producing the necessary kind of blood cells. She nibbles on food and becomes stronger. The physical restoration of the human body is amazing. I wonder why emotional recovery is so much more difficult. I have no answer.

Discharge arrives without much fanfare or announcement, after a tumultuous week of highs and lows. I am ready to vacate my cramped room at the boardinghouse; the tiny single bed and the shared bathroom help me appreciate my many blessings. I am ready for a bit of space and place that is mine. To be a whole family again is almost too good to be true. We have all endured, and come a long way these past seven months. Victory is within our grasp!

The homecoming is a grand event! We barely make it in the driveway, and the boys are out the door and into their Mom's arms. Tired and beat as she is, their spirit lifts her up! I am at a loss, and can't quite describe how this feels. I have this newfound internal glow, the kind that inexplicably touches your heart and warms your body. We all move in mass to the house and get Natalie to her recliner. A great homecoming!

We settle into a somewhat normal routine. Our wonderful church family has planned a fun-filled fundraiser, an Ice Cream Social. On point is a wonderful

Christian spirit, Carli, who has been working tirelessly to help ensure our family is well cared for and is helping us prepare for any unexpected treatment costs in the battle against the monster.

It is a beautiful August night, just perfect for ice cream. We gather at the gazebo in the center of town, and it seems as if the entire community has come out to support us. Natalie and I mix with the crowd, feeling like celebrities. We have a chance to thank so many for their help and support. The boys play with friends and other children and are all smiles. The highlight of my night is watching Natalie eat a bit of ice cream. The demons that once haunted her are now just a distant memory. I dread their return, though, and can see them drifting our way. They beckon from both the past and the future.

I jump back into the world of the living and return to work on a regular basis. I know it is going to be short-lived. While my company has been so gracious to me during these many months, I want to be sure I continue to deliver value. I am going to need my job more than ever, especially the health benefits, the ones giving Natalie access to the treatments and care she needs.

A home health nurse visits Natalie several times a week, just to keep a check on blood levels, to make sure everything is staying in a normal range. As with many things in life, time passes all too quickly, and as we head toward the end of August, we find ourselves getting the green light for the next treatment. We will return to Boston for the final monster beat down! While I get the science behind what is going to happen, I can't help but wonder just how tough this is going to be, and how any one person can endure this kind of beating and live to share the tale. Especially the one I love. "Lord Jesus, it is into your hands I place my love. Thy will be done. Please Lord, let that will be one of victory. Amen."

The last and final treatment is here. Not sure I am ready. Dr. Weston informs us that as a result of Natalie's tremendous weight loss, the little waif that is now my wife is going to need an additional port, or access point, through which she can receive nutrition. The additional port is inserted into Natalie's neck, and with all of these lines coming and going out of her body; my ladylove looks like a scientific experiment or a sci-fi movie gone wrong. Something makes me think that this round of the beat down is going to be particularly rough.

As we begin day one, Natalie is heavily medicated with a potpourri of drugs that will keep her just below waking consciousness. The plan is to keep her body stable and her mind restful. There are many many visits from the nurses during the beginning of the treatment. Everyone is closely monitoring her vitals. I sit quietly in a recliner designed to be anything but comfortable. While I wish there were a different way through this, I am confident we are going to win the battle and declare victory.

I saddle up and settle in for the long haul. It is so quiet, except for the steady drip of those horrible, but necessary poisons. For three consecutive days, it seems more of a punishment than a cure. Natalie is well cared for, her pain well managed, and her nausea under control, for now. Meals show up as scheduled, Natalie is not interested. The nurses offer them to me since I have been hunkered down. I nibble a little bit here and there; I don't have much of an appetite either. I am anxious; the thought of food makes my stomach jump.

It is day two, and daylight slowly trickles into the darkened hospital room, announcing the beginning of a new day. I realize I need to move, the hospital room consuming me, and I feel so grungy. I head to the boardinghouse so I can grab a quick shower and change up my clothes. The bright sunlight is nearly blinding after 24 hours in a darkened hospital room. If there is such a thing as a vampire, I decide I would not be a good one. I need sunlight… it warms my soul.

Cabin fever hits me hard. As we begin day 3 of our harrowing journey, I feel the walls closing in on me. I need to escape before they consume me whole. I head to the boardinghouse once again, and once there, turn on the small black and white television and catch some national news. The newscasters are foaming at the mouth, *Andrew*; a powerful Category 5 hurricane, is hammering the state of Florida. There are early shots of the devastation, and it is incomprehensible. It is almost too much to absorb. My heart breaks for all those impacted by the storm. As I watch the raw footage, I can't help but compare this storm to the horrible storm that is taking place inside Natalie's body, and the ravages that will be left in the wake of the storm.

As day 3 closes out, the doctors come into Natalie's room en mass. Dr. Weston begins with, "How is my favorite patient?" Natalie pulls herself from her groggy haze and says in a light voice, "Good." The doctor then asks, "How are things going and how are you feeling?" "I am doing just fine doctor," a small lilt in her voice. That's my Natalie, always thankful, and the last one to complain about anything. The doctor smiles, and says, "You probably don't understand what a treat it is to work with a patient who is so understanding and appreciative. There aren't many." These kind words bring a quick smile to Natalie's face. I am proud of this courageous woman, who appreciates every day as the gift it truly is.

The doctors do their final evaluation before they hang the bone marrow! It is a quiet affair as they do. I am not sure what I was expecting. I thought there would at least be a parade of some kind! Nothing really happens, so after some time passes, I bid my love adieu and head back to the boardinghouse for a shower and a nap. I have been up forever, or so it seems anyway, and I am beat. Beat by all of it!

I return to my post feeling a bit better after a few hours of sleep and a shower on my side. I suit up at the hospital with a gown, gloves and such, and as I push the door open to Natalie's room, I feel the swish of air rushing in my direction, brushing against my face. It is chilly, and it sends a chill of its own down my spine. The room is eerily quiet. The bone marrow bag is gone, and now the waiting game begins! Natalie is still well medicated, but greets me, just the same, with a smile.

I sit by her side and hold her delicate little hand. It is so white, almost translucent, and a bit chilly to the touch. This is a different sensation. Usually, right after chemo, her body is warm to the touch, almost hot. I am not sure what this chilly feeling means. All I know is that the hand I am cradling is weakened and frail. It saddens me to think about all she has been through. She looks my way, smiles, and asks, "When can I see my little boys, I miss them so?" Don't we all.

As dark spirits ravage the land, Natalie's blood levels tank, and it is time for crazy to kick in. A transfusion of blood plasma and platelets begins, but the platelet transfusion does not take, which is not a good thing I am told. The plan, try another infusion of platelets. It does not take this time around either. They do a DNA matching, hoping for a different outcome, and work with the blood bank to find a good match.

A match is found in Pennsylvania, and when the platelets arrive, the nurse hangs the bag, the whitish fluid owning the moment. The platelets go in pretty quickly. We need success this time out; Natalie's body is now in a precarious place. The news is good; the matched platelets bring about the much-needed improvement in lab results. A huge crisis averted, praise God!

Dr. Weston finds me in the hall, and suggests, given Natalie's improving condition, that I get the boys to Boston so they can see their Mom, and more importantly, so their Mom can see them. This lifts my spirits; I can only imagine what it is going to do for Natalie.

My brother Matt and friends Adam and Becky bring the boys to Boston, and we all stay at a local hotel. I am excited for Natalie to see the boys. Although she is still in isolation, the boys will be able to see her through the window in her hospital door.

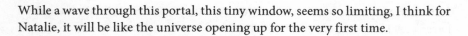

While a wave through this portal, this tiny window, seems so limiting, I think for Natalie, it will be like the universe opening up for the very first time.

The boys have messages and pictures for their Mom, and Ryan and Jake sweetly hold them up to the window on their tippy toes. Heartwarming! I am not sure who needed to see whom the most. It seems as if Ryan and Jake understand the reasons behind the veiled view, but this stuff just does not make much sense to William. No surprise! Got to be hard for him to wrap his little boy heart around all of this.

I pick William up and hold him to the portal connecting his world to his Mom's. He waves his little boy hand to Natalie, and when he sees her, he starts to cry like a little boy might for his Mommy. I could see his Mommy crying on the other side of the portal, just like a Mommy might for her little boy. It is like bridging two different physical planes within the universe. Just the same, I can see a glow in Natalie's eyes. Bringing the boys here was the right thing to do.

While Natalie rests, Matt, Adam, Becky and I take the boys into the city. I feel as if I have rejoined the land of the living. We traverse the Freedom Trail, visit some historic sites, eat out and watch the boys swim like a bunch of fish in the hotel pool. For these brief moments, I pretend like my life is normal, and I push the constant threat of disaster away. I need a respite, and this chance to be with my kids is it.

Like so many things in life, the good has to come to an end. So it is with the weekend. It is hard to say goodbye to the boys; I don't want them to go. We go to the hospital and are surprised to see Natalie up and about, best she can. Ryan and Jake put their hands on the window, and Natalie places her weary hand on the other side. She then smiles down at William. I bring him up to the window, and as I hold him, a single tear rolls down Natalie's cheek. She smiles at William, and mouths, "I love you." We watch as she returns to her bed, where she collapses in sheer exhaustion. I am not sure if it is physical or emotional exhaustion. Might be both.

The next day brings good news. Natalie's body is beginning to produce blood cells. Praise the Lord! This is the moment we have been waiting for. The moment in time that said that Natalie has made it through the treatment and is about ready to come out the other side in one piece. The most exciting thing! Goodbye isolation and good riddance to all of that stuff associated with it. We make an event out of it. I say, "Goodbye mask," and drop the one I am wearing into the garbage! "Goodbye gloves," and drop them next into the garbage. "I never want to see you guys again! Nothing personal, but I am over you!" Natalie smiles.

I find harmony and sleep in that horrible, clunky chair. I feel a kind of serenity I haven't felt in weeks. I am encouraged and looking forward to Natalie's discharge. I know we still have a long way to go, yet I remain encouraged just the same. Why shouldn't I be? I think to myself. All indicators seem favorable!

I return to work for a few days in the Boston office. Everyone there, and in the Regional Operation I manage, continue to carry the weight, allowing me to focus on the fight with Natalie. Everyone is genuinely concerned about Natalie, the boys and me and asks all kinds of questions about the latest part of our journey. It is so reassuring knowing just how much they care. They are a special group of people, and they all mean the world to me in this crazy moment in time.

The other emerging crisis in my world is this notion of consolidation and relocation. As if I don't have enough to worry about, I have this in the mix now. Can't even begin to wrap my brain around it! The company has offered me 3 locations to consider: Boston, Detroit, and Dallas/Fort Worth. I struggle to find the right words to tell Natalie, who is in the fight for her life. How I wish we could get through the battle with the monster before we have to deal with something else. It looks like the Lord has a different plan in motion for us. I am not so sure I like His plan.

The doctors want Natalie to gain some weight before discharging her. I do not see that happening anytime soon. I break the rules and sneak in some of Natalie's favorite foods, especially things in her favorite food group, chocolate. One day I pick up a sweet card and a couple of Kit Kat Bars, and surprise her. She takes both of my hands in hers, smiles that smile, and says, "Thanks, couldn't have made it this far without your love and devotion. Thanks for being you." We hug, and she holds on tightly. I can feel her frailty.

Discharge comes without a ticker tape parade, but the news is music to my ears just the same. It is time to say goodbye to the tests, ports, blood transfusions and waiting games. Time to say goodbye to the world of cancer and claim our victory! Ahhh, what a sweet notion it is. We will have to stay in the Boston area for at least another week. There is going to be daily blood draws, and if something were to happen, immediate access to the facility is a must. Natalie is going to join me in my little room in the boarding house. What a lucky gal! I know she will love the shared third-floor bathroom!

It is the beginning of fall in New England, and we decide to do a couples thing and drive a bit south to Plymouth, Massachusetts to watch the harvesting of cranberries from their bogs. It is a beautiful fall day, and it is nice to get away, if only for the day! The colors are just spectacular! It tells of the beauty and gift of life. While it is an easy outing by my standards, it tires Natalie out. It is obvious her recovery is going to take time, maybe a very long time.

It is with a heavy heart that I share the news with Natalie as we snack at a diner close to the boarding house. Keeping it bottled up has been killing me. She catches my eye, and I know now is the moment. "I have something I need to tell you, and it just might rock your world." She grabs my hand and says, "No matter, after all of this, all that we have been through, we can handle just about anything."

I give her all of the gory details, the consolidation, the impending relocation and the options available to us. After I finish, she looks me square in the eye, and says, "As long as we have each other, and the boys have their health, what difference does it make where we live, as long as we are alive to enjoy?" And there it is, just like that. All that matters is that we are together. I know she is right, but I sense the burden of the move is going to be mine to carry alone, and a heavy one it will be.

After a week of daily check-ins, we are finally given the all clear to return home. After being gone for over a month, the drive back is oddly reassuring, like we might get to experience a taste of normalcy, if only for a bit. I am so looking forward to having a bathroom I do not have to share with the masses!

God bless my parents! They stayed with the boys the entire time we were in Boston fighting the fight. You can see the joy in their eyes… well… maybe it is the relief I see. I know they are ready to escape the craziness and return to their once quiet lives in Maine. And it's well deserved.

We get back in the saddle pretty quickly and are off to the races. Natalie is really beaten down, and is feeling the effects of all the chemo on her heart. The loss of heart capacity is now playing out in our real lives. Fatigue seems to own her day. It is extremely frustrating as she was once so active. New day, new realities! So we decide to get some daytime help, someone who can help marshal the boys when they get home from school, maintain the house, and take care of important tasks like laundry.

October melts away quickly! It is over before it starts, or so it seems. We have been living normal lives and with it the return to normal affairs. With the shortened days of fall, come the longer nights, and a growing depression I just cannot seem to shake. Maybe everything is catching up with me now? Not sure, I can't pin it down. I just keep pushing myself forward, fearful of the past and all of the havoc it has played in my life. I feel a bit like Humpty Dumpty, and after the great fall, I am having a hard time getting all of the pieces of me back together again.

It is time for our follow-up visit with Dr. Davidsen, and she seems pleased with where Natalie is post-treatment and thought she looks great considering all she has been through. Then, she puts the moment of truth right out there. "Time to evaluate the disease and the effectiveness of the treatments. Time to declare your victory."

We are both anxious to finalize our destiny. Where will we be heading as a result of the consolidation? Dallas/Fort Worth is certainly the most promising to me. But what do I know about Dallas/Fort Worth, never been to Texas? It's tough to make such an important decision sight unseen. My company is quick to resolve that. I am going to fly to Dallas/Fort Worth to meet with Steve, the local key executive, and the business team. I'll also get a chance to visit local communities and schools, so that I can guide my family in the right direction.

As doctors collect and analyze test results, I am off to the great state of Texas! It is the beginning of November, and the blue skies and warm breezes are a surprise and a welcome treat. I marvel at how wonderful it feels. I think that Texas just might be a good thing for us, might even hold some promise. A tour of the area, a boat ride with Steve on a gorgeous lake, is all the convincing I need. I know this will put us all in a new land, but the promise of sun filled days is just too tempting to pass up. Maybe the promise of a new beginning is what entices me?

I call Natalie from Steve's boat and tell her of my boat ride in the warm Texas sun. She says she doesn't believe me. I don't believe me! It is just unbelievable! I describe the blue skies, the warmth, and how great it feels to be away from the gray and depressing feel of the northeast. Without me prompting, Natalie says, "We need to do this thing." Done! Don't need to convince me. I am already there! Goodbye New England and the cold, dreary days of winter.

The excitement of the Texas journey carries me forward into our Friday appointment with Dr. Davidsen. The news on all testing fronts is very positive and encouraging. Gone are all signs of cancer, and Natalie is declared *clean*. We are all high fiving and celebrating this great news. "But," said Dr. Davidsen, and all the joy I had been feeling starts shifting, and an uneasy feeling settles in my gut.

Dr. Davidsen goes on to state that there is still something visible at the primary cancer site. She takes us to a monitor, and throws the test up on the reader, and points to the area of concern. I can see it for myself. Unsettling! Dr. Davidsen

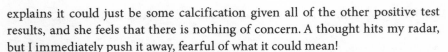

explains it could just be some calcification given all of the other positive test results, and she feels that there is nothing of concern. A thought hits my radar, but I immediately push it away, fearful of what it could mean!

Dr. Davidsen tells us to get ready to celebrate Thanksgiving in a really special way because Natalie is now a cancer survivor! How we have waited for this moment, to be cancer free, to be declared the victor! The monster is gone, GONE! But the word calcification keeps creeping into conscious thought, trying to wreak havoc, the demon what if, active at work! I lasso him and tie him down. He will not rain on my parade! Not today! I am going to focus on making Thanksgiving something really special. After all, we have so much to be thankful for!

Thanksgiving is a great holiday! We celebrate our reasons to be thankful, and give all the glory to God for getting us to this place! It feels different this Thanksgiving. So many unknowns last year! At least we know where we are and what we are up against, or so I try to convince myself. As November comes to a close, we turn our sights to Christmas. We do so with immense joy in our hearts.

Natalie tries to participate in Christmas best she can, but it is still tough for her to rally higher levels of energy. The damage to the heart has been significant; it seems a permanent reminder of the incredible journey we have made. Much of the Christmas burden falls my way. Compared to the burden already carried, it is a piece of cake. Getting all caught up in the spirit of Christmas does so much for my weary soul; it focuses me on the right things, the things that matter most. The birth of my Lord, Baby Jesus, and all that He has done to get us to this place. There is much to celebrate.

We are not slated to return to see Dr. Davidsen until after the first of the New Year, so we begin this New Year in a different way. Happy! Encouraged! Ready for new beginnings! The feelings of dread and fear from last year are all a distant memory. They have no place in this New Year. The reality of our changing world takes shape when the For Sale sign goes up in the yard. It is going to be a big year for us! Texas, here we come!

Inspiration...

When you pass through the waters, I will be with you; and when you pass through the rivers, they shall not sweep over you. When you walk through fire, you will not be burned; the flames will not set you ablaze.

Isaiah 43:2

Reflection ....

Moving pieces and parts, swirling all around me! I struggle to keep my head wrapped around all of it. Every time I think I am in control, something else enters the fray and knocks me off track. I am struggling to manage it all. The fight against the monster! Funding the cost of treatments! And now a move, thrown into the mix! Selling a house! Buying a new home! Moving a family to parts unknown! Seriously! How do I manage all of this and not lose myself in the process?

Is my struggle really about all the pieces of my life that are in flux? Or is there something else in play for me? Is this about control? That I want to control that which cannot be controlled? Is it that I want to control events and outcomes? Is it that I don't trust that God is in control? That I am not sure I am going to like all of the outcomes that He has planned for me? So far, His plans have not lined up with mine.

If God's goal is to bring me to my knees, I am there. The fight against the monster has been a heavy burden to carry. Now, a new challenge enters the mix right in the middle of the insanity that is my life. It hurts my head just to think of all of the complexities it will bring. On top of everything else... a move to a distant land... Texas.

Who would arrange this, surely not a loving and giving God? How can God expect me to balance all of these challenges? My little 'ole part of the world is already volatile, and now there is more trauma in the mix. I want all of this and I do mean all, just to go away, quietly disappear into the horizon. No harm, no foul. I don't have the fortitude to take all of this on!

God must see things differently than I do. Is it possible that God sees something in me that I don't see in myself? I knew there would be challenges as I journeyed through my life, and like any journey, I knew there would be potholes, obstacles, and roadblocks along the way. But I am beyond them. Suffering should not be part of the journey, part of the challenge. It is not fair. No one should have to suffer. Surely suffering is not part of the plan?

Do I need to stop trying to figure everything out? Do I need to relinquish control? Ah... there it is... that control thing again. Do I need to turn control over to God? Is God really in control? Does He have an aerial view that allows Him to see all of the variables and particulars about my world? My struggles? My fears? My life?

There is a reason for everything that happens in this life; so they say! I have heard this so many times at this point I could slug the next person that offers up that bit of wisdom. I know I need to trust, and give up on the control thing. But I want to know; I need to know, all the reasons why these things are happening in my life. How can I give up control if I don't understand the why? Why, a perspective that has haunted the ages, and certainly haunts my waking hours.

I know part of the struggle is the rate of speed at which things are happening. I get the science and the intellectual aspects of what is happening, and can easily assimilate these events, or facts. Unfortunately, I am wired with these things called emotions, and they don't seem to move at the same rate of speed. What happens? My overpowering emotions hold me hostage, locking me in a place, interfering with my thinking. Does my emotional state, interfere with ability to manage the events taking place in my life, seemingly out of control. Do my emotions interfere in my relationship with God?

So many questions are rolling around, and I never know what is coming next. Things keep coming my way, no end in sight. My life is out of control, my control. Am I afraid to let go, and give up control? Is loss of control my struggle? Has this fear become an enemy of my faith? Have I unconsciously given fear control of my life?

If fear owns my life... do I need to turn it over... put my trust in God... and truly relinquish control? Give up control, why is that so hard for me to do? Is it that I am afraid that the outcomes I pray for, are not the same outcomes my Lord has planned for me. Wow! There it is! I said it. If I relinquish control, I want a guarantee. I want to know life will play out my way. That Natalie will be well, that the move will be a good thing, that we will all adapt and survive the turmoil.

It seems my lack of trust is about outcomes I can't control. Does lack of control create too many uncertainties for me? Is uncertainty the big white elephant in the room? That the outcomes I hope and pray for are not certainties, nor will the outcome I want be the one I will see? Does the Lord have something different in the works for me? That's it! That notion makes my insides shake and my heart quiver. He would never cause me that kind of pain.

Surely not, right?

BOOK 5

Unbridled Fear

Contemplation..

Yesterday's Past

Day is long; night is cold
Fearful against morning daylight gold
Difficult at times to corral and mold
The days of yesterday's past
Work to hold me in a cast
Fearful life's blessings may not last
The quiet of a moment is but a trace
Of soulful melodies longing grace
The precipice of life, a frightening place
Angel wings making a precious sound
Dream of a day, darkness to be bound
Courage when sought, can be found
Fear's hallowing light a beam
Strength it hastens, losing steam
Providing life pieces of a dream
Wisdom and secrets to be told
Life's deep soul never to be sold
Harkens my belief against the cold
Life's internal light burning bright
Darkness becomes weak, losing might
For my will is a powerful sight
Choice is seems, is offered to me
Belief in self, a light to see
Courage over fearful circumstance, just maybe

By: Robert Mapes

The Story ....

The holidays slide right on by, and it is time for our January appointment with Dr. Davidsen. I am excited about this one. Coming off of a Christmas high, I feel like we have made our official return to normal life mode. And why should I be anything but uplifted? Our last appointment with the good doctor included the words *clean and remission*. I like how those words sound. They are music to my soul, a soul that had been ravaged by the storms of life.

Dr. Davidsen is very reserved as we enter her office. Odd I think, she was so excited and encouraged at our last appointment. I chalk it up to it being a rough day. I am sure she has them from time to time. This daily battle against cancer and all of the chaos it brings to the world just has to be a drain on the human spirit, her spirit.

After a brief seasonal catch-up, and a rather somber physical exam of Natalie, she jumps right in. "I have reviewed all of Natalie's recent test results with various doctors, including Dr. Weston. There is collective concern about the image we found in Natalie's left breast. While it may be nothing but some calcification, we believe Natalie should undergo a radical mastectomy, purely as a proactive measure."

I can't think. I can't move. I can't feel. A blow to the human spirit, it feels physical, a direct hit to the abdomen. Hard! I can feel the color draining away from my face... I am afraid to look Natalie's way! How can this be? My head falls back against the wall; I close my eyes, and my spirit looks to the heavens. Lord, please, not this. No...No...No... not this! Anything but this, after everything! No, Lord, please! Dr. Davidsen quickly brings me back to the present, stating that it would be best to move quickly on this, just in case. I think to myself, "Just in case of what?"

The good doctor suddenly becomes very scientific and describes what will be involved in the radical mastectomy. Suddenly, I feel like I am right back where we started. The joy of the past two months quickly evaporates and is replaced by sheer, unbridled fear. I try to corral my escalating emotions and reach for Natalie's hand. It is cool, damp. I can sense her turmoil, her fear running wild! I work to remain in the moment, determined to know specifically what is going to happen. I have some preconceived notions about a radical mastectomy, and it is frightening! I need to work with facts so that I can have a clear understanding. I listen, I learn, and it is not going to be pretty, ugh!

I am caught off guard. I think back to our last appointment with Dr. Davidsen, and I remember being slightly uneasy, unsettled actually. The notion of something remaining in the left breast just didn't sit right. Guess I had every reason to feel that way. Is it possible that Dr. Davidsen knew where this thing was headed? Is it possible she did not want us worrying about something so traumatic, both physically and emotionally, over the holidays? Was this a gift she gave us, a chance to have some joy?

Dr. Davidsen recommends a breast surgeon, Dr. Cotter, to do the surgery, and Dr. Monnix, to do the reconstruction surgery. Okay, slow it down here. I am trying to wrap my head around the idea of surgery, and now this notion of breast reconstruction. This is happening way too fast... so slow down here good doctor, slow down. Can I get a ref to blow the whistle here? I think I need a timeout... from life!

As I quietly walk to the car with Natalie, I feel the weight of the world slamming down on me! My head feels like it just might explode. I reach for Natalie's hand, the silence palpable. Our home is already on the market. We have a move date, April 1st. This thing, this radical mastectomy, is not on the radar, not part of the plan. What are we going to do? How will we ever survive this?

Natalie is so tough through all of this turmoil! Her family is her first priority. She is determined to get everyone ready for the move. As always, she is the witty one, uses humor to bring ease to those around her. Everyone is traumatized by the notion of the upcoming radical mastectomy. Not my gal. "It's not like it is my arm or anything," she says, "I really can live without it. Maybe I can make a deal with the reconstructive surgeon, get myself a new and improved set."

It is time for the pre-surgery mammogram. The tech has the previous tests to look at, so finding the little monster this go round is not as difficult. It is a quick test and it seems that the small mass in question has not grown, indicating perhaps, that the image is not cancer, and is just calcification. I should feel elated, but I am not feeling it. Everything but elated!

While all of this kind of chaos is going on, we have an offer on the house, and our plans for an April 1 move date fall eerily into place. Strikes me as odd how those things came together so easily. Is someone helping these things along? I wonder. Now we have to lock in on a surgery date. Yeowser! Not ready for that one! But then again, can you ever be ready?

Surgery day finally arrives, a mere three weeks before the big move. I try praying for a miracle, or wishing it all away. Neither seems to work, and I wonder where my God is in all of this. Dr. Cotter, the surgeon, said he expected the surgery to take about two hours or so. I lock in on this as my reality, and as Natalie and I say a strained farewell, I say to Dr. Cotter, "Bring her home safely."

I look out at the world from inside the hospital waiting room. It is a cold March day. The gray of winter dances on the horizon. I've been here before. Winter is desperately trying to dominate while spring tries to make its way in, with the promise of new beginnings. My spirit is not feeling the promise of anything, and it is in complete alignment with the long, gray and depressing world I know as winter. The piles of snow seem to stifle my spirit, imprisoning me.

I find myself up against the two-hour mark, and there is no doctor! Different hospital, same game! I glance around the room, wondering who here is struggling against the odds. I know I am not alone. My thoughts run wildly, and they take me to a dark place. I get myself up and start doing the pacing thing, which seems to unsettle those around me.

I take it to the halls, where Dr. Cotter finds me pacing nervously. He gives me a reassuring smile, grabs my elbow and says, "Let's find a room where we can sit and talk." Oh no no no! I've been here before. "Natalie is doing well, and she is resting comfortably in the recovery room." Whew! Maybe I am overreacting to things! The good doctor continues. "But, we found active cancer, and it is evident throughout many areas of Natalie's body."

I sit there, looking but not seeing, I have nothing. Words escape me! I am horrified! What does this mean? Mortality charts and survival rates randomly bounce through my consciousness. My eyes quickly fill to the brim and my head falls forward, chin hitting my chest. I feel defeated. I don't sob... I can't.

Dr. Cotter explains that he removed all of Natalie's breast tissue, all the way down to the muscle wall, and then did something called an auxiliary lymph node dissection. I am numb, and Dr. Cotter can see it on my face. He then goes on to explain this is a somewhat common practice when there is evidence of cancer. The lymph nodes removed all tested positive for cancer.

I am just numb. Words are still elusive. Dr. Cotter asks quietly, "Are you okay?"

My voice shakes a bit when I respond. "No... I'm not okay. This isn't fair. This is not how this is supposed to play out. None of this is supposed to play out this way!"

"Mr. Mapes, I am so sorry... and for what it is worth, I had hoped for a very different outcome."

I like the good doctor; he is so compassionate and caring. I get my heart together, and say, "Thanks for taking such good care of Natalie!" All I can get out. I need to get out of here! I can feel the walls, the world for that matter, closing in on me. I am feeling boxed in and wonder where God is in all of this? After all, I gave Him control.

As if knowing I was in trouble, my brother Thomas shows up at the hospital just as the doctor is leaving. He is a welcome sight! I am a blubbering mess. He knows something is up, and says, "Let's get out of here for a bit." We walk the cold, gray wintry streets of Concord. I am angry! I am mad! I am betrayed! I have so much anger bottled up inside me that I randomly start kicking snow and whatever else I can find as I sob uncontrollably.

I am embarrassed to be crying like a fool. I try to tell Thomas what is going on, to no avail. The poor guy can't understand half of what I am babbling! We continue our walk and eventually, I get my act together. I take a deep breath and launch into everything that has just happened. Thomas listens quietly, dealing with his set of emotions. I am so thankful he is here! Not sure how this would have played out of I had been on my own.

Thomas and I return to the hospital, and I head directly to the recovery room. I go to Natalie, unsure of what to say, or how to say it. Although she is still a bit groggy, she easily smiles at me through the meds and the pain. She grabs my hand; it is warm, tender, and she caresses it lovingly. Her eyes catch mine, and in a fuzzy whisper, she says, "Dr. Cotter has been by and he explained everything. I thought we won the war, but it looks like we live to battle another day." I lean into the bed, hugging her delicate frame, careful not to get all tangled up in the tubes, lines, and cords all around her. I whisper in her ear, "I love you. I am so sorry we are here in this place… that you are in this place. I would give my life to spare yours; I would. I don't want this; I don't want any of this."

I break away, and she smiles up at me, weakly, my hand still in hers. I can see her fighting to stay in the moment, the meds pulling at her mind. I mention that I plan to stay the night, and will work things out with the nurses. My ladylove has a different plan. I am to go home and be with the boys as we promised. I try convincing her otherwise, to no avail. Decision made! I hang around long enough to make sure she is in a room resting comfortably. I watch her sleep, machines and pumps doing their thing. I kiss her forehead, her warmth oddly reassuring.

I try and calm my insides, and convince myself that things aren't as dire as they appear. The nighttime commute calls the spirits from their darkness, and they

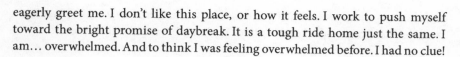

eagerly greet me. I don't like this place, or how it feels. I work to push myself toward the bright promise of daybreak. It is a tough ride home just the same. I am… overwhelmed. And to think I was feeling overwhelmed before. I had no clue!

It is reassuring to see the warm glow of lights as I pull in the driveway. I am not sure I can face the boys… anyone for that matter. I need a moment or two for an internal attitude check. I quietly creep to the window in the family room and peek inside. There I see three, beautiful, tow-headed boys popping up and down, playing, as little boys should. A kind of sadness settles on me, darkening my already dark mood. What does all this mean? It hurts too much to think about it! I push the thoughts aside for the moment. I think I need a hug or three. I push open the door… the boys do not disappoint.

I step out rather sheepishly into a partial sun filled March morning. Maybe the promise of spring will win out over winter, finally! I head to the hospital on my own. The surgery was grueling, and I think it best to leave the boys at home. We'll be moving in a few weeks, and they already are dealing with enough traumas. I am ready for the move, ready to leave all of this crazy winter nonsense behind me! Enough is enough! I think of Texas, and warm sunshine, and pleasant winters, and it makes me smile.

Natalie is alert, and greets me warmly, almost confidently. There is a special sparkle in her eyes today. I want to talk about Dr. Cotter, and what news he shared during rounds this morning. Natalie wants no part of it. Odd I think! Is this her coping mechanism? Her escape? She is all about the move and the new house, though. She wants an update on the movers. Too funny! Like I have nothing else going on in my life. She is clearly focused.

Discharge day finally arrives, and it feels like I've been in this place before. It feels heavy, weighs heavy on me. William is home from preschool when we get to the house. He barrels out the door and into Natalie's arms, embracing her tightly! Mother and son reunited. As I watch this from the sidelines, I go to a dark place and consider what our life might be like in the future. Don't even want to consider that thought, and send it away.

I return to work, knowing that Natalie is in good hands with friends and family, everyone is helping manage the house, and getting us ready for the move. I get home, a bit earlier than planned. The visiting nurse's car is parked in the driveway. I greet the boys happily and head down to the master bedroom. I tap lightly on the door and push it open slowly. A grisly site greets me! It grabs hold of my heart and squeezes tightly. Standing before me is my beautiful wife, surgical bandages removed, her body stapled and bruised. My heart breaks into little pieces!

Natalie catches my eye, and looks at me warily! I know this will be a defining moment for me. With a light voice, I say, "What are you ladies up to?" I push my way to the side of the bed, sit myself down, and watch as the nurse finishes changing out the dressing. I did not bargain for this. I stay in the moment, though, panic running wildly. The nurse collects her things and informs us that she will be back in two days. I go to Natalie, hug her warmly, afraid to hug her too tightly. "I love you; you are the most beautiful woman I know, and one of the most courageous. How about I help you get dressed?" She smiles and says, "I'd like that. You know Bob; I could not have done this… any of this without you. You have been my light, my hero." Funny, I feel anything but a hero!

Friday arrives all too quickly for me. I am dreading this particular Friday, as it is our follow up appointment with Dr. Davidsen. We sheepishly enter her office. Dr. Davidsen reads us pretty quickly, and says, "This is not at all what anyone expected. Everyone believed it was a bit of calcification, not cancer." Well, guess what, that is exactly what it is, and it sucks. All the suffering and pain. I press forward and ask the tough question. "Dr. Davidsen, what do we do now?" Dr. Davidsen explains to us that while the surgery did reveal cancer, all other tests leading up to the surgery were clean and showed no signs of cancer. Given this, she and her colleagues agreed that the best way forward would be to treat the area with radiation.

Being the good doctor that she is, Dr. Davidsen indicates that she has contacted a medical oncologist we can work with in Dallas, a Dr. Dalton. She said Dr. Dalton would pick up with Natalie's care and arrange the radiation. I can't believe this is the last time we will be seeing Dr. Davidsen; move day is just around the corner. It is a bit melancholy for me, she has been right with us through the battle and wanted a victory as much as we did. She has become a friend, a member of sorts, of our extended community. I find it hard to say my goodbye.

The journey home is just that – a journey! I am quiet, unsettled, and heavy of heart. As if sensing my inward move to a place of gloom, Natalie jumps into reality check mode! She says, "Remember one of our earlier appointments with Dr. Davidsen, where she told us how long I had to live?" I say, "Of course I do, how could I ever forget?" She continues, "I've already beaten the odds, and we are so fortunate to be starting a new and exciting chapter in our lives. It is a blessing from God! We need to make the best of it, whatever it is, and whatever it becomes, and live in the moments we do have, and not dwell on the moments we might not." Now that is called a shutdown!

I am in a panic! No surprise there. It is a chilly March 30th, and it is moving day just the same. It does not take the movers long to figure out who is in control this moving day. Natalie, her arm in a sling, is calling all the shots. I am a smart man and know to give her the berth she needs to run the day. It warms my heart to see her in motion and think being in this place gives her the strength to be in this place. She seems stronger than I think possible.

Amidst all the chaos that is moving day, a little voice calls out to me. It is William. "Daddy, where are my trucks?" What is he talking about? His trucks? I am not sure where my car is at the moment! Then Ryan and Jake jump in the mix. "What trucks?" I say to the brothers three. William is clearly on top of this. "The big yellow trucks I play with Daddy, where are they?"

"Okay guys, okay. What is all this about trucks?" Leave it to boys to worry about trucks. Ryan pipes in. "Dad, for real. We were outside playing with the trucks before the big snow storm." I try to get the uptick of what they are talking about, and then bam, I get it! A huge snowstorm hit the northeast a couple of weeks back, and it must have buried their trucks… the trucks are buried beneath the snow.

With little warning, big tears start flowing from my sweet little boy's eyes, and he is howling about his trucks. Well, something just has to happen here. We can't just leave the trucks behind now! How are we going to find them? Snow and all! Ryan, the practical and handy son, comes to the rescue with an incredible idea! "Let's use the bottom side of a rake Dad, and poke around in the snow until we hear a thud." Why not? Better than the anything I can suggest.

It is a sunny morning, and the last of our lifetime here is loaded onto the truck. The truck is ready to pull out, taking with it a few of our dreams. It is with mixed emotions that I watch the truck pull away. We say our goodbyes to friends, as Thomas and Christina shuttle all of us to the hotel at the airport, where we will spend the night before jumping on a plane tomorrow. All of the activity gets the boys into high spirits! While they are up, Natalie is down. The dark circles under her eyes tell me how beaten down she is. She is oddly quiet, almost reclusive and introspective. I wonder what she is thinking?

Christina, David and Alicia, our nephew and niece, are going to spend the night with us at the hotel so they can give us a grand send off in the morning. We go out to dinner and have fun together. As we put the boys down for the night, snow starts to fall. Natalie and I watch this through the window in our room, we snuggle in close, as close as we can, and watch the white flurries fall from the sky. I am so happy to be moving away from this stuff. I am looking forward to the sunny days of Texas, warm afternoons and blue skies. Good-bye to the depressing, gray winter days!

There is a dusting of snow as we gather for breakfast. The boys are having a blast with their cousins, and it is great seeing them so happy, it is refreshing. There is something off this morning; there is a grayish pallor to Natalie's face. I notice she is moving a bit slower. Alarms start sounding; I work to turn them off. I smile at Natalie. "Hey, hon, how ya feeling?" "I feel winded this morning; I'm having trouble catching my breath." She tries to smile at me, but it is obviously forced.

Without warning, they are calling for us to board. Natalie and I decide to divide and conquer on the flight to Texas; I sit close to Ryan and Jake, and Natalie sits with William. The boys are directly in front of me, so I can keep my eyes on them both. Natalie tries to stay alert and in the moment, but that just is not going to happen. She dozes off and on. Little color returns to brighten her grayish hue.

The adventure continues, and before we know it, we are landing in Texas. We all jump up when it is time to depart. Well, most of us anyway! Natalie, although awake, does not make a move. Odd! She is just kind of stationary. The boys and I hang back with her while passengers disembark. All eyes are now on Natalie. I say, "Babe, how about I help you get off the plane and into the terminal, and we kind of rest along the way?" Before she can even respond, a flight attendant approaches and asks Natalie, "Will you need a wheelchair?" Natalie smiles and says, "No, thanks, I'll be fine. I just needed a moment. I think I am ready now. There is no way I am touching down in a new land with anything except my own two feet." Ah, there she is, my witty wife!

I am not sure where she is getting her strength; she digs deep for sure. She pushes herself through the terminal, baggage claim and jumps on the tram with us to the car rental agency, determined. While I play the wait in line game with the boys, Natalie heads to the restroom. She is gone a good while and eventually returns. If she was gray before, she is now twice as gray. Not a good sign. "You okay?" I say. "I'm fine," she says. "Something must not be agreeing with me; I got sick a couple of times. I think I am okay now. Don't worry." I am not so sure about that.

The boys help load up the van, and we are off. It is time to check out the new house. The boys jump out of the car, running to the house. Natalie, however, is moving a bit slowly. She stands in front of the house, taking it all in. It seems to ground her; she nods her head approvingly, and it lifts her spirits. We walk through the fields to the elementary school, the boys frolicking along the way. They grab from the many wild flowers, and with fists filled, they run to their Mom. They gingerly hand them to Natalie. She stoops down and gathers the boys up in her one good arm. Not wanting to be left out, I join the group hug.

We finish our walk to the school, and peak in a window or three. We take off to Sonic, a first time for all of us, and eat in our rental van. The boys are beyond themselves. Burgers, fries, shakes, eating in the car, what else can you ask for? This is not something you would get to do on an April 1st kind of night back in New Hampshire. It is just a marvel for us! "Welcome to Texas," I say to myself. After dinner, it is off to our furnished apartment, and we do our best to get the boys settled in for the night. It has been a long day indeed.

The moving van shows up early Saturday morning, and drops off our car and a bunch of clothes and such. We will be able to keep the van for a month before we have to return it! It is just enough time to get our footing and figure things out here in Texas. The routine will be simple; Natalie will drive the boys to and from school while the builder finishes the house. On Monday, game on! We jump into our new routine in a new land. Natalie is off to school with the boys, and I am off to work.

My first official work day in Texas is a good one. It is good to be here and focused on the business at hand. Natalie greets me at the apartment with a warm hug. I can see how worn she is. Dinner is well under way, and she is doing her best to keep three young boys corralled in our small apartment. According to all reports, the first day of school in Texas goes great. Hallelujah, I think. The rest of the week melts away, is normalcy settling in for us? Could be nice.

Our appointment today with the oncologist, Dr. Dalton, has me a bit on edge. Is it that a bit of the unknown is heading my way perhaps? Or is it my demon friend? Doesn't matter, we meet with the doctor just the same. Dr. Dalton is entirely up to speed, and shares with us that he had a very thorough conversation with Dr. Davidsen. He goes on to explain the treatment, and Natalie will get radiation every day for six weeks. Déjà vu clubs me up the side of the head. I think I've been here before!

Logistics call out to the weary. Eventually, we will be a one-car family. I walk Dr. Dalton through my upcoming logistical concerns, and he is most understanding. Here is the plan we land on. Natalie will drive into Irving where I am working, and pick me up around lunchtime. We'll take advantage of my lunch hour to make a quick jaunt to the hospital for treatments. We'll jump back in the car and head to

Irving, where she will drop me off. From there, she will grab the boys after school, and head to the apartment, settle everyone in and start working on dinner. It sounds simple enough, right?

So the new rules for life begin, and we are off to an okay start. I have myself convinced anyway. Until… Natalie calls me one afternoon at work out of the blue.

"Hey, hon, how ya doing?" There is hesitancy in her voice.

I try to be upbeat in my response. "Holding my own, I think you have the tougher job, though."

She laughs a bit, and then the line goes eerily quiet. Something is up here. Oh boy, here we go.

"… I am worried about Jake." I hear the concern in her voice.

"What ya got going on with Jake?"

She pauses slightly. "I've noticed him dragging his left leg, and I mean dragging. I checked it out; it is really swollen, even has a hint of purple coloring. Not sure what's going on."

"You think it could be a sprain?" As active as he is, seems like a good explanation to me. "Let's take a look at it together when I get home. That work?"

"Yeah, that works. The Mom in me tells me something is going on."

Natalie jumps into Mom mode. Tired or beat down mattered not, she finds a pediatrician and gets an appointment pretty quickly. Mom has this kid on a fast track to getting well. During our initial appointment with Dr. Traverse, he does an exam, some blood tests and an x-ray. He rules out Lyme disease and a fracture. He suggests we try and get the swelling down by limiting Jake's physical activity. We leave with a prescription for a steroid, and directions to use ice packs at night to try and manage the swelling.

Natalie develops a limp of her own, complaining of a pain in her hip. It's hard for me to keep everybody's everything square in my brain. During our appointment with Dr. Dalton, we discuss this new development, and he examines Natalie thoroughly. He can't detect anything, but orders an x-ray to be on the safe side.

He thinks she might be developing a bit of arthritis. No big deal. The x-ray comes back while we wait, the report is good, and there is nothing to worry about.

Not worry? Me? Not likely! I am the skeptic, and I am not so sure I am buying what the good doctor is trying to sell! Something is going on here. I see it in Natalie's face, which has gotten paler by the day. While her hair is growing back, she is having trouble eating, keeping things down, and often struggling with an unsettled stomach. Vomiting is making a repeat appearance. Something is not quite right, and it gnaws at me.

The house is getting closer to being completed. It is fun to visit the site, and we do it as often as we can. During today's visit, future neighbors, Tom and Samantha, come out and introduce themselves. They are fun and lively, and we have an immediate connection. They are a welcome sight, and I welcome new friends into our world.

Dr. Traverse is perplexed. During our follow-up appointment, he indicates displeasure with Jake's progress. Clearly, restricting use of his leg has done little to improve his limp. Given the lack of progress, he wants Jake to see an orthopedic surgeon. Maybe it is something structural, and maybe an orthopedic can figure it out. Thankfully, Dr. Traverse both recommends and sets up an appointment for us. One less thing!

School comes to a screeching halt, and now our daily jaunt into Dallas includes the boys. Oh yeah, the joys of life! I am worried about Natalie's stamina. I see the toll life is taking on her poor body; her weight loss and gray pallor are a cause for concern. Valerie, a friend from work, was transferred to Texas with me. Her teenage daughter, Rose Lynn, is looking for a summer job! I waste no time and offer her a summer job taking care of the boys. She readily accepts. Hope she knows what she is in for!

The appointment with the orthopedic surgeon, Dr. Frampton, finally arrives. I take Jake, and the boys with me. Thought it would give Natalie a chance to rest. Dr. Frampton exams the functionality of Jake's left leg. He reports a significant loss of mobility. Tell me something I don't already know. So there will be no answers today, which is a bummer. Jake and I leave with some therapy exercises to do at home, and a follow-up appointment in a couple of weeks.

I feel as if I am back on the hamster wheel, running to and fro, doctor to doctor to doctor. No answers are coming in on any front. The doctor of the day is Dr. Dalton, and Natalie and I are in a holding pattern in the waiting room, along with three young ones. They eventually call Natalie's name, and I leave the boys in the waiting room, under threat of life. The doctor exams Natalie's body, and indicates he wants to do a full blood work up. I think I'm happy about this, but I'm not so sure. I have been worried for months that something big is in motion.

A nurse comes in and begins the blood draw, and Natalie goes white. She becomes woozy and sways a bit sitting on the exam table. I jump up, but the doctor beats me to the punch. He gently gets Natalie to lie down, and they finish the blood draw. The good doctor then finds an empty bed nearby where Natalie can rest while we wait for the results. For some reason, dark spirits swirl, dragging me down, squeezing tightly on my heart.

Inspiration..

The LORD is close to the brokenhearted and saves those who are crushed in spirit. A righteous man may have many troubles, but the LORD delivers him from them all.

Psalm: 34:18-19

Reflection ....

I thought I had already climbed the mountain of adversity, my own personal Mt. Kilimanjaro! Everything coming at me from all angles like a gathering storm atop the mountain peak! Overwhelmed is my operative word. Funny, a year ago I thought I was overwhelmed. What little did I know back then? Overwhelmed is where I am right now. Jake and Natalie both hang in the balance. Where are these things headed? I fear no good will come from these things!

A year ago, I was clueless about the difficulties of life. I had no idea what adversity really meant. Thought I did, but I didn't. Not even close. Every week life seems to throw something new and unexpected my way. I journey forward, whether I am ready or not. As I journey, I notice a correlation between my circumstance and my spirit. The more challenging the circumstance, the more beaten down I feel. My spirit is now fatigued. I am afraid I can't make the ascent, this time out, to the mountaintop. My energy wanes and victory taunts and teases, just outside my reach.

Life has done little to help ready me for my perilous ascent. Cancer is the monster lurking in the shadows. The mastectomy is downright horrific. Jake... beckoned from the wild unknown. It has been tough to watch all of this happen around me, adversity owning the day, and seemingly my life. I feel helpless. I want to fix it all;

make it better for everyone. I want it to be me, not them! Oh Lord, can you please make this be about me and not those that I love.

I have tried to be the courageous one, to be unwavering in my faith, and in my determination to prevail, against all the odds. I can't help but question the why... why? I find myself seeking to understand, yet I find no answers. I ask God, but I only find silence. How can He be so silent? How can He not see Natalie suffering at the hands of a monster? And Jake? And me, struggling to hold it all together, a family together. Why won't He intervene and work a miracle or two? Maybe He could arrange to deliver a few to our house. Seems like a reasonable request.

Is it possible there is a plan in place, and God isn't quite ready to share it all with me? Maybe He has told me the plan, and it is not what I wanted to hear, so I ignore it. Maybe God has answered my prayer, but I ignore His response because it is not the answer I want. God has to answer my prayers, right? And the answer has to be the answer I want. That is how it should work – my prayer, my answer. It seems simple enough to me. Maybe God is quietly protecting me? Watching out for me? Is He there for me and I just think He is absent?

Relationships can be tough sometimes; there are high and low points. My relationship with God is no different. Right now it is at a low point. No surprise there, it is strained. It would be tough for it to be at a high point for me. I am overwhelmed and spiritually fatigued. No God present in the chaos of my life. Not my choice, my life just the same. It forces me, though, to turn away from God, instead of turning to Him. As I turn from Him, I can see the dark shadows gathering at the edge of the mountainous slope. They are calling out to me, forecasting a fate I don't want to see or consider. The thought of it hurts.

As I work to make sense of all of this, I wonder if my response to these challenges will be the mark by which God judges me one day? Will a life well lived, against the mountains of adversity, be measured by what I do with what I learn as I make my perilous ascent. What did I learn about myself? What did I learn about God? As I stare straight ahead into the face of the storm, I wonder how I will be judged, especially on that most important Judgment Day?

I have learned so much about myself. I have tried to become a more vibrant spirit, one that is more aware of the world, the people around me, their pains and needs. These things are hard to do though when the rules of engagement are constantly changing. It is still difficult for me to find my way forward. I guess I'll just keep muddling along, making my ascent, working to find answers to life's most difficult questions, hoping God will weigh in soon.

Whenever He does, I hope the answer I am praying for is the answer I get. The plan I have landed on has to be the plan He has in store for me. Has to be, just has to be. It hurts too much to consider what actually might be in God's plan. Not sure I want to climb that mountain!

I hear a quiet whisper... no... no... that isn't it. It isn't a whisper. It is the quiet beating of a drum.

BOOK 6

The Darkest Hour

Contemplation...

Journey's Fate

I wait for fate with tearful eye
While the sun shines behind a blood red sky
The monster's grasp is strong and grows
Controlling life and shattering dreams
Hopes and fears become as one
As the dusk of life grows ever nigh
A hallowed feeling I have inside
As I shed a tear for love's last dance
Randomness beckons what's left of a rainbow song
Happiness now a shattered illusion
While life's burdens hurt a hallowed soul
I struggle against the growing storm
Facing dark spirits that steal pieces of my heart
Bearing witness for what's left of journey's fate
Creating pain beyond life's spiritual gate
A promise was made and asked of me
That love and honor be strong
A promise to be fulfilled by a heart's saddened song

By: Robert Mapes

The Story ....

With the boys in tow, we settle in with Natalie and wait quietly for the blood results. The boys are good as gold. A bit out of character even. I wonder what their read is on all of this? Are they scared? Fearful? Is their heart heavy like mine? I sure hope they aren't getting a read from me. That would not be a good thing. I don't have a good feeling about this, not at all. Can't put my finger on it, though, I just can't.

The doctor tracks us down, and pulls me aside, which sets off all kinds of alarms. He reviews the labs with me; it is just more noise in my head. It seems Natalie's electrolytes are all out of whack, and that he needs to get them squared away. He also wants to do a blood transfusion, which will help her a bit with the energy thing. Okay, so we are good here doc, I think to myself. But find myself saying, "Doctor… what does all this really mean?" He smiles, trying to downplay things perhaps, and says, "This means we'll need to keep Natalie overnight, maybe a few days, possibly. There are some additional blood tests I would like to do while she is hospitalized."

The boys and I hang with Natalie until she gets a regular room, and then I haul three active ones out of the hospital. We get back to the apartment, and it is pretty late. I rally the troops, and everyone gets ready for bed. We do story time. The stories are a necessary diversion for me, a distraction. My thoughts are jumbled. Should I be worried here? I disappear inwardly, but the boys bring me back into the moment. "Dad! Dad!" I jump back into the story, sort of.

Thank goodness for Rose Lynn! She shows up bright and early to be with the boys while I race to the hospital to be with Natalie. I want to be there during rounds. I feel like we've been in this place before. Wait a minute, we have! I am encouraged when I first walk in and greet Natalie. She has a bit of color and seems slightly more energetic. Maybe this is nothing but a thing, and some periodic blood infusions will become part of our new 'normal.'

There is a quiet tap on the door, and Dr. Dalton sheepishly enters the room. He smiles or attempts to smile anyway. He greets us kindly, and as he starts speaking, he oddly works himself backward, up against the wall. "I have the results of the blood work… I'd like to tell you what we found." And then, an awkward silence descends. It becomes eerily quiet. He tries smiling again, failing miserably.

"As you know, we did a number of tests… and I am afraid that what we found is not very encouraging… Mrs. Mapes's cancer has spread, and it is very active in her body." I hear these words. They hurt. I feel the blood drain from my face, and a warm sensation moves throughout my body. My lungs feel heavy, and so does every breath I take! I take Natalie's hand in mine; it is cool, clammy to the touch, much like my own. I am numb, unsure, scared! There is an awkward silence, again. Someone say something, anything. I think I can hear everyone's heart beating. I inhale; take a deep breath to find my voice. "So… what does this mean, exactly what do we do from here?"

Dr. Dalton continues thoughtfully. "Given that the cancer has spread, radiation is doing very little to hold the cancer at bay!" He pauses just a moment, giving us time, perhaps to absorb some of this. My heart is racing, and my thoughts are spinning, my skin feels prickly, and my hands are damp. Every nerve in my body is on high alert. I want to go somewhere, anywhere, to escape this moment.

In a quiet voice, Dr. Dalton presses forward. "Since Natalie has already received such aggressive chemo, and the cancer is active, I don't see starting another round of chemo doing much good." No-o-o-o! This can't be the death sentence that it sounds like. Please, not this!

Internal panic grabs my gut, and I find myself saying, "Doctor... if chemo and radiation are not going to work, then what do we do? What will we do?" Dark thoughts are tumbling, my spirit is afraid to interpret what is happening! The doctor smiles sadly, takes a second or two, and comes back with his thoughts. "I'd recommend that you forgo any treatment, and live the best life you can for as long as you can."

La la la la la la la la... I don't want to hear this, not now, not ever! His words are sharp, like a knifepoint. There is a dissonance deep in my soul, pushing me to the edge of the unknown. How is it we are even here? This can't be. This is not how things are supposed to end. There is a victory yet to be celebrated, and a life well lived. What is this all about Lord? Why this ghastly sentence?

Dr. Dalton brings me back from the precipice, and says in a soft and caring voice, "I'd expect Natalie, given her current condition... to live about 60 days, maybe 90 days best case. I'm so sorry to tell you these things. I know you have fought long and hard. I know you have young children. I cannot imagine being in your place."

There is that silence again; it hangs over the room like a wet blanket. Dr. Dalton moves on. "I'd like to put you in touch with Hospice. They can help you through the difficult days ahead."

Days, did he just say days? My brain scrambles to make sense of all of this noise. From some unknown part of my soul, I hear my own voice. "I think we'd like that Doctor." He doesn't respond; he quietly walks out, the door softly closing behind him. My tears overcome me; a sob catches in my throat, I have no control over it. It escapes; the sound is raw, primal in a way. My body begins to shake at the horror of it all. I can't speak. I go to Natalie to comfort her; we grab one another in a tight embrace. We end up comforting each other if you can call it that. I jump in bed with her and lay alongside her tormented body. We hug tightly. She sobs softly against me, her body shaking quietly.

From behind her tears, Natalie says, "All I ever wanted… was to live long enough for all of my children… to read me a story… just a story, that's all! I knew… I knew I would never… make the distance. Was I asking… am I asking… is it too much?"

I wipe the tears from my eyes. "No… you were asking for the things we all want… things we all take for granted. You weren't asking too much… you weren't."

I snuggle in close to her in the hospital bed, and we lay there, our sobs eventually easing. The nurse comes in to check Natalie's vitals. She grabs Natalie's hand, placing it in both of hers, and says, "I am so sorry… so very sorry. Please let me know if there is anything you need." I lay quietly with Natalie; we are a broken part of humanity! Time seems to slow, giving my dark spirits a chance to set up shop. I feel a tremendous burden and a heavy pain.

Parental duties beckon me from our dark hour and call my name. As my tears begin to subside, Natalie looks at me, and says, "You might need to get a giddy-up in that ride if you are going to get Jake to his appointment on time. We need to know what is going on with this kid." I suggest a cancellation; Natalie quickly nixes that notion. Off I go, back on the hamster wheel.

I am not sure how I get to Jake and the boys or get us all to the doctor's office. Must have been my autopilot kicking in. It is packed at the doctor's office; Jake and I check in and we all go to the waiting area. The boys are so quiet; can they sense something is off? Can they sense that I am on autopilot? Do they know the birds of prey are circling their world? Do they sense the hammer of fate has started to fall? How will I ever tell them, how? The thought hurts my heart.

After what seems an eternity, they call Jake's name. I bring all of the boys along with me, and we make our way back to the exam room. The doctor gives Jake's leg a complete work over. He looks my way and says, "Let's go take a look at that x-ray one more time." He takes me to the white, fluorescent image reader outside the exam room, and puts Jake's x-ray on it. He points to a grayish looking area on Jake's ankle and says, "This is what concerns me. I am perplexed… and worried about the deterioration in functionality. Based on my exam, and the result of this x-ray, I think we need to do an MRI… and rule out cancer."

I can feel the bile rising from the pit of my stomach! I shoot to a clammy state quicker than possible and feel myself turning green. I think I am going to be sick.

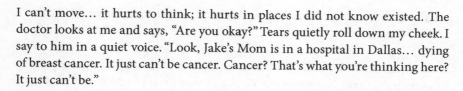

I can't move… it hurts to think; it hurts in places I did not know existed. The doctor looks at me and says, "Are you okay?" Tears quietly roll down my cheek. I say to him in a quiet voice. "Look, Jake's Mom is in a hospital in Dallas… dying of breast cancer. It just can't be cancer. Cancer? That's what you're thinking here? It just can't be."

He grabs my elbow, and gently guides me toward his office, leaving the boys in the exam room. He says to me, "I am so sorry to hear that. This must be so tough." He continues kindly. "You take a minute, wait here, I'll go collect those boys, and I can explain to all of them what we are going to do." Good, I think, because I am in no position to explain anything to anybody! My psyche is spinning, dark shadows closing in! I can't be here. I can't! Please, not this. Please! Not my little boy, not Jake too! No-o-o! Not cancer, please not cancer!

The doctor returns with three unruly young boys, sits them down and miraculously gets control. He explains that Jake is going to need a special test that will take a picture of his ankle and help him figure out what is going on. He delivers the message carefully and thoughtfully and it comes across as a nonevent. While the doctor is delivering his message to the boys, I am contemplating a very different message that I need to deliver. Just the thought makes my heart race!

I gather up the boys and we head to the hospital to visit Natalie. I know I cannot go all weepy-weepy when we get to the hospital, so I bottle everything up and put a tight lid on it. Just got to do it! Good thing! The boys run into Natalie's room and shout, "Mommy, Mommy!" That could have done me in.

Natalie is all smiles! I go in for a hug, and she holds on a bit longer than usual, a bit tighter. I can tell she is scared. I'm scared. Who wouldn't be scared? The boys keep things moving, though, and are all about Jake's visit to the doctor and the upcoming MRI. They don't even give me a chance to queue it up. Natalie looks at me with concern, and says questioningly, "MRI?" I decide that maybe less is best. I spin a tale of sorts. I just have to. I can't bear to tell her the complete truth. I am fearful that the truth would destroy her. Besides, we don't know anything for a fact yet. So, no harm no foul!

I put on my best smile, and say, "The doctor wants to rule out something mechanical. He thinks it might be a torn ligament or simply a bone chip." She holds my eyes for a second or two, and I am afraid she is going to see right through me. She moves on to Jake and says, "Jake, an MRI is so much fun. You get to go in this really cool tube, and you'll hear all this banging around. I remember times when you were trying to help your Dad fix something. It sounds exactly like that." Jake is all smiles.

Some things are easier said than done, calling everyone and sharing this painful news is one of them. Not sure I can do it. Not sure I want to do it. How do I even begin to tell Natalie's Dad, Fred? How do you tell a parent their child is dying? I pick up the phone; hold it in my hand… stare at it. The high-pitched wail brings me out of my reverie. The only way here is straight through it. It is tough, forget the tissues, I use a towel! It is the only way I can get it done. I'm not sure I'll ever be able to breathe normally again.

No sleep comes my way! I am filled with jumbled thoughts and feeling, all uncorralled, wreaking havoc on me. I fear sleep will elude me in the nights to come. Tonight, I pace. Tonight, I cry. Not sure I can shed one more tear, but tears flow just the same. I try to watch some television; there is no escaping the reality that is my life! I pray to the Lord God Almighty, and ask Him to help me understand. How do we find ourselves here Lord?

After a restless night, I get the boys up and ready for Rose Lynn's arrival, and myself to work. I have a few things I need to get done before I go over to the hospital, hopefully, to pick up Natalie. It is a bright, warm, sunny kind of Texas day. But there is nothing bright and sunny for me. I finish up a couple of deliverables; ensuring things are in good order on the work front, just in case.

I pick up the phone and try to dial Hospice. I end up disconnecting before the phone rings. I try one more time, but it ends with the same outcome. I know that calling Hospice means I am acknowledging a known fate, a fate I don't want. I quickly realize how much I don't know about the uncharted storm waters I am entering. Having wise counsel seems like a good move. I make the dreaded call to Hospice. Ugh, I am not ready for this, any of this.

Next, I call Josh, our builder. Our home is not scheduled to be finished until mid-late July, which by my simple math is cutting things a little close. I am all too aware of the 90-day clock that is ticking away. Tick, Tick, Tick, Tock! We are now at day 89 according to my count. I bring Josh up to speed, and he tells me how sorry he is to hear about Natalie. I ask him, "Is there anything you can do to speed up the process so we can get into the house sooner than planned?" Josh pauses slightly. "We'll do everything in our power to get you and Natalie into the house as soon as possible." I think he is doing some math of his own.

I have one last thing to do before I head out to the hospital. Time to update Steve, my boss. My world is going to get downright squirrelly, and he needs to be in the know. Steve is a compassionate leader and has become a wonderful friend. I walk into his office and ask if he has a couple of minutes for me. He always does, and today is no exception. I quietly close the door, take a big breath, my heart hammering in my chest! I know I need to own this moment.

Steve is so understanding and tells me how sorry he is, then says, "I will do anything you need me to Bob, to help you and your family out. All you need to do is ask." I decide to take advantage of his kind offer and ask, "Would it be ok… if I worked, kind of… half days… you know, until… well… before Natalie." Steve grabs on before I have to finish my thought, and caringly says, "Of course you can."

I quickly move to my office, grabbing my keys. I need to get out of here. I don't dally, I am right on the edge of a meltdown, and I have to get out of the building! The walls begin to close in on me; breathing has become difficult. I jump into the elevator, still in one piece, but can feel myself starting to shut down; my brain is racing and is oddly out of sync with the rest of my body!

"Hurry!" I shout at the elevator as the world begins to darken around me. I hammer at the button for the lobby. "Hurry!" I push myself up against the back of the elevator; the doors slowly, painfully close. I feel as if I could go down, face first. The universe continues to darken; I am consciously working to get air into my lungs. Finally, I am at lobby level, and as the doors spring open, I bolt out of the elevator, crashing into any poor soul in my way! I feel like I am spinning, I am losing a sense of time and motion. The physical world seems to be crumbling around me, the pieces seemingly falling beside me.

I continue my push toward the lobby door. Out, I have to get out! The pressure on my lungs is growing and breathing is more difficult! My conscious being is a jumble of words and images. Nothing seems to make sense. One word, though, keeps coming to the surface. It is unrelenting! It won't let go, try as I might release it to another realm. It floats again toward my consciousness, determined. The word is *death*!

I get my frenzied self through the lobby doors… look toward the heavens, the warm sun on my face. I shout, "How can You do this…. how… can…. You?" I put my face in my hands; a sob quickly greets them. I fall to my knees, head down, with my chin against my chest. My meltdown has begun.

Time has lost all meaning. People come and go, many trying to be kind, others offering a helping hand. I refuse them. I am completely alone, so very alone. Abandoned by all, especially by a God I thought loved me! Eventually, the sun becomes a bit too warm, and my sweat begins to mix with my tears. I am a certified mess. I inhale deeply and pick my sorry self up. Pity party over! There are more pressing matters for me to deal with, ugly as they are.

I make it to the car; I am feeling a bit better, at least in better control now. I find my way to the hospital, although I remember nothing of the journey. I stop in the main lobby restroom, and splash some water on my face! It feels good. I know I need to look fresh and in control! The water reminds me I am alive. I think about baptismal water, and question my faith, and where my God is. I look at the man in the mirror. He looks back at me sadly. I tell him to be the unyielding one. I'm not so sure he hears me.

I take the stairs to the third floor and quietly enter Natalie's room. It is so quiet. At first, I think she might be asleep. She hears me, and looks my way, with that easy smile of hers. How does she do that? No words are exchanged. Our eyes lock, and I bravely return the smile. I can do this! I kiss her, and we embrace caringly, each in our own way being a lifeline for the other.

Eventually, she pushes me back, looks me in the eyes, and says, "We need to talk."

I say, "Might be a good idea."

"I need you to promise me some things."

"Depends, I reckon."

"Bob, I do need you to promise me some things."

"What if I don't want to? What if I just want this all to go away... just disappear?"

"I still you need you to promise me some things."

"Natalie, I'm not so sure I am in a position to promise anybody anything."

"Look, I don't want to be in this place any more than you. I cannot imagine saying goodbye to you, or the boys. A forever kind of goodbye."

I look at Natalie, and a big ole' tear slowly travels down her cheek. I know, I'm being selfish, but I can't help myself. The tear is my reality check! Time to be the courageous one. I go to her and hold her while she cries quietly onto my shoulder. More than I can stand!

She says, "I am not sure how to tell the boys I am going to die."

There it is, that horrible, awful, no good word, and it makes my heart go whomp, whomp, whomp in my chest.

"Not exactly the kind conversation either of us wants to have with the boys."

"Well, we are going to have to figure it out pretty quick like. We won't have the luxury of time."

"Yeah, I know! I called hospice… they said they could help us with all of this. Let me call them and make an appointment. You good with that?"

"No, I'll never be good with that, not now, not ever. But given our circumstance, it is what I think we need to do."

"Ok, I'll do it once we get you out of here and back to the apartment."

"I still need you to promise me some things."

"Not letting go of that one are you?"

"Not a chance."

And there it is, that reassuring smile of hers. Her life hangs in the balance, and she is smiling and wanting me to make promises. It is clear to me that this is going her way.

I try to smile back. "Okay Natalie, what kind of promise do you need me to make?"

"Well, it is not one promise, it is more… like *promises!*"

"Ah, I think I can see where this is going. Not so sure I am your guy for promises these days."

"You are the only guy that can deliver these promises."

"Okay then Natalie, hit me with your best shot!"

"Promise me Bob, that you will continue your spiritual journey no matter how angry you are or become and that you will help the boys in their spiritual journeys."

"Wow, are you kidding me here? That is a huge promise!"

"I know – but promise me anyway."

"Seriously?"

"Seriously!"

"Aw, man… Okay, I'll do it!"

"I didn't just ask you to do it; I asked you to promise."

"Come on Natalie. You honestly want me to say I promise?"

"That is exactly what I want you to say."

"Okay, okay, okay. I promise. Cross my heart. Hope to die… right along with you."

"Not going to happen, you have too much yet to accomplish, and there are more promises to be made."

"You have got to be kidding me!"

"Not kidding."

"You drive a hard bargain kiddo. Okay, Natalie, got the first one… what else ya got lined up for me?"

"Promise me that you'll make sure the boys all graduate from high school. That they will get some kind of advanced education after graduation!"

"Okay, I can do that."

"I know you can do it; I want you to promise!"

"Okay. Okay, I promise the boys will graduate high school and will get an advanced education of some kind."

"Promise me that you will let the boys all explore the sports that inspire them?"

"I can work that one out. No Natalie, I promise to help them explore sports."

"You're doing good Bob. Now promise me that you'll expose the boys to culture and that they'll have a chance to explore cultural kinds of things, whether music or art, whatever floats their boat."

"Okay, okay – got it! I'll make it happen".

"No – promise me! It is not the same thing."

"Umm… I promise!"

"Promise me that there will be no drugs, alcohol, smoking or promiscuity while the boys live under your roof."

"Are you kidding me here Natalie? This will be me against the world you know! I am struggling with meeting the first promise. I hope this is your last one!"

"Not a chance Bob… there is one more, and I want you to listen to this one carefully."

"Okay, but I have got to say… you've got me worried now".

"Promise me that you'll move on one day…….and that you will share your love with another."

I don't hesitate. "No, Natalie, no, no, no!" Tears spring from my eyes. It hurts to take the next breath. I cannot believe what she is suggesting. "I can't, Natalie. No, I won't, I won't promise this. I refuse! It is you I love, and I cannot imagine… imagine ever loving another. How… can… you… ask… this of me?"

Barely above a whisper, she says, "Bob… look at me."

I glance her way, and can see just how serious she is about this. Her eyes are filled with compassion, an easy smile on her lips. "Look, you are a great guy Bob, and someone else deserves the kind of man you are, and that someone will make you happy. That someone will love you the way you deserve to be loved."

"I cannot make that promise to you. I can't! I'm still trying to imagine a world without you."

"Promise me, Bob."

I have nothing. If I admit this here and now, it brings me all too close to my ugly reality. I am not equipped for any of this.

"Bob… promise me!"

I look into her eyes. "I promise… to one day consider the possibility, just the possibility! That is it, just the possibility. That's all I can do."

Natalie smiles like she has won an Olympic event. "You do realize… that where I am going… I will be able to see how well you live up to all of these promises! And guess what? I will be with my Heavenly Father… and will be pain-free!"

"Okay, Natalie… got it, got it. So are we all done with this promises thing here?"

"As long as you live up to the promises you made, I am done with promises. I won't mention them again, and remember who will be watching you ever so closely," she says with a Cheshire cat kind of smile.

In an excited voice, she says, "Time to check out of this hotel. I want to spend as much time with the boys as possible."

I talk with Josh once we get to the apartment, and the news is good. All subcontractors can meet an accelerated timeline, meaning we will be able to be in the house before the July 4th weekend. Whew! Great news! This is 30 days ahead of schedule. I feel a bit of worry roll right off my back.

My next call is not as easy, hospice! It brings me a bit closer to the mighty hammer of fate. Hospice indicates they can help us, but want to get to know the family before landing on an approach. Makes sense, so I set up an appointment for them to come out to the apartment and meet all of us. This is going to get ugly real quick like.

With the calls behind me, I head to the pool where Rose Lynn is with the boys and give them the good news about Natalie. Is there good news here? I think not! But here in this moment, the fact that she is home is welcome news to them. They are on their way in a flash, and are ever so happy to see their Mom. There are wet hugs galore. I do some quick math; I don't like the magic number.

There is a great joy as we head out to dinner. We sit outside, in the waning summer sun! It is fun to be together and to laugh at the boys and all their crazy boy antics. They push the boundaries, and we let them. Things are going to change in a big way, and I want them to have some reasonable kind of fun with Natalie. These moments will have to sustain them over a lifetime!

Natalie is up early and very alert! I am impressed! Just knowing what the cancer is doing on the inside makes me marvel at her spirit. She makes breakfast, determined to make what little bit of life she has left, as meaningful as possible. We agree I will work half day today, and when I get home, we will all go off together, and pick out appliances for the new house. Just like a normal family. Funny what I consider normal these days.

Time to leave work; it went quickly. I head to the apartment to pick up one and all. Natalie is all dolled up; this is going to be a big outing for her. She is putting on a good front for the boys. Off we go to the Home Depot. It feels good walking together across the parking lot, everyone hand in hand. We barely get in the store, and Natalie makes a mad dash to the restroom. She is gone a good bit of time. I panic. She finally comes out, and is pale, gray even, and a bit unsteady on her feet. I rush to her, the boys right at my side, and I ask, "Hey, Hon… you okay?"

She smiles easily, taking in the worried looks about her. "I'm just fine. I say we go pick us out some brand spanking new appliances." To which the boys cheer!

As we make our way to the appliances, I quietly whisper, "You sure you're okay? We can do this another time you know."

She shakes her head vehemently. "No… I'm good. I just lost what little I have eaten today, and I am feeling a little out of sorts. But nothing to worry about, though. I'll be fine. We don't have the luxury of time on our hands." Well, that about sums it up, doesn't it?

Natalie stays in the moment, but it is clear she is not feeling well. We make selections rather hastily and start our journey back to the parking lot. As we near the restrooms, Natalie makes another quick beeline. She is gone awhile but does return to us. If it is possible, she lost what little color she had. The boys become quiet, and walk up to her, grabbing her hands. It seems like a million miles to the car. Makes me wonder what is headed our way.

The drum beats loudly this morning. I try to silence it... but it continues just the same. I wish I could push it away. It is the death march! It calls out the days remaining on the clock of life. I am new to this game of life and death and am not sure what to expect. Who does? Besides, what I wanted and what I got are two different things!

I wait for Rose Lynn to arrive before I head to work. My heart just isn't in the game; it feels burdened with the pain yet to come. With a future that is grim, I remind myself that I need to keep my heart in this game if I want to keep my job. The last thing I need right now is to find myself jobless. A part of me doesn't care... what is one more thing? Does the Big Guy even care anyway?

The chance to decompress during the commute is a good thing. It is a warm, sunny day, and I am growing to like this change in climate. It is so different from the world of New Hampshire. I think about winter, and then it hits me... Natalie will never be with me to experience a warm Texas kind of winter. I feel myself start to tumble downwardly. This is going to be a tough one!

I close out a couple of meetings and call Josh to see if he has a closing date. He does, hurrah! I thank him for his kindness, care, and compassion. It is nice to get good news now and then. The closing date is Friday, June 25th, meaning we can move June 26th. If all goes according to plan, we will have time left on the death march to make a few memories before the monster claims victory!

I have a few minutes alone with Natalie when I get home, outside of prying ears and eyes. I give her a big ole hug; she feels mighty tiny in my embrace. I share the good news about the closing and move date, then the grimmer news - the appointment with Hospice tomorrow. She catches my eye at the mention of hospice and is quick to put a smile on her face. How can she manage a smile knowing everything hospice represents to our world? Her message to me is clear, get on board mister!

I am dreading the meeting with hospice, and Kally, the counselor that will be working with us. Dreading it in a big way! I am going to be forced to confront my ugly reality and talk about death in new ways. Ugh! Has to be a better way! There is no way this wonderful and beautiful creature is going anywhere. It just

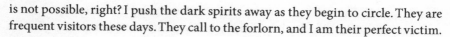

is not possible, right? I push the dark spirits away as they begin to circle. They are frequent visitors these days. They call to the forlorn, and I am their perfect victim.

The meeting with hospice arrives whether I am willing or not. Kally is a young woman who clearly loves what she does. I cannot imagine working in that kind of world all the time. I quickly come to appreciate what hospice and Kally might be able to do to help all of us with the dark days that are just ahead. Kally explains that hospice is all about end-of-life care! I learn quickly that the goal is to manage Natalie's end of life pain and symptoms. The death march continues.

Kally, Natalie and I talk about the boys, Ryan, Jake, and William. We explore all the factors surrounding our move to Texas. It is clear she is trying to get to know the boys, and understand our lives in advance of our official family meeting. I mention that we are not ready to have a conversation today with the boys to Kally, just so she's clear! I am not ready now and might never be ready for that one!

"Kally," I say, "Since we have a little bit of time, when do you think is the right time to tell the boys?"

She asks, "How much time do you think you have?"

I explain about Natalie's recent hospital stay, and what the doctor shared with us about the 90-day march.

Kally smiles warmly, and in a soft voice says, "90 days is just a number, let's say a doctor's best assessment based on what they see. There is no science to it. You need to know that things could happen sooner, or they could happen later. There is no real way to know for sure. I just want you to be aware that you might not have 90 days."

What? WHAT? What is she talking about? But the doctor said 90 days, so in my simple brain, it means we have 90 days. There is no way we don't have at least 90 days, right? No way! No way! It has to play out that way! It just has to! Please! Doesn't it have to play out according to what I want?

Kally senses my internal retreat, and says, "Mr. Mapes, I know how tough this is, and the thought of saying goodbye to a loving and caring wife, a life partner, is tough, but we have some important things to discuss."

Silence quietly descends; I can feel it pushing down from the ceiling. I am in no position to break it either. Luckily Kally does. "What are your thoughts on sharing this news with your children?"

Seriously! My thoughts are to ignore all of this and hope it goes away! Maybe we don't tell the children anything, how about that? How about this bad dream evaporates into nothingness, and we can continue on with the great lives we were living before the evil monster arrived on the scene!

Natalie jumps in. "We are kind of new to this, what do you recommend?"

Kally explains that the best way to break this kind of news to children is for us to be together, as a family. Kally would join us, and be ready to do whatever is necessary to help the boys understand what is happening, and to help them with the devastation they will feel. Oh, I have a bad feeling about this. It is going to be ugly, isn't it? But the boys, I've protected them from harm their entire lives. Now I will be subjecting them to the greatest of pain.

I say, "There is never going to be an easy time, or a right time, to deliver news as devastating as this. I think we need to do something sooner, rather than later."

Kally jumps in. "I agree."

"How about tomorrow afternoon, late?" Did I just say that? Tomorrow afternoon? Where did that come from? It doesn't matter. The world will stand down tomorrow afternoon, and the world will never be the same!

It is a restless night for me. There have been for far too many as of late. Natalie has a magic pill that helps her sleep, so she is out for the count. Just as well, that way I can toss and turn all I need. My insides are spinning like a top, random thoughts finding their way into my consciousness, making it near impossible to clear the debris field in my head so that the soft hush of sleep will find its way to me.

I give up on the notion of sleep and slip out of bed. I make my way to Jake's bedroom and quietly open the door. Just enough light from the hallway makes its way in, and I can see his face. My little boy rests in a sleep felt lull, at least one of us does. Not a care in the world. How little he knows. Tomorrow the news will shake his world to the core. On top of that, he will find himself stuck in a big tube, with all kinds of banging and clanging going on around him. While I watch him sleep, I wonder what will be next in his journey.

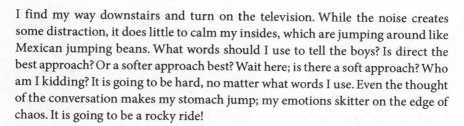

I find my way downstairs and turn on the television. While the noise creates some distraction, it does little to calm my insides, which are jumping around like Mexican jumping beans. What words should I use to tell the boys? Is direct the best approach? Or a softer approach best? Wait here; is there a soft approach? Who am I kidding? It is going to be hard, no matter what words I use. Even the thought of the conversation makes my stomach jump; my emotions skitter on the edge of chaos. It is going to be a rocky ride!

I crawl back into bed in the wee hours of the morning. I snuggle up next to Natalie, and spoon right on in. The way I figure, time for this special kind of intimacy has a shelf life, and I need to take advantage of it here in the now. Sleep still seems only a promise, but eventually I fall into a troubled slumber. Images and thoughts collide into a chaotic world where dreams are dark and heavy. Eventually, the alarm screams, beckoning me into a new and dreadful day.

Natalie gets up with me, and after a warm kiss, asks me to help her get dressed for the day. Rather odd, she has been doing that mostly by herself. I'm not sure what to make of it, if anything. I do the gentlemanly thing, and help her out. As I help her slip on her top, I notice small gatherings of little blackish and bluish dots on her body. I don't remember seeing them before. Wonder what they are all about? Odd.

The day weighs heavily on my heart. I do my best to keep my feelings out of the way and focused on the moment and the boys. After our conversations with them later this afternoon, things will never be the same, for any of us! It saddens me, hurts my heart to think about the days ahead!

I head into work for a bit before heading back to the apartment to pick up Jake and head off to the hospital for his MRI. Work is a good diversion, if only for a few hours. It feels good to be part of something other than the world of cancer and all the havoc it brings with it. Time moves by rather quickly, and I dread that it does. I'd like time to go into a holding pattern, like forever! I know that is not ever going to be possible, so I gather up my sad spirit and head off to tackle one of the monumental challenges for the day... Jake and the MRI.

Jake is at the apartment with Natalie, and he is ready. Natalie seems a bit peaked to me, off just a bit for her, maybe not as alert as she usually is. I wonder if things are becoming more painful. I give her a quick wink! She smiles in return. Trying to make light, best I can, knowing what awaits us just around the corner.

The techs at the hospital are so kind to Jake and do their best to put him at ease. They walk him all around the MRI, and explain things to him, trying to get him comfortable. Jake holds my hand the entire time with a vice-like grip; I think my son is a bit scared. Jake says little, even when the tech tries to engage him in conversation. At the end of our little tour, we are sent off to get Jake changed and into a lovely hospital gown.

I try to hand Jake off to the tech, and he is having no part of it! I get down on my knees so I can be on eye level with him and Bamo... tears are streaming down his face. Aw man, I think to myself! I say, "Everything is going to be okay Jake, I promise. This test will help the doctor figure out how best to care for you. Don't you want that?" I receive a deep, blue eyed, stare, and a slow side-to-side shake of the head. Just great, I think to myself. I ask the tech if I could help get Jake loaded up, and then leave the room for the actual test. Thankfully, she agrees.

I get Jake up on the table and buckle him in. I tell him I would be waiting right outside while they do the test. Jake still has a vice-like grip on my hand and makes no indication that he is about to let go. Before I can even begin to step away, he says, "Daddy, don't leave me, please don't leave me. Daddy, please, please, don't leave me." Big tears escape from his little boy eyes and roll down his cheeks. I look to the tech... and she smiles and says, "Sure." I could have hugged her!

I wait at the head of the tube, talking to Jake, and grab his hand as soon as I can. He holds on tight, what a grip! He is as still as a rock and does not move. Before we know it, the knocking sound is over, and Jake is moving on out of the tube. Hallelujah, we made it! Jake jumps off of the table and gives me a great big hug. I am not sure who is comforting who, it doesn't matter, and it just feels good.

I stop at Sonic and get Jake a milkshake, a little something to pick him up. It was quite the deal for me; I can just imagine what it was for him. As we drive back to the apartment, I am ever so anxious; it's hard to describe the feeling. If I had to choose a single word, it would be hurt. I have an open wound that won't heal, and it hurts. And to make matters worse, I will soon be hurting my children. What parent ever wants to do that? Someone, somewhere, tell me there is an easier way! Lord, are you out there? Please help me. Help us all Lord, through this day!

Time moves along just the same, propelling me toward a finish line I do not want to cross. As I sit poolside with the boys, I try to envision a world without Natalie and come up empty. Mostly, because I don't want to have that kind of dialogue with myself. There is another dialogue hanging on the horizon, and it is rapidly approaching like an incoming storm, promising to leave chaos and troubled souls in its wake. Our time with Kally is just around the corner. Ugh... my heart hammers away in my chest just thinking about it.

Natalie and I sit with the boys watching TV while we wait for Kally. The soft knock on the apartment door sounds like a stick of dynamite going off in my mind. It brings an immediate sense of dread. Not like any sense of dread I have ever felt. I move to answer the door, feeling like I am moving in slow motion. The boys are on high alert as a stranger enters the apartment. I do a quick round of intros, and the boys shake hands like the gentlemen they are.

I get Kally situated, and say, "Boys... we have some important news to share with you, and Miss Kally is here to help us."

A dead on stare greets me, unease obvious on each of their young faces. My heart is hammering in my chest – thump, thump, thump. I've never been so nervous in my life. I don't want to be in this place. I don't want to have to say the words I have to say... to share words that will cut like a knife... words that will steal joy. I don't want to do this, I don't.

I begin just the same. "You all know how sick Mom has been."

My heart is racing, wanting me to jump into an alternative universe. I am afraid I am going to come unglued here. Okay Bob, breathe... hold. One more hold. I don't want to do this! I don't want to hurt them.

There is an unexpected touch; I look down to see that Natalie has grabbed my hand. It calms me a bit, maybe soothes me. It brings me back into the moment, a moment I don't want.

I draw in another big breath. "Sometimes, boys... cancer can be tricky; tricky to treat and sometimes it comes back."

I see the unease in their faces; I can see their wheels spinning, panicking, and trying to figure out where all of this is going. Certainly, having a stranger in the mix is sending its own kind of signal. It seems like they are hanging on every word I say.

Okay Bob, here goes. "You know how we thought Mom's cancer was all gone? Well... Mom's cancer is back. It's back and the doctors say there is nothing... they can do... nothing..." Tears quickly spring to life, even as I try with all my might to keep a lid on them.

I wait for a reaction. I'm really expecting one, in a very big way. There is nothing. What is going on here? This is not at all what I expected.

Kally, in a low-key and soothing voice says, "Ryan, Jake, and William… this means that your Mom… is going to die. I'm so sorry. I'm so sorry!"

And there it is! Die! Death! Ryan screams, "Nooooooo… not Mom," and leaps to Natalie and throws his arms around her. He sobs for a second, a painful kind of sob, and then runs up the stairs to his bedroom.

Natalie is doing her best to maintain control, soft tears are falling from her cheeks as William quickly goes to her, tears flowing from his little boy eyes, and they grab hold of each other like they will never let go.

Jake is just sitting there, numbed by it all, tears running down his face as his reality sets in. I go to him, and he collapses into me and sobs - the kind that hurt when you breathe. I pick him up. What a day he has had, and we head for the stairs. I want to go to Ryan, to try and comfort him, if that is even possible, but don't want to leave Jake all alone.

Kally touches my arm softly, and says, "You stay here with Natalie, William, and Jake. I'll go to Ryan. This is why I am here. I can't make it go away, but I can help with what I can."

Right about now, I need every bit of the help I can get, and her light touch is a reminder to me of the frailty of the human spirit. With Jake in my arms, I go to Natalie and trade him out for William. William, his big teardrops falling endlessly, puts his arms around my neck and holds on tightly. Jake melts into his Mom's arms, and haltingly says, "I… don't want… you to… dieeeeeeeee Mommy!"

Time loses all meaning, and after a bit, William, Jake, Natalie and I all gather together on the couch, grounding each other in the moment. No words shared. Thoughts are too painful to process and are running rampant through everyone's mind. Eventually, Ryan comes downstairs with Kally and joins the crying mass of humanity. I can feel their raw pain.

After a bit, Kally says, "I think you guys should all go do something special tonight. It has been a tough day." Tough ya think, I say to myself.

Somehow, I get my wits about me, and say, "Hey, let's go to Sonic, and then we can go over to the house, and you guys can all show Mom your bedrooms. I bet they have made lots of progress."

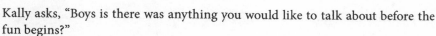

Kally asks, "Boys is there was anything you would like to talk about before the fun begins?"

As I would imagine, they have nothing. They are overwhelmed. So am I. I hurt my children today. I hurt them! I hate that I hurt them. Life shouldn't be like this. It shouldn't. I shouldn't have to hurt them.

Sonic, once a fun affair is anything but fun this night. It is quiet and somber. There will be no spirit lifting tonight! We make our way over to the house. Josh and his team have been busy. The house is further along than I could ever have imagined. Then I guess it has to be if we were going to hit our move-in date and beat the mighty hammer of fate.

The boys each have a turn walking Natalie through their room, telling her in great detail how they want their rooms to look, and where they will put all of their stuff. I stand in the doorways and watch from a distance. I try to imagine what the boys are feeling. I try to imagine a life without a Mom! I try to imagine what the days ahead will be like. I try to imagine a world without Natalie. I shiver at the thought.

I toss and turn all night; no sleep comes my way, again! Natalie gets up early with me, and I notice she is moving a bit slower. I could see it last night at the house too. It took almost everything she had to make it up the stairs with the boys. I can hear it in her breathing. I try to picture what might be happening on the inside of her body. I know the battle continues, and that the evil monster is winning. Surely it can't be gaining a stronghold already? We still have plenty of time left in the death march, right?

Once at work, I call Jake's doctor, to see if there just might be some MRI results. Of course, there are none. Dang it! I am stressed... I need to know... I have to know. So instead of playing the game of *catch*, I set up an appointment with the doctor. While I do not relish another doctor's appointment, it is a good plan.

I talk to Josh, telling him of our visit to the house last night, thanking him for the great progress. I am feeling better about us getting into the house before tragedy strikes. Josh reports we are still on target for June 25th. Wow – coming up quick.

Time to call the moving company and finalize plans. While I should be happy about this, I am anything but happy!

Inspiration...

The cords of death entangled me; the torrents of destruction overwhelmed me. The cords of the grave coiled around me; the snares of death confronted me. In my distress I called to the LORD; I cried to my God for help. From his temple he heard my voice; my cry came before him, into his ears.

Psalm: 18: 4-6

Reflection ....

I am not ready! Not now! Not ever! My heart is heavy in ways I never imagined possible. It hurts to breathe sometimes, to take that next breath. How will I ever overcome? How will I manage without her? I can't! I won't! No, that's not it, that's not it at all. I don't want to! I don't! I don't! I don't want to live life without her, alone, raising three boys in a strange land. This is not what I signed up for. This isn't my life's destiny.

I think, God, you've made a mistake here. I am not your man. Not me! I can't do this; I can't. You must have confused me with someone else - someone who could cope with all of this and come out the other side in one piece with his heart intact, a bit bruised maybe, but still intact. I am clearly not your man.

I thought that the battle against cancer was about as bad as things could get. But this? This, I am not prepared for. Not a chance. Death in a strange land? Come on now! I don't belong here, not now. I don't want this and all this stuff with Jake hanging in the balance. What is this Lord? The word cancer whispers a second time. Just how much is one soul expected to carry? Just how much?

It doesn't seem to be too much for Natalie though. How can she be so courageous? Natalie, forever the one based in reality, is the courageous soul. No pretense enters her sphere. Natalie knows things are not going to be all right and that time cannot be wasted pretending otherwise. She knows what is going to happen and how best to prepare for it. How to prepare her family for the dark days ahead. What she will do to ensure her loved ones are well cared for before she answers heaven's call! She has faith that there is a plan, and she holds onto it tightly.

Me, I feel stuck in some twilight zone. A place between denial and reality. The doctor's words, my reality, echo endlessly, all the while I build a wall of defense that says, no, not happening. To survive, sometimes I live in a Land of Pretend, where Natalie is not dying, and everything is going to be okay. I have to believe, now and then, that there will be a different outcome. I know these thoughts are misguided. It is the only way I can cope some days. To take a breath that doesn't hurt. To move myself forward, one minute at a time. It is all I can do. Is it possible that my tomorrows will be better than my today? Nice thought, but who am I kidding? I haven't even hit the darkest of days!

As I consider my journey, I realize I have conquered a few of my demons along the way. And maybe, I have coped with the things life has chosen to throw at me. Maybe I should give myself some credit here. I could have quit at any point in this journey, but I didn't! I stayed valiant, the best I could, against overwhelming odds. I have held my family together, while Natalie's life hung in the balance. I cleaned wounds and administered medicines, feeling ill-equipped to do it, but doing it just the same. Kept my job and coordinated a move to a strange land. And now Jake trying to get him through whatever lay ahead. No matter what is happening or happens, the drum beats and the death march continues.

I am ill-equipped though for the surge of emotions that overtake me like the raging storms of Texas, unannounced. I am angry, fearful, worried, betrayed, resentful, exhausted and sad. All of these wrapped up in a big ole package of despair. There seems to be no right or wrong way for me to feel, or think, and the raging storm clouds my ability to think, to think clearly.

It is all too easy for me to hang out with the dark spirits. They beckon, and I come running. Despair owns me in the minute to minute of my life. It is hard for me to reconcile, to figure out a way forward when life keeps kicking me back! I try to keep the dark spirits at bay, but it is easiest just to let them in and let them run wild with my spirit. They dance as the drum beats wildly.

In rare moments when I do have clarity of mind, I settle on three things I need to do to get through the dark days. Others will be looking my way, and following my lead. So I guess the first thing is for me to be courageous so I can help others along. Secondly, I need to help Natalie get ready for her journey home, to be with her Father in Heaven. It is a painful thought, but I am determined she will leave this world in peace, knowing her family is well cared for. The last thing, which is maybe the toughest, is that I need to get the boys prepared for their own dark days. I think if I can make these things happen, I can take care of my family. This can't be about me, my suffering; it can't. I have important things to get done.

I take a liking to my thinking. I do. By putting others first, I can put myself last. I can put their pain ahead of mine. Oh yeah, this can work for me. I am not ready to deal.

I will need my own time for that, and right now, others are more important. I need to get them through. Whatever it takes, whatever it takes.

When my emotions are running rampant, and my heart feels pummeled, I will press forward just the same. Although I am exhausted being everyone's everything, I will press forward just the same. While I am mourning the loss of the battle, I will press forward just the same. As the shadow of death draws nigh, I will press forward just the same.

Is this willingness of mine to press forward a bit about hope? Is that even possible for me? Will a bit of hope help me through? Maybe hope will make for brighter days. Maybe hope will get me out of bed in the morning. Will hope help me believe I can prevail? That I can get us all through this thing, as ugly as it will be?

It is with a heavy heart and troubled soul that I prepare for the dark days ahead as the death march continues on. I will work to keep my looming shadows at bay, hoping and pressing forward just the same. It is not easy to manage the spirit's influence, especially as the dark hour draws closer. As the dark spirits tighten the noose they have around me, I will work to push them away; using hope as my sword, and the joy of a life well lived, as a barrier.

My problem with the dark spirits is that they move in so stealthy, no advance notice provided, always catching me off guard. It takes hard work; it takes energy, the energy I sometimes feel I don't have. I push them away just the same. After all, I must be the strong one. I know I have to be determined, a life hangs in the balance, and I am determined to make the days ahead for my family as beautiful as possible. They will have to carry me through a lifetime.

But can they? Will they? Will they carry me and inspire me through the dark days I know are just ahead? Is it a choice? "Lord, will you join me in this? Will you help me through the dark days ahead? This is too much for one soul to bear Lord. Can we dial this thing back a little bit?"

Boom, Boom, Boom. The drumbeat continues... nothing will stop the march and the mighty hand of fate!

BOOK 7

Precipice

<u>Courage Has New Meaning</u>

Courage has new meaning
As I watch you fight for life
Hallow breathing, not but a whisper
Of the battle you must face
Into the dark unknown
You walk without hesitation
To battle against an enemy
Known only within your being
As the battle rages wildly
Your spirit reigns supreme
Proof that your life
Will defeat your unseen foe
You laugh in the face of despair
The spirit for life never warries
As you struggle to endure
The challenges of your pain
Love and friendship you sustain
Your faith never questioned
As you bring your strength to bear
Upon your quest for life
The enemy battles relentlessly
Thriving within your being
Your strength begins to diminish
The desire to love lessened
With all the courage of a hero
You prepare to leave this life
Words of encouragement you deliver
To those that gather close by
You bid farewell with dignity

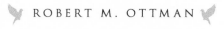
To a life filled with heaven's certainty
For every life you have touched has learned
Courage has new meaning

By: Robert Mapes

The Story ....

Julie, Pastor from our Plymouth Church, calls as she often does to check up on Natalie, the boys and me. It is a pleasant break from the rigors of work. Her voice is a reassuring one today. She shares that our church family is supporting us with thoughts and prayers. I'll take it. I give her the low down, most of it ugly, and talk about the 90 days. Julie is interested in the conversation we had with the boys, especially their reaction. Julie is relieved to know that we are working with hospice and that the counseling and grief team is already plugged in, especially for the boys.

I mention how happy I am that we'll get into the house earlier than planned. As I talk, Julie becomes oddly quiet. "Bob, have you ever heard the term nesting before?"

It seems like a rather random question. "Can't say that I have Julie."

"Well, it is a pretty simple concept. Natalie, as a wife and mom, will be focused on getting the boys and you to a place where she knows all will be well, safe and settled. A kind of nest, actually."

"I got ya Julie. Makes sense."

Softly she says, "You need to know that this nesting desire can be so strong that it can give individuals at the end of life stage, the drive to prevail, to endure pain and suffering, and to live to ensure their loved ones are cared for."

I start to retreat, not sure what all of this means. Julie quickly reads me and says with grace and compassion, "Bob, you need to realize that Natalie… might not have 90 days."

This blows me away. Nesting… what is this craziness? Not going to apply to my world. It is near the end of the workday, so I decide to call it quits. I head to the parking lot to begin the journey home. My conscious world spins on its axis, my thoughts colliding with the harsh realities Julie lay before me. The same truths Kally put out there for me! We aren't even at the 30-day mark. Is it possible I have

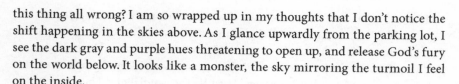

this thing all wrong? I am so wrapped up in my thoughts that I don't notice the shift happening in the skies above. As I glance upwardly from the parking lot, I see the dark gray and purple hues threatening to open up, and release God's fury on the world below. It looks like a monster, the sky mirroring the turmoil I feel on the inside.

I find my way to a low wall surrounding the parking lot, and take a seat, just as the skies become eerily dark. Clouds seem to get both tall and low, and I feel as if I could reach out and touch them. In the distance, I can see the big swords of light, as they shoot from the heavens earthward. The flat land makes today's view of the incoming storm spectacular.

I watch as the storm gains strength and ferocity. I think about my life, and how much my life is like the growing storm. The dark gray and purple skies remind me of my bruised spirit. Like lightning's randomness, so it is with my life. Everything, absolutely everything, seems so random and unpredictable. Are you painting this portrait Lord, to show me what is to become of my earthly life? You have captured all that I am feeling.

On the way home, the skies open up, and a deluge quickly follows. Lightning strikes quickly, and thunder seems to own the land. It is a full-out storm by the time I get to the apartment. The skies fill with bright flashes of light and intense roars. I make a wild dash toward the apartment, and glance up, and see just a few sets of eyes watching my wild run. I am pretty wet, actually more like soaked, and a wild thought flashed before me. I slow myself down a bit so I can live in this moment. As buckets of rain fall to the earth, I launch into some crazy, wild dance, spinning and jumping around like a madman. I see the boys watching me at the window; I can see their smiles. I continue with my wild man jive until the next clap of thunder. BAM! I make a wild dash up the stairs to the apartment.

I am completely soaked and greeted by howls of laughter from all interested parties. Seeing this light moment for what it could be, I chase the boys around the apartment and give them all soaking hugs. Natalie watches from the couch, with a big grin on her face. It is great to see her smile. I gather up the boys, who are now good and damp, and we all give Natalie a big ole hug. Damp as we are, we go out on the porch, and we all watch the storm. Thunder roars and lightning flashes. Without warning, there is a bright flash and a loud roar of thunder. The power is gone, and the lights blink an early good night.

We all make a dash for the porch door, and to the safety of the apartment. Natalie tells us all to get some dry clothes on, and while we all race up the stairs, pushing each other down and out of the way, she tracks down some playing cards and candles. By the time we return, she lights the candles and we are in for some family fun. The dim of the candlelight throws different shadows, though, and I can see just how thin Natalie has become. If I thought she was pale and gray before, it is nothing compared to what I see now. Must be the candlelight. There is nothing to worry about.

As the dark skies subside, the late day sun speaks to the earth below. We gather again on the porch, and a cool, gentle breeze dances about us. Gone is the hot, humid summer day. It is refreshing. Out of the blue, William shouts, "Look, Mommy, a rainbow… a rainbow!" Off in the eastern sky, is a spectacular rainbow. The colors glimmer over the landscape, highlighting God's promise, a promise to all of us, a promise of peace after the storm.

Morning dawns before I know it. I sleep fitfully again, dreams and realities all rolled into one subconscious and chaotic mess. There's so much to worry about. Natalie asks me for some help getting dressed; getting something up over her head on her own is now a real challenge. As I step in to help her, I notice that the black and purplish spots are much more prevalent, and spreading. What are they anyway? I choose not to explore the possibilities. No good will come from me finding an answer.

My rock, my sister Grace, has helped me hold it all together. She and her husband Rick will be staying with us for a couple of weeks. Together with the help of my Mom and Dad, we decide the entire family, my seven siblings and their spouses as well as a childhood best bud and his sweetheart, would head to Texas on Friday, June 25, to help us with the move on June 26. It is the best of news. Having so many helping hands is going to be a blessing.

Time presses forward, not waiting for anyone, especially me. It is a sunny afternoon when I return home from work. I push the apartment door open, thinking I might get a grand welcome of sorts, instead…. reality… slaps… me… hard! A cruel blow to the spirit! I am confused by its presence. Perhaps there's been a mistake? I look about, and see Natalie, so of course, I am in the right place. I still question the reality of what I see. Surely, it has no place in our world. Not yet anyway.

The red, four-wheeled transport mechanism graces the wall in the living room. A wheelchair… exactly what does this mean? Whatever it is, I am not ready. Natalie sees my confusion, and softly says, "Hospice thought it might be good to have a wheelchair handy, in case we need it." I push the swirling dark spirits away and put my best foot forward. I throw a soft smile on my face, and go to Natalie, and take her in my arms. I say, "This world is not going to be the same without you! I cannot even imagine! How will I ever go on?"

Natalie gently pushes my shoulders back, and looks me square in the eyes, and says using force in her soft voice, "You will go on, and you will heal, and you will be the man I know you can be. You are stronger than you give yourself credit for!"

I kiss her forehead, and we return to our hugging state. I am not so sure I believe her, as all kinds of conflicting emotions swim within me. As we hug, she whispers softly in my ear, like a mother to a child. "It will be alright. I promise you; it will be alright." Oh, how I needed to hear those words. Now if only I can convince myself that it will be alright.

Natalie breaks away and mentions that she got a call from the elementary school, William's kindergarten teacher to be exact. The teacher said she had some concerns about William, and thought it might be best if we set up a parent-teacher conference. The appointment is tomorrow. Yikes!

We meet with William's kindergarten teacher as planned. She is a gem. As sweet as the day is long and very interested in William, and all that is going on in his world. She indicates to us that she is concerned about his development, and his readiness for first grade. Surprised? NOT! How could William be ready? It doesn't take long for us to realize William isn't equipped academically or emotionally to successfully conquer the first grade.

Mrs. Gellens suggests, perhaps, that William repeat kindergarten. She explains that this would give William the foundation he needs to be successful in first grade. Natalie wants to make sure we make the right decision here, and softly launches into the world we have been living in for the last two years. The teacher looks at Natalie sadly, and says, "I am so sorry for all that you, and your family, have endured." I think to myself, you haven't heard anything yet Mrs. Gellens. Without much fanfare, Natalie covers the road yet to be traveled, and with grace and dignity, she tells Mrs. Gellens that she will soon die, in answer to the death march, and that William may start the new school year without his Mom.

Well, that sucks all of the air out of the room. Mrs. Gellens puts her hand on Natalie's arm and tells her how incredibly heroic she is, to battle such an incredibly powerful disease. How resolved she is to come to the school and plan for her son's future. Natalie is courageous, and how she can hold it together here in this moment, is a testament to that strength.

Natalie says, "Given all that we have shared with you, and what you know of William, what would you do if he was your little boy?" The teacher pauses for just a second and gracefully responds. "I'd have him repeat kindergarten." Done! That is all Natalie needs to hear. The teacher in her is of the same opinion. Natalie briefly looks my way, like I have any say in the matter. I do some quick math, but don't ask me why. According to my calculation, it looks like William will be stuck alone with his Dad for at least 13 school years! Poor kid.

Once we get to the car, I can't help but smile. Natalie was on her 'A' game during the meeting with Mrs. Gellens, and I just let her roll with it. She seems more energetic than I have seen her in days, and this is a welcome sight to me. She dressed to the nines, and even though her hair is growing back, she wore a wig and makeup. With the clock ticking away, I think that just maybe, the doctor is wrong. Maybe, we will get well beyond the 90 days. You never know!

Natalie notices my smile, and says, "Why the Cheshire cat kind of grin?"

"You were pretty remarkable back there."

She smiles and says, "It is the right thing. William is going to need the time and so are you."

"Yeah, Yeah, Yeah!"

"Remember Bob… you made a couple of promises to me, and I want to be sure you are able to deliver, promises made are promises to be kept. Hey, I have an idea of something I'd like to do Saturday."

I say with a smile on my face and in my voice, "Oooooo… should I be worried?"

Natalie's idea was to take the boys to a lakeside retreat at Lake Grapevine for a picnic. Why not? I'll take any opportunity that will make us feel like a family. I smile. "Great idea, it will be a blast. How about I get you back to the apartment, and I hit the grocery store and get all of the things we will need for our little outing?"

I get Natalie home in time to rush off to Jake doctor's appointment. Talk about balance. Time to get the scoop on Jake. I need the calm. It is an eerie feeling walking into the waiting room alone. Is this a sign of things to come? It seems like a million years pass before a nurse calls my name. As I stand up, I feel a bit on the woozy side from lack of sleep. I jump into self-talk mode, telling myself that I can do this, as I walk down the hall to Dr. Frampton's office.

Dr. Frampton greets me warmly, and asks all about Natalie, where we are in our journey against the hands of time, and inquires about all of the boys. We talk about everything it seems and spend a good bit of time talking about Jake. He wants to know all about his activity level and to see if I have noticed any change in his left leg. While the care and concern are heartwarming, I am about ready to jump out of my skin! I need the bottom-line… on Jake. Finally… we get to the results of the MRI. Dr. Frampton begins. "The good news is there is no sign of cancer or any other kind of growth. While this is good news, the bad news is that I am perplexed as to what is happening."

I do not hear much of anything after 'no sign of cancer.' I disappear somewhere inwardly, not sure where. I am so relieved. I say a quick praise God as my thoughts start wandering the lands. Dr. Frampton continues talking as if I'm listening. I'm picking up pieces and parts, and reel myself back into the conversation when Dr. Frampton asks, "When would be a good time to put the cast on Jake's leg?"

I try to catch up, but find myself thinking, what cast? I am not tracking with the good doctor. Recovery mode, where are you, Bob? So I ask the doctor, "Why… exactly… do you think a cast would be helpful for Jake?"

I focus now as the doctor explains that immobilization might do the trick, let whatever is happening in Jake's leg settle down, and maybe even heal. Okay, got it now. All I know is that it isn't cancer. Hallelujah! And it isn't a growth. Hallelujah! I am on board to do whatever the doctor thinks is necessary. I make an appointment for Jake to get his cast the following Monday. Hallelujah!

I stop by the grocery store and pick up all of the things we will need for a great outing to Lake Grapevine. I am pretty excited about it. I am worried about Natalie though. I worry about her energy level and her ability to keep up. I sense this is pretty important to her, and that she will do whatever it takes to make this the special outing she has in her mind.

Once at the apartment, I track down Rose Lynn and the boys at the pool, and get them to help haul in the groceries, and to help surprise Natalie with a lounge chair I bought her. A good resting place is exactly what she needs! The boys are all about the surprise, and we have fun surprising Natalie! She is all grins and the boys are all hugs! I freeze frame. How I am going to miss these moments.

I get up early Saturday and check out the weather. Natalie stirs as I get up, and asks what I am doing getting up so early. I tell her I want to try and get everything ready and the car packed. I want to hit the Lake early, and get a great picnic spot.

I want to be sure we are in the shade somewhere. I want Natalie to be cool and comfortable. It tends to be a bit warm in Texas in the summer.

The boys get up early too; they must have heard me moving about. I know they are excited! They help pack up the car, and before I know it, we are ready. Natalie gets herself dressed, no need for my help today. Maybe she is gaining some strength or is it just my wishful thinking. It is a warm day already, lots of sunshine, blue skies and a mighty breeze coming from the southwest.

Lake Grapevine, we are amazed by the size of it. It is HUGE! It seems like it goes on forever. High cliffs partly line the shoreline. Its beauty simply enthralls us. The boys are excited. I park the car, and we all head toward the Lake. William is just teeming with excitement; he is dancing up and down! The boys love the water, and love to swim. I think it is going to be a great day. As we near the Lake, I can see the Texas breeze at work. Large waves are hitting the rocky shoreline.

William takes one look at the shore and the waves, and yells out, "Look, Mommy, it's the ocean… it's the ocean!" Too funny, I am about to bust out, but Natalie gives me the ole evil eye, telling me it is best if I don't go there. She stoops down, grabs William in her arms, and kisses him on the forehead and says, "Yes baby, look at the ocean, isn't it beautiful!"

As she stands back up, she loses her footing and teeters just a bit. Before I can even react, a total of six hands are in place and have her steadied! Once she gains her footing, Ryan, Jake and William walk her to a spot under the trees where there is plenty of shade. Freeze frame. A memory for a lifetime. I am not needed. Ryan makes a quick dash to the car to get the lounge chair, and Jake and William hang with their Mom until they all have her comfortably situated.

Then all bets are off as the three boys race to the shoreline where there is immediate splashing and yelling! It is good to see and it feels normal. You would never suspect, looking at this family, that a death march is now under way. I sit on the ground by Natalie, enjoying being close, watching the boys play in the water. She is tired, I can tell. She lies down and is asleep before I know it, a kind of special contentment on her face. I kiss her forehead and make my way for the craziness. I get myself right smack in the middle of it all.

The day passes all too quickly, and before we know it, the sun is getting low on the horizon. Natalie slept off and on most of the day. She did her very best to be present and in the moment. I go down to the shore to collect stuff so we can get packed up and ready ourselves for the journey home to the apartment. I notice I have lost the boys somewhere along the way and glance back toward Natalie. There they are, all gathered around their Mom, talking about their day, talking about who did what to who, and was she privy to all of it. I can't help but wonder if they have a clue that a train wreck is heading their way?

Eventually, we make our way home. It is a quick jaunt and everyone is so quiet. Obviously, we're all worn out by the day, even the boys. My forehead is pounding, not sure from what, but it is letting me know it is not happy. Ryan jumps out of the car when we arrive at the apartment, taking point on getting his Mom get up the stairs. Jake and William help me unload the car. I look up and see Natalie sitting on the stairs, with Ryan standing close at hand. I panic, thinking something is wrong. I make a mad dash. Natalie assures me that all is well; she just needed a break before climbing the rest of the stairs. Not a good sign I think to myself, not a good sign at all.

Monday dawns as surely as a new day! It is time for me to head back to work. I have some things I need to tidy up, and I need time to make a few phone calls. I check in with Josh first and confirm that the house closing is still set for the 25th. While the house will be ready, I am not so sure about Natalie, not so sure she has the strength to get through it. Life gave me some lemons; I'm going to try and make some wine.

I call Patty, our realtor, and tell her about Natalie's weakened condition, and suggest we move the closing to the apartment. Patty, given the circumstance, agrees to check into it. She calls me back pretty quickly and has great news. The closing will be at our apartment. Great glory! I just hope Natalie will see this as a good thing, and not a sign that she is losing the battle.

It seems pretty quiet on the home front. I can tell the boys are at the pool with Rose Lynn, so I quietly let myself into the apartment. Natalie is sound asleep on the couch. I sit in the chair next to the sofa and watch her sleep; her breathing seems so shallow. She is so much thinner and pale than I remember from just the other day; I can see it in her face now, the dark shadows. Is this how it is at the end? As that thought flitters briefly across my consciousness, I push it away immediately! I am not ready to go there.

I get a book to read, and sit quietly with Natalie. Eventually, she stirs. "How long have you been there?"

"Not too long. How are you feeling? You get a good nap?"

"I feel so tired all the time. I want to be with you, Bob… with the boys, live what life I have left."

"I know Natalie, I know. I think being well rested is part of that life."

"I guess."

"I talked to Patty. She's arranged to have the closing here at the apartment."

Natalie looks at me sadly, and quietly nods her head. Breaks my heart.

"Hey Natalie, how about we swing by the house and check it out. I bet it is almost finished. Could be a fun field trip?"

She smiles broadly. "I think I'd like that."

Time to load the boys into the car and head to the doctor's office for the grand casting event. Natalie is tired, so I am running solo, a sign of things to come I am afraid. Dr. Frampton greets us all warmly and takes us all back to show us what would be happening with the casting. At the end of the demo round, he lets Jake pick out the color he wants for his cast and he picks fluorescent pink! No surprise there.

I can see Natalie's presence here in this world slipping through my fingers. Try as I might to slow it down, it continues to rush by. The days are long and hot, and though the skies are often blue and filled with bright sunshine, there is a kind of grayness that hovers just outside my reach. It is the day before the closing, and Natalie is just too tired to make it to the walkthrough. I am not alone during the walk through; a sense of gloom is there to accompany me. Funny, the gloom feels welcome.

The closing is a quiet affair and goes without a hitch. Not that I expected one. Moving the new house closing to the apartment is a good thing. Natalie is really worn; I can see it in her waning energy level. Just the same, she does her best to get all dolled up for the big event. I help her steady herself as she puts on a bit of makeup, trying to bring some color to her growing gray pallor. I help her get dressed and notice that the shades of purple and blue own more of her body. It saddens me, having to accept that the evil monster is waging a battle against a caring soul. Does the battle ever end? Might not like the answer to that one.

Moving day is a special event. It is so great to have all of my brothers and sisters, their significant others, special friends and my parents with us. Natalie is adamant that the house is going to be completely set up complete… finished! Julie jumps to the forefront of my mind, along with the notion of nesting. It bounces around for a moment, but I quickly push the thought away. I don't even want to contemplate the notion of nesting and what it can mean to my life.

Somehow, like magic, breakfast arrives at the house. The moving truck arrives as planned, and my Dad takes point as the inventory control man. Mom says, "Good job for him, it will keep him out of everyone's way!" Only Mom can get away with saying that! Friends I had made in the short time we have been in Texas find their way to the house to help with the move. It is, as near as I can tell, an all hands on deck kind of event. Who knows, maybe we will get everything set up, complete, finished!

It is evident that there is only one queen in this kingdom this day. Natalie is up and about best she can, directing and guiding, organizing and placing. No question. Everyone takes their orders and then go about doing the business at hand. Miraculously, lunch, like breakfast, just shows up. I am SO thankful that I do not have to worry or think about it. It is one less thing; I have plenty of other stuff to worry about.

It is early afternoon when the truck pulls away, and Natalie asks me to go upstairs and try to get the boys and their rooms situated. I am not even sure where to start. Stuff is piled and stacked everywhere. Others offer to help, and I gladly take them up on it. After a bit, I head downstairs to check on things. As I turn the corner into the family room, I see my beautiful bride, working to stay in the moment. She looks so tired and frail, a former shell of herself and appears lost in the wheelchair. The site shocks me and catches me unprepared; I can see fate casting a wider web.

I roll with it just the same. "Hey, Hon, how are things looking down here? The boys' rooms are coming together slowly, but we're making progress."

"I forgot about the couch, Bob, I forgot."

I'm afraid where this is going. "What about it?"

With a strong emphasis, Natalie says, "We need a couch."

"We can pick one out later… we have so much yet to do today."

This time out, she is adamant, forceful. "We need a couch. We have to have a couch. Maybe we shouldn't have given ours away?"

My sister Grace, always on the ready, is getting a quick read on the situation, and says, "How about if Bob and I go out and buy a couch for you?"

Natalie immediately relaxes and smiles warmly. She clearly likes the idea. She is determined! So, Grace and I collect our marching orders, and away we go. It is late afternoon by the time we get back. Natalie is completely spent, and has fallen asleep in the master bedroom. I peek in and watch her quietly sleep. I decide not to wake her and tell her of our success in the quest for the perfect couch. That can come later. Right now, while things seem to be under control, I sneak away to my car and take off to the grocery store. I realize I have not done anything special for Natalie, chaos owning my life. It is time for a couple of Kit Kat Bars and some flowers!

I knock softly on our bedroom door, and quietly open it; I sit down bedside, close to Natalie.

"Hey, hon, how ya feeling?"

She smiles; "Just a bit tired, kind of like a truck hit me. It has been a busy one."

"I'll say. Grace and I got the couch all set. They will deliver it on Monday!" She smiles broadly. I smile back at her, and say, "I brought you a gift or two."

I bring out flowers, and she takes them in her delicate hands, and pulls them in close to her, snuggles with them. She doesn't say a word. She doesn't need to. I bring out the Kit Kat bars; this brings a big ole grin, and it warms me from the inside out.

"Remember our first Kit Kat bar?" I say with a smile of my own. "Who gave it to whom first?"

She giggles lightly. "I gave it to you first. It was our first Easter together, senior year of college. We had just started dating. I'll never forget."

She takes my hand in hers; it is delicate like fine china, thin, it feels like it could break. She smiles. "You have been so valiant... so faithful... so caring... so courageous through all of this." Barely above a whisper, she continues. "I could not have made it... done it, lived through it, without you. You are my... rock!"

"No… it is you, Natalie! You have been my inspiration! When I felt weak, you were strong. When I thought I couldn't bear it any more… you brought me peace. When I thought I couldn't endure… you smiled and lightened my load. I am a better man… because of you."

Her eyes close, her grip tightens slightly. "I love you… and I am a better woman because of you."

I lean in to hug her, to hold her frail frame, with what strength she has; she says, "It won't be long now."

Tears flow from my eyes, I work to hold back a sob, and it catches in my throat. It is hard to speak. "I'm not ready… I'll never be ready… for a life without you."

She places her hand on my cheek, with her thumb she gently brushes my tears away, and smiles that easy smile. "You'll be okay, Bob… I promise… I'll always be with you." And with that, she places her hand on my heart. "I'll always be with you."

She closes her eyes, clearly drained by it all; she is still snuggled up with the flowers and Kit Kat bars. I kiss her forehead lightly; it is cool to the touch of my lips. "Get some rest, my love, tomorrow is another busy day."

I don't know why time refuses to stand still, if only for a moment or two. It presses forward, taking me with it, whether I like it or not. It is Sunday just the same, time for my parents, family, and friends to depart! It is a somber event. It is not a typical goodbye as in "see you later". This is forever goodbye! It is gut wrenching to watch. One by one, everyone hugs Natalie tightly; tell her how much they love her, all the while having a personal meltdown. It hurts to watch, the pain palpable. The boys stay close to me, snuggling in. Christina is last, and leans in for her goodbye; she and Natalie grab hold of each other. After a bit of sobbing, Natalie somehow chokes out, "I'll never get to hold… my niece or my nephew." That is all she wrote. No recovering from that.

Monday comes like every Monday before it! No slowing the hands of time, as much as I want to. Natalie is BEAT! She barely stirred all night long and doesn't even move as I get out of bed this morning. I wonder if this is 'it,' that the time is now. Nah, I quickly dismiss the notion. I'm not ready! Not ready for love's last kiss!

As I head off to work, I do so with a heart that is heavy. Grace and Rick are staying with us for a couple of weeks to help us get settled I am elated. I have been so worried about balancing all the stuff in my world. Today, Grace is going to be on point to work with the boys, to get rooms squared away, and tackle some things on Natalie's wish list. I leave knowing Grace has it all under control. Glad someone does. It clearly is not me.

It is a tough workday for me. Having the gauntlet of death hanging over me, it is hard to concentrate. Painfully… the hours pass me by, and the workday is over. Whew! It feels good pulling in the driveway. The boys run out and greet me warmly, but man, they are highly charged! They cannot wait to show me their rooms. Grace has been a busy one. After the tour of rooms, Grace tells me that hospice had come to the house and that they are going to start coming every day. Oh boy, no good can come from this. I am not ready. Death, go away, you have no place here! The death march continues anyway.

Tuesday is a repeat of Monday! I work as much as I can, feeling as if I am not contributing my fair share. I try to focus, but it is extremely difficult. I am jumbled up mess of thoughts and emotions. Dark spirits are constantly on call, and I can feel them tightening their grasp on my heart. Natalie is sort of up when I get home. I should feel elated, but I feel anything but elated. She does not look well, not well at all. She is weak, lethargic, and so very pale, and gray. She is as gaunt as I have seen her. She smiles at me from the new couch just the same. Grace takes me aside, and tells me Natalie struggled all day trying to stay in the moment; she seems disconnected from the world.

Grace and I think it is all about the stronger pain meds. What else can it be, right? Yeah… it is the meds. I go to her on the couch, sit by her. She barely notices my presence. I take her hand in mine, and squeeze but she doesn't squeeze back. I kiss her on the cheek; she is cool to the touch. She announces weakly that she'd like to go back to bed. I help her up from the couch; she is light, like a feather. She is uneasy on her feet; placing one foot in front of the other seems to be a struggle. We move slowly to the bedroom, and I get her settled in bed. She is wearing her favorite navy blue polka dot pajamas.

The boys tire themselves out poolside. They even take themselves to bed. Who would have thought? Been a busy few days. Once they are all settled, a collective sigh of relief is felt throughout the house. Soon after, Grace and Rick call it a night. I head off to bed myself. I crawl into bed, and say a quick goodnight to my lovely bride, and give her a light kiss on her forehead. She is still cool to the touch, maybe more than she was just a bit ago. She doesn't stir, doesn't move. No response. Odd I think. She must be exhausted. I can only imagine!

I get up before the household. I want to get into the office early so I can get out early, and be home with everyone. I have lost track of time, and I am not sure where we are against the clock of life! All I know is that the death march continues, and the drum beats loudly this morning. I lean in to kiss Natalie goodbye, and she is in almost the same exact position and spot she was in last night when I said goodnight! Come to think of it, I don't remember her moving much during the night. I don't even think she stirred.

I try to focus on work. It is tough. The phone comes to life, startling me, bringing me back from the brink. It is Grace, her voice telling me she is in a state of panic. I know something is wrong.

"Bob... oh, Bob! You need to get home. You need to get home now, like NOW!"

"Hey, Gracey, what ya got?"

"Look, Bob, hospice is here, and they just checked Natalie's vitals, they think this is it."

"What... what?" I am confused, unsure. "What do they mean... this is it?"

"This is it, bucko, you better get home, get home fast. Natalie is fighting for every breath... you can hear it! Go, go, go!"

"Noooooooooooooooo... this cannot be it Grace! It can't be!"

"Get it together Bob... you don't have time to dally!"

Okay, what to do, what do I do? Okay, got it, think, think, think! That church, yeah that one close to the house, the one Natalie and I talked about joining, what was the name of it? Come on Bob! Think... think! Got it! Where is a phone book when you need it? Panic, panic! Find a phone book! Screw it; I call information!

I get a phone number and start punching numbers. There just has to be someone there at the church that can help me, help us! The phone rings a couple of times, and finally, after what seems like hours, someone answers. I ask if there is a minister available, I am told yes, and then immediately passed through.

I try to calm myself. "Hi, this is Bob and I am in a desperate state, and I need your help right now." My words tumble out haltingly, seemingly falling all over the place. Every nerve in my body is on fire, and I am scared. Really scared!

"This is Jacob, and I am the senior pastor here at the church. Can I ask what you so desperately need help with?"

"I don't have much time here Jacob. So in a nutshell, we moved into our new house on Saturday. It is just around the corner. My wife, Natalie, she has cancer. Hospice just called and said she is being called home. She is about to leave me, to leave us, the boys and I. Will you help me... us?"

"Okay, got it, Bob. What is your wife's name, and where do you live?"

I give the info to Jacob, and he is on his way by the time I hang up the phone.

I run out of my office, telling Steve's executive assistant, "This is it," and run out the door to the elevator. I don't have time to be emotional; I have to have all of my faculties if I am going to make it home to Natalie in time. I am not ready! I put the pedal to the metal, racing home! I make it in record time.

Grace greets me at the door with a big hug. "Bob, hospice is still here, they will be staying. Natalie will be leaving us shortly... she is fighting, fighting to hold on until all of her family is gathered with her."

The word gathered throws me off, and an internal alarm puts me on high alert. "Okay Grace... so what's the problem?"

Panic clearly owns the moment, and Grace says, "The boys... they are off with Rick at the movies, we had no idea we were in this place, no idea."

"It is okay, Grace... it will be okay! You know Natalie, she is not going anywhere until the boys are here, of that I am certain."

I force myself forward and introduce myself to the hospice nurse in the bedroom. She quietly says, "I'm so sorry... you have a beautiful family." I look at Natalie, and she seems so serene... angelic. There is a kind of softness about her now. It is hard to describe. I watch as she fights for every breath. Long... hard... and labored breaths. It is clear she is fighting the fight.

Then it hits me hard! This is it! This is really it! I am not ready. I am not! Can you ever be ready? I am not! Please, isn't there an alternative here? Isn't there? If not Lord, can you please, please stay with her, stay with her Lord until the boys get home? Let the boys get here, Lord! Please let them get here before You carry her home! I am so focused on the moment that I don't take in the strangers in the

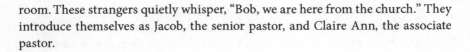

room. These strangers quietly whisper, "Bob, we are here from the church." They introduce themselves as Jacob, the senior pastor, and Claire Ann, the associate pastor.

I take their hands. "Thank you… thank you so much. Thank you for being here with us."

I am glad to see them. Never done this before. Don't want to do this now, but that is not an option. Natalie is still in the fight, taking very labored breaths. My own breathing cadence shifts, and I find myself breathing every breath right along with her. Willing her to live, to live until the boys get home.

The hospice nurse looks to me. "You need to know that Natalie is very much alert in her mind… she knows everything that is going on." She turns to Natalie. "You keep right on fighting honey; we're working to get your boys home."

It seems like days before the boys get home, and finally, there is a welcome slamming of car doors, the garage door opens. I take a big breath, and greet the boys at the door, stooping down to eye level.

I take another deep breath. "Hey, guys … you know Mom has fought a great fight, done everything she can to make sure we are all set, but I have to tell you… that it is time… for Mom… to go home to heaven."

They look at me, confused. Tough to absorb, I get it. I'm in that same place. Another deep breath. "This means guys… that Mom is dying … she…"

I can't do it… my head falls to my chest; I work to bottle up my emotions. I force myself to finish. "… she will be leaving us soon, very soon… it is time for us all to say our forever goodbyes."

They storm past me, into the bedroom. They glance briefly at the strangers gathered, and seem confused by their presence, but a glance at the bed prompts them to action.

Ryan jumps on the bed, straddles Natalie's body, and falls into her, hugs her tightly, waits for her response, there is none. "Mommy, Mommy, please don't die… please don't die!" A flood of tears springs to his eyes.

Natalie continues her fight for life, the spark dwindling quickly. Her breaths are shorter, further apart. This is it. I am not ready. Okay, Lord, bring her home safely!

Jake moves in closer to his Mom, unsure. He haltingly reaches for Natalie's hand, holds it briefly, and when he doesn't get a response, he returns to my side, falling into me, rivers of tears running down his face. I put my right arm around him; try my best to console him.

William, on my left side, is trying to crawl up me. I bend down to pick my little man up, and he falls into me, crying. He wraps himself tightly around my neck; I hold him close in return. I want to go to Ryan; there is only so much of me to go around.

Grace is quietly sobbing and is close to both Ryan and Natalie. She tries to soothe Ryan, telling him everything will be okay. Will it be, I think to myself, will it be? It hurts to see Natalie fighting so. She has fought so hard and for so long. I want her to have peace, to be at peace, for the pain. Yes, for the pain to go away for good.

I am surprised when I hear a voice break the imminent doom, especially when I realize it is my own. I choke back a sob, forcing myself to give her the all clear. "We love you, Natalie… we do and we are all here, all of us, the boys - your Ryan, your Jake and your little man, William. We are all here. Grace and Rick, they are here too… it is… okay… to let go… my love… it is okay to let go… to go home, home to your Heavenly Father."

I sense tranquility about her now. She continues to fight the fight. Her breaths begin to fall off slowly and over the course of minutes they become erratic. They are short, barely a breath at all now. With all of us sobbing and breathing right along with her, Natalie takes a very shallow and labored breath. I wait for the next one. It never comes. It never comes! She is gone! She is gone! It never comes! I try to will her to breathe but to no avail. Just like that, she leaves us, and this earthly world for a better place in heaven - the perfect place for my angel. I draw little comfort knowing this.

My insides hurt, and not just from crying. It feels like someone has kicked me in the ribs. I can't move, just can't. Jake and William have a fearful stronghold on me. Someone, I am not sure who goes to Ryan to soothe him enough to get him off of the bed and over to me and his brothers. I put William down and hug all my boys, my sons, my little men, knowing that they will never be quite the same and that life will never be the same. Grace and Rick join in the group hug and somehow we move as a single entity out of the bedroom.

I comfort the boys the best I can, and head back to the bedroom, hoping this is still a bad dream. Reality slaps me hard; the Ministers are administering last rites.

I could puke! How can this be happening, and how did I ever end up in this place? As Jacob finishes the last rites, I grab Natalie's hand. It is so frail, pale, and gray. I give it a squeeze, hoping for a return squeeze… it doesn't come. It will never come again! She is gone. She… is… gone!

Jacob turns to me and suggests that we prepare Natalie for burial. He said it would be easiest to do before the hearse arrives. I can't cry, I can't respond! I can't do anything! Jacob, sensing that I am just numb by all of this, recommends that I pick out one of Natalie's favorite outfits for burial purposes and that I go and sit outside, let them take care of things with Natalie. I am not sure what to do; I decide to go with his plan.

Jacob quietly says, "Before you go, Bob, you need to decide what to do with Natalie's jewelry." What, me decide? Surely he is kidding? I don't want to have to decide anything; not a thing, this is too much. Oh, she can't be gone. She can't be!

I look to Grace, and she says, "I think you need to keep it. Think about the boys one day. It might be nice to pass a bit of their Mom on to them."

I am frozen in place. I don't want this. Why can't everyone see this? I take a deep breath. I dig deep, remembering that I must be strong, realizing that Grace is right! I gently reach for Natalie's left hand, and gracefully slip her rings off. They slide off all too easily, a reminder that the evil monster has claimed victory. I think back to the words we shared on our wedding day, till death do us part. It is too soon, this death thing. It should not be here and now. This is not how this should have played out.

There is a ring still on her right hand, and there is someone special I want to give that ring to. I gently slide this last one off her hand, and turn to Grace. "I think Natalie would like it if you had this one." All I had to say, we fall into each other, each grounding the other's heart.

Grace gently escorts me out of the room, and onto the small porch off of the master. Someone, I'm not sure who said they would come and get me when everything is done. I am not sure what that means exactly, but I am beyond trying to figure stuff out. Pointing me in a direction is the best bet at this point. I find myself outside, sitting on the porch, watching the sun dance in the western sky, as it considered its options for a sunset, as it had for all of the millennium. I hope it would be a spectacular one, in Natalie's honor this day.

I sit in the warm June sun, watching the clouds play in the sky, wondering where Natalie is. I lift up a single prayer. "Lord, this is just too much, way too much. I miss her already… please bring her home safely, Lord. Please, Lord, let me know she is okay. I need to know; I have to know. Help me Lord to live in a world without her. Amen." And with that amen, I sense the dark spirits gathering. They foretell of a great darkness that will come upon my lands. I try to push them away. Interestingly, they have gained strength.

The door opens quietly. I hear soft footsteps. I don't turn around. I don't need to. I feel Grace's soft touch. She sits down quietly beside me. She drapes her arm across my back, her head gently falling against my shoulder. We sit quietly. No one speaks. No one has to. Isn't that how love works sometimes? You just know the love is there! Is that how it works with God? As the clouds continue their dance in the sky, the hearse pulls away. I can't cry. I can't feel. I am numb!

Inspiration

The Lord is my shepherd; I shall not be in want. He makes me lie down in green pastures: He leads me beside quiet waters. He restores my soul. He guides me in paths of righteousness for His name's sake. Even though I walk through the valley of the shadow of death, I will fear no evil, for you are with me; your rod and your staff, they comfort me. You prepare a table before me in the presence of my enemies. You anoint my head with oil; my cup overflows. Surely goodness and love will follow me all the days of my life, and I will dwell in the house of the Lord forever.

Psalm: 23

Reflection

The drum speaks to those weary of spirit, the beat of the death march calls to the mournful. It calls to me. I feel the beat… of the drum. It is loud, pounding at my consciousness, beckoning me. The anticipation is ghastly. How do I prepare for the end of the march, and the inevitabilities heading my way? How do I prepare the boys?

Truthfully, can you ever be prepared? When it comes down to the end game, what can you do? Sadly, all I can do is wait. So it begins, the waiting game. The counting and waiting and the hoping and praying! It seems it is all I can do. I try to enjoy the last bit of life we have on this earth together, but I hear the drum beating in the background, it is constant… endless. I am painfully forced into a reality that does not match the desire of my heart.

I think Natalie knew right along when she would leave this world, but she didn't want to burden me, so she hid her dark secret. She knew her time was limited. The mastectomy was the sign that closed the deal, told her life was coming to an end. Life taught her what to value most, maybe a lesson for us all. She set her sights on the priorities that mattered most, little space in her world for the trivial, the common worries that plague us one and all. Her spirit, focused on love, love of God, love of family, and love of friends. Her goal, prepare her family for a life without her. How do you do that? How did she do that? Focus so intensely knowing the death march would eventually end.

Me, I was in denial. I knew the angels would come calling, but believed they would arrive according to my timeline, the one I had set in my head. When I left for work and said my goodbye to Natalie, I never dreamed the end game was here, that it was time for her to be called home. I was surprised when Grace made the dreaded call to me at work. Once home, I could tell immediately that the line dividing this world and the next was already blurring. I think she was ready to move on to the other side. But Natalie is strong, so strong, and is determined to stay on this side, this world until her family is gathered. Am I surprised? Not at all. She has fought long and hard without complaint, and with faith in a Lord she knew was standing by her side.

The drum beats one... last... time... and I watch Natalie take her last breath and she becomes quiet, still. I try willing her to take another breath, but there isn't one. None! I can feel, almost sense, something leaves her body. It is hard to describe. I feel as if I am in the land of the living, and also in the land of the dead. As that something left her body, I also felt something leave mine, a part of my soul I think. Together we had become one. It hurts, a physical pain I can't quite explain.

And as one... we had built a life... and a family. We had children, three beautiful boys. It has been a struggle for me knowing that all of this, everything, would hurt them in ways I could never imagine. They don't want their Mom to leave! Their cries for her are palpable and hurt my heart like an electric jolt. I want to soothe them, but I don't know how. It hurts to think, to move. But move I do, to best comfort them. They grab hold and hang on for dear life. Their sobs racking their bodies... hurting me! There will be a wound on their heart that they will carry for the rest of their lives.

I think about Heaven, and what it is like to enter Heaven's Gate. What it's like to see the face of God? Wow! Hard to wrap my earthly bound head around that and what it might be like, to see God, to stand in His mighty presence. I take comfort knowing that in His presence, she is pain-free. She needed to be pain-free. But me, I have a kind of pain I have never felt before which kind of makes me question this notion of heaven. Heaven. If I can't see it, or feel it, is it real?

As the dark hearse pulls away, I struggle to see what might come next. It hurts even to consider. Darkness, like the hearse, is already swirling and is grabbing pieces of my heart. The pain, so intense, makes me think I want to die as well! I don't want this life, a life without Natalie. I don't. I even question who I am at this moment. I am confused, disorientated. I am frightened, overwhelmed, already lonely and exhausted. Exhausted by it all, much more than I realize.

I am lost! A speck of humanity, floating in the middle of the universe, wandering. I stand now at the fringes of that universe. So where from here? I am not sure. This is all new to me. The storm that is my life has been all consuming and difficult, and I suspect the days ahead are going to be difficult for me. And the boys have suffered a terrible loss, too. How will I get them through their tough days? Such a burden to carry. I'm not even sure how I will get through mine.

I think I'll try and live one day at a time, which is all I get anyway, right? But the thought of a day is just overwhelming. A day is a long time. I think I'll focus on the minute-to-minute and just get through the day. One minute at a time. That is about all I think I can endure anyway. Minute to minute! Just might work. Let's see how the next minute works. Surely, it has got to be better than the last minute. It can't get any worse!

Dear God in Heaven, it can't get any worse, right?

BOOK 8

Solstice

Death

Death
You have no name
You have no face
I've never met you
Yet you guide me to your embrace
Death
I've seen your tragedies
Shed many a tear
Believing I have a life to live for
Dark spirits paralyze me with fear
Death
You are a stranger
Curing illness too great a feat
You care little for the pain
Pledging warmth when we meet
Death
Your eyes tell the tale
A burden heavy upon my heart
A simple nobody to you
A love you beckoned from me, must depart
Death
You hide in the darkness
Reaching to me with open arms
You encourage me to your will
With evil intent and sinister charms

By: Robert Mapes

The Story ....

I need to escape the noise in my head. Loud thuds, the galloping of horses hooves. The pulsating sound syncs up with my heart, centering in the middle of my forehead – thump, thump, thump. It hurts! I move to the bedroom, trying to hold myself together and bring relief to the growing pressure. I collapse on the bed, a kind of exhaustion I've never felt before tries to claim my body, my soul. I lay in the ebbing daylight, the sky turning purple and bruised, like my heart. I try to go to a kind of numbing place where time and feeling have no meaning. It is my escape, my way of coping, at least for now. The sun continues its dance against the blue skies of the day. As I work my way into the present from a whirlwind of emotions, I sense a thought circling my consciousness. I pull myself from my numbed state, realizing that self-pity was not going to help those that I love most. Tonight, the boys need their father.

I work myself out of my sorry state and head out of the bedroom. It feels funky. First stop, aspirin, I've got to get control of the horses, their gallops still pounding loudly. As I step into the family room, it is oddly quiet. Something is missing. Everyone is on edge. The emotion is raw, palpable; it seems to be emanating from everyone, even the boys. I muddle through dinner, going through the emotions on autopilot, I think.

I move from my sorry state into the now, the present. I need to circle around with Ryan, Jake, and William, to say goodnight. I am dreading it! I want to fix their pain, make it go away. I know that they will need a chance to mourn and that I will need to help them figure out what that looks like. Interesting I should think this. I am not even sure how to mourn myself. Guess it is a good thing that Kally and Hospice, will be working with the boys. Okay, here goes, show time!

First, I go to Ryan and sit on the side of his bed. In a quiet, soothing voice, I say, "Hey buddy, I am so sorry Ryan that you lost your Mom today. I can't imagine how much that hurts. You need to know how much she loved her oldest, favorite son… and how special you are to her."

I am not sure where the words come from, or how I manage to say them without falling apart. I know that this is not, nor can it be, all about me. Ryan sits up, grabs hold of me tightly. "I miss her already."

"I know you do. I miss Mom too." I work to stay in the moment, Ryan holds on tightly! We pray together and send messages of love and care heavenward.

"I love you, Ryan."

"I love you too, Dad."

I move quietly to Jake's room and sit on the side of his bed. That's all it took. He jumps in my arms before I can say a word. "Hey, Jake… your Mom loved you so much, Jake. You were her special middle son, her favorite middle son. I am so sorry that you lost your Mom today. I know it hurts pretty bad."

We embrace tightly; I am not sure how long; time seems to have lost meaning for me. From out of nowhere, Jake asks, "Dad, who is going to take care of Mom now?"

Wow! Did not see it coming, but respond just the same. "God has Mom now, and He is going to take great care of her. Mom is free of her pain, Jake. No more ugly cancer to hurt her and no more pain."

We sit together; eventually his tears subside, and we say a prayer together, and send messages of love and care heavenward!

"Love you, Jake."

"I love you, Dad."

I am dreading being with William. Not sure why that is. I gently push his door open; there he is, crying quietly into his pillow. It breaks my heart. I remember that this is not about me. I go to him, sit on his bed; he easily falls into me, tears streaming down his face.

I hug him tightly, and whisper, "You were pretty special to your Mom, William… and she loved you so much. You were her youngest, her favorite youngest son, a very special son. I am so sorry that you lost your Mom today, William. I am so sorry."

We hold each other, and eventually the tears subside. William says, "Dad, what if I forget what she looks like… what if I forget?"

It is a full-on kick to the side. Not sure what I expected, but it certainly was not going to be something like this. I stay in the moment and say quietly, "You will always, always remember your Mom, William. I promise! I will help us all remember, I promise!"

I sit with him, the silence almost too much to bear. I break it anyway. "You okay, kiddo?"

No response. Who am I kidding; of course the poor kid is not okay.

"How about we say a quick prayer, and send some messages to your Mom."

Surprisingly, he smiles. I'll take it!

"I love you, William."

"I love you, Dad."

I stop at the top of the stairs, needing a moment to gather myself. I look back at the boy's bedrooms and slowly shake my head side-to-side.

Downstairs, Grace is working the phone. It is like command central! Friends, family, new neighbors, everyone, wants to know when things are going to happen. Don't they know that I am not ready for anything to happen? Can't they see that? And know that? I am in no position to deal with the difficult decisions that lie ahead. A part of me still believes this is a bad dream.

I sleep fitfully, tossing and turning, in various stages of sleep and turmoil. I spend a good bit of time in prayer throughout the night asking in many ways and manners that God help me make the right decisions, and that He strengthen me, prop me up, gather me in His arms, and get me through my tomorrow. That's all I feel I can handle, and it's a stretch goal at that!

Dawn brings a new day, sunlight glistening through the window, throwing shadows that seemingly dance about me, hovering. I lie in bed, waiting for the right answers to find their way to me. By the time I drag my beaten body and tired soul out of bed, I have a pretty good idea of what I need to do.

Grace and I talk first thing, not on a list of things I want to do, but things that I have to do. Natalie and I did talk about plans briefly, at her insistence of course. The courageous soul that she is! She was emphatic about a couple of things. One was that her children not see her humanly form in a box! She told me she would come back and haunt me if I put her earthly vessel on display for all to see. Makes me chuckle! Hmm, haunt me, she would! The other was that she be buried in a simple pine box.

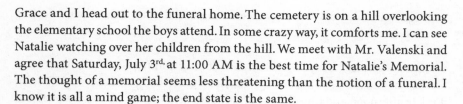

Grace and I head out to the funeral home. The cemetery is on a hill overlooking the elementary school the boys attend. In some crazy way, it comforts me. I can see Natalie watching over her children from the hill. We meet with Mr. Valenski and agree that Saturday, July 3rd, at 11:00 AM is the best time for Natalie's Memorial. The thought of a memorial seems less threatening than the notion of a funeral. I know it is all a mind game; the end state is the same.

We decide it best to receive guests at the Church before the service. We will drape Natalie's casket with some of her handiwork, her handmade quilts. I am going to try and unearth some pictures of her, our family, and the boys from any of a million unpacked boxes. Good luck with that, I think to myself.

Selecting a casket is overwhelming. Why are there so many choices? Caskets, one and all, end up in the ground, covered with dirt! And, for the pleasure of covering something in dirt, you pay a pretty penny. Seriously! Expensive is an understatement. I ask the funeral director for the pine box options. He is quick to tell me that no such pine box option exists. I wonder who made that decision? I sense a conspiracy here. I feel forced to select some costly option, and will wait for Natalie to reach down from the heavens and smack me upside the head!

Whew, it is tougher than I thought. I must make so many decisions quickly. This thing is on a fast track. It may be on a fast track, but my emotions aren't. By the time Grace and I get back to the house, I'm pretty spent. Wiped out. Toast as you might say. I hope Natalie is proud of me as she gazes down from the heavens.

Back at the house, flowers, meals, snacks and all kinds of things are arriving. Neighbors I have yet met are working to support the new family in town. This caring and compassionate response helps ease my burden. It tells of the kind nature of humankind, and that as God's people, we are all called to be kind and to help one another out. Why doesn't this notion play a larger role in life? Kindness seems pretty basic.

Time jumps on the fast track, and before I know it, things take on a life of their own! The family starts showing up, Natalie's and mine. They left just a few days ago, and here they are. It is a glorious reunion, considering the circumstance. I am thankful for their presence.

Ryan, Jake, William, and I step carefully into the garage, ready for the hunt! Where to begin? Boxes are everywhere. We all just grab any box and see where we end up. It is a good distraction. After a couple of hours of searching, we hit the jackpot! A huge box filled with all kinds of pictures. Hurray, hurray! Together, the boys and I go down memory lane, have a few laughs and share a few tears, selecting our favorites.

Friday is absolutely crazy! With so many siblings and friends, there is constant movement and things going on. All in all, it's a great distraction. Before I know it, it is late afternoon and time for us to meet with Jacob, so he can learn a bit about the daughter, wife, mother and friend he would be memorializing. A woman he has never met, but whom he would meet through us. It is reassuring to be with family, remembering the fun times together. The boys chime in often sharing stories of their Mom.

I wake up early Saturday morning, before the rising sun, with dread in the very pit of my stomach and my soul. The burdens of the day cause my heart to race, thumping loudly in my chest. It is beginning to hit home, that I am now alone in this game of life. I step out the door and sit on the patio, just taking in the quiet of the moment. I try to wrap my head around the day. I think self-talk is going to be king today! So, I jump into my valiant mode. I know I have to keep it together, well, sort of together, anyway. Maybe I can avoid being a blubbering mess. I tell myself, "You can do this Bob... you know you can." Not sure I am convincing myself of anything. She just can't be gone; she can't!

The boys and I are resplendent in our navy blue suits, white shirts, and ties - a mighty handsome bunch indeed! I purposely busy myself with getting them ready, a nice little distraction. It leaves me little time to dwell on what we were getting ready for.

My heart races as we pull into the church parking lot. The boys are somber and quiet; I can see them struggling with their own internal demons. I walk into the church and BAM! There is the coffin. It steals my breath! The thought of Natalie inside some dark box, devoid of light, sensory deprived, seems wrong to me, and I struggle to reconcile it. I look at the boys, who are surrounding me, William and Jake holding my hands. I could have a meltdown, but I dig deep and call myself to be the powerhouse I need to be. It works. I somehow manage to keep it together, at least for now.

I say to the boys, one and all, "Mom would really like what we have done for her. She would like the pictures you guys chose for her. I think she is smiling right now." They all smile. Maybe I can get through this thing.

The funeral director queues the family up for their entrance into the service. The organ sounds, a sad call to the mournful, and the procession begins. The director guides the family down the aisle, leaving the boys and me watching. Once the family is in place, he comes to the back of the church, to the boys and me. I see his approach, and I begin to feel anxious, unsure, and ill-equipped for this moment. I reach out an invisible hand to my Lord and ask that he take my hand, and help me get through this.

The director gives the boys and me the all clear to make our way down the aisle. But there is an immediate problem, I'm frozen, I can't move. Maybe I don't want to move. Panic begins to set up shop, and all eyes are on me, on us. The boys quietly sob. I somehow will myself forward, one painful step at a time. The boys are so close to me that we move as one. William reaches for me; I stoop to pick him up, and carry him down the aisle. He melts into my arms, his tears rolling onto my neck. I keep it going, one footstep at a time.

Jacob does an awesome job with the service; you would have thought he had known Natalie his entire life. There are quiet sobs all about me, and somehow I manage to stay in control of my personal pain. It is difficult, as the boys' sobs rack my body! The music is awesome; a member of the church family sings 'Morning Has Broken.' Rose Lynn lifts the theme to Ice Castles to the heavens, but becomes so burdened by the painful tears of the boys that she stops midway through the song, never able to regain her foothold and continue.

The boys and I are first in line in the recessional. I would have preferred to go last. The funeral director guides us to the limousine, and we head out. Our bright headlights become a beacon of pain to an unknowing world. The limo parks close to the cemetery plot. The casket looks so forlorn, so alone there on the hillside. The mound of dirt nearby seems to scream at me. This the final curtain call on her life.

The director opens the door for the boys and me, and we sheepishly get out of the limo. I kind of hang back with the boys; I am in no rush to get to the casket, no rush at all. Everyone is getting out of cars, and they seem to be hanging back, milling around, no one heading to the gravesite? I wonder what they are waiting for? The funeral director comes to me, and whispers in my ear. "Whenever you are ready." I think on this for a second or two, and say back to him, "Don't give me that option, I'll never be ready."

He whispers in response. "Everyone will be waiting for the family to lead off." Oh, isn't that just great, I get to be the first one to the gravesite. Aren't I the lucky one? I look to the boys; they are waiting for my signal. I take a deep breath... hold it in for a couple of seconds, and will my right foot forward, then my left. Remarkably, they move. It seems like it is a million miles to the casket, William finding his way back into my arms, watching with eyes wide open. I make it to our seats in the front; my stomach decides the time to do flip flops is now.

At the end of the gravesite ceremony, we all hang back for a bit. Violet, my sister-in-law, purchased roses for the family to leave on top of Natalie's casket. The boys and I walk up last, softly placing our roses on the casket, and gather together for a moment. I have no tears left and feel an emptiness I have never felt before. I pray to God to keep a watchful eye on Natalie and to please let me know that she is at peace. I just need to know, Lord, that she is okay.

In a quiet moment, my Mom tracks me down and puts her arms around me. "I would do anything to take this pain away from you and the boys." Through my tears, I say, "I know you would Mom." And at that moment, I am a little boy again. I quietly cry as Mom holds me, knowing she is at a loss at how best to help me, her son. I know that feeling all too well.

The day seems to drag on. I spend some quiet time with the boys and pray together with them. Like me, they just want to know that their Mom is good up there in Heaven with God and Jesus. I am not sure that doing another memorial service in New Hampshire is a good thing. What was I thinking? Peter, our pastor in New Hampshire, helps plan the Memorial Service, gets the word out to friends and family that Natalie's Plymouth Memorial will be on July 10th.

Touching down at the airport in the Northeast is a bit melancholy for me. It seems rather odd; it feels like we just left. Who would have thought lives could change so quickly? Not me! My brother Matt is at the airport to offer assistance, and the return to the Northeast brings a flood of memories to the surface of my heart. It makes me dread the Memorial. I'm not sure reliving the experience a second time is going to be any easier.

It is a beautiful, sunny Saturday in Plymouth, New Hampshire. The service, although painful to endure, is as beautiful as I had hoped, lead by pastors Julie and Peter. The boys and I, along with the family, gather in the fellowship hall of the church to greet everyone after the service. People came from all over to be with us, and I stood proudly with Natalie's Dad, Fred, and the boys, as we thank the multitudes for attending the service. I am not sure how many came out, but I am on my feet for hours. At some point, I shift to autopilot; I just need to push through and get to the other side. There is one high point that lightens my heavy heart. The boys, who are just worn down by all of this, go off and play with their friends and cousins. A freeze frame moment!

On Sunday, we make a jaunt to Maine. We are going to spend some time at my parent's home. I am ready for an escape, just a few moments to try and collect myself before I return to Texas, to an unknown life.

The boys and I head to the Lighthouse at West Quoddy Head with my parents. It is a favorite haunt, and we have a picnic right along the cliffs and the rocky shoals of the coast. The breeze and sea air feel good on my face today, kind of soothing. There is something missing today, and it hurts. After lunch, I end up wandering the trails that run along the coast. I follow it for miles, high along the bluff; I can hear the roar of the sea crashing against the rocky shores below. I think briefly about tossing myself into the tumultuous seas. I think we would be good company for each other. My greater sense prevails.

As I traverse the coastline, memories again flood my waking moments, and the loss of my love becomes so intense, it hurts to breathe. It forces me to sit on the ground. I think of the boys, and the days ahead for all of us, and I sob, try as I might to hold it together. Maybe it is being truly alone for the first time, but I feel the freedom to openly feel what I have been carrying inside me. As I continue to wander the trail, I find no easy answers to calm my hardening heart, so I decide to head back. Realizing that I didn't tell anyone I was going to disappear. Selfish, I think!

On my way back, I see several bright colors on the shore just ahead of me. It is a somewhat familiar sight. It is oddly comforting and brings a smile to my face. It is a lobster buoy. As I continue my journey back, I see something else very familiar on the trail. There is sudden movement, and before I know it, the boys are upon me, with smiles and hugs. It is so great to see them happy and smiling. I kneel down and show them the buoy I found, and collectively, they shout, "Let's find another one... for Mom."

Time in Maine passes all too quickly, and before I know it, I am helping the boys pack for a return trip home to Texas. I am not ready. I do not want to confront my reality. Is this what life holds for me? My big entrée into the newly single parent kind of life will be a flight home to Texas alone with three young boys? Giddy up, cowboy, I tell myself. It is time for me to get on the wagon train or be left behind.

Matt brings all of us to the airport and, the good news, is that I hold it together and get the boys and myself onto the plane and make ready for our journey. I am missing the extra set of hands in ways I cannot even describe! As I get all settled in, a tall guy approaches me. He introduces himself as Kevin, and as chance would have it, he is a former swimmer from my brother Matt's swim team. Kevin tells me how sorry he is about Natalie's death. Kevin then offers to help with the boys on the flight! Now what are the chances, seriously? Chance, maybe not! Lord, is that you?

The hot Texas sun beats down on all of us as we work to haul our luggage into the house. We've been gone for a few weeks, and Grace isn't with us, and I am already missing her steady hand. Being in the house is a bit overwhelming. Everything kind of closes in on me, reality starts to shut me down from the inside out. Suddenly, without warning, a thought comes to me seemingly out of nowhere. We've been gone so long there is no food in the house! None, nada. It's time to go grocery shopping, just me and my three amigos.

Ryan, Jake, along with his crutches, William and I head out to the grocery store. Oh, joy! Jake quickly tires of the crutches and shopping thing, so in a moment of despair, I put him in a shopping cart so I can push him around. Jake fits fine, but his crutches, which he uses off and on, hang out of the cart. I have another one already filling up with groceries. It is my three amigos, me, and a couple of shopping carts. Crazy!

I realize I passed a few things that I need. I tell the boys, "Stay right here; I'll be right back." I dash a couple of aisles over and grab the items. As I start my way back, I hear a loud crash a few aisles over. Nah, I think to myself, they know better. I dash back to the boys just the same.

I turn the corner, and there is Jake, his cart at the opposite end of the aisle, his crutches and cart jammed into the Jell-O display, with boxes of Jell-O all over the place. It is a certified mess, and William and Ryan are frantically trying to pick it up. I think to myself, single parenthood, it's gonna be a long journey!

They all see me, the panic is evident on their faces. They know they are in trouble. I have two choices - I can either cry or laugh. I decide to go with the second option and laugh at them from the top of the aisle. We have cried enough to last a lifetime! Their relief, priceless! We laugh together as we clean up, and some kind employees come to our aid. I can't wait until my brother Matt gets here to help me out. All hands on deck!

Matt's arrival is a big deal. Matt is great with the boys, and the extra set of hands allows me to get back into the workforce and get things settled before the boys start school. The big task before us; find a nanny. We run an ad and Matt spends hours scouring the applicants to find the best match for us. It ends up being a harder process than I thought, and after a series of interviews, we find the perfect nanny.

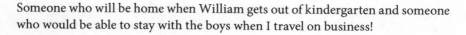

Someone who will be home when William gets out of kindergarten and someone who would be able to stay with the boys when I travel on business!

I rise early to greet the day, and the day greets me back with light blue skies painted with hues of burnt orange and pink. It is a beautiful sunrise. I am excited about today. A feeling I don't have too often as of late. It is time for Jake to get his cast off. I know he is ready, I know I am. I am ready to hear some good news, too. The cast comes off without much fanfare, and Dr. Frampton does a complete exam of the ankle. He is surprised that the swelling has not decreased. Frankly, so am I. The thought that this thing is not resolved overwhelms me.

The doctor puts Jake through some physical motions, and although I am not a doctor, I can quickly see that there is absolutely no improvement in function. Not the news I wanted. Not the news I needed. Dr. Frampton looks my way and says, "This is not at all what I was expecting." Me either, so I ask, "Dr. Frampton, what do you recommend as our next step?" He looks my way. "I think we need to do exploratory surgery, get in there and see what is really going on." As we leave Dr. Frampton's office, I do so knowing less than when I arrived. The good news, Jake's surgery can be done before school starts. I guess that is good news?

Valerie agrees to watch Ryan and William while I take Jake to the hospital for the surgery. In the pre-op area, a nurse approaches Jake with a needle to set up his IV, and man, he comes unglued. He starts screaming, fighting with the nurse. I go to him, try to soothe him, calm him down. My words have little effect. He wants none of what is happening! I carefully climb into bed with him, lie down next to him, and gently hug him. I can feel his body begin to relax, quickly followed by tears. The nurse sets up his IV while my little boy sobs in my arms.

As the marvels of modern medicine kick in, Jake becomes groggy, and before they take him back, we have a chance to hug. I walk along with him as far as I can. Jake is gone a very short time before Dr. Frampton tracks me down in the waiting room. He walks me back to the pre-op area, and says, "We can't do the surgery today. Jake has an open wound on his ankle."

Seriously, I think to myself? I don't need this! The doctor gently pulls the sheet back and shows me Jake's scraped up ankle. I had lectured the kid about going easy on the ankle! I didn't even think to look before heading off to the hospital. When Jake finally arrives back from the land of induced dreams, I tell him what the deal is. My first reaction is to lecture him right then and there, but my better sense kicks in, and I hug him, and the little guy just melts in my arms. It looks like we will have to conquer this monster on a different day.

Nighttime brings quiet to my world, the quiet that is reflective, a chance for the noise in my brain to ramp itself up, screaming to me that something is different, that something is not quite right. Nighttime is a monster! Dark spirits wait for me, hiding in the shadows. They pull on my heart, taking me deep into the caverns of sorrow and grief. At times, I think I might not be able to find my way back; their life force is so strong. I am alone, and loneliness now defines my world.

I live in the minute-to-minute that is my life and go through the motions until Jake's rescheduled exploratory surgery. I am watching him like a hawk, and he knows it. He is extra careful this time around. The surgery is upon us quickly, and before he surrenders to the land of slumber and dreams, I get a chance to hug him and reassure him that all will be well. I walk him back towards the Operating Room until a nurse stops us. I worry as I watch my little guy disappear behind big swooping doors that seemingly swallow him whole.

A child, so helpless in the world, creates an entirely different kind of worry for me. Maybe it is the association of all that has happened over the last two years; I just have this sinking feeling I cannot shake. It seems like eons before Dr. Frampton comes to greet me in the waiting room.

"So," I say to the good doctor.

He smiles a bit and says, "The results of the surgery are inconclusive. I could not find anything physiologically that could be causing the deterioration."

What now, I wonder? Dr. Frampton continues. "I did remove a good amount of questionable fluid."

Okay, time to freak! I don't like this one bit. This is like déjà vu!

He must have seen the panic in my eyes, and goes on to say, "I think having a pathologist take a look at the fluid is the way to go. Again, I don't think it is anything cancerous. I didn't see anything that would make me think anything like that."

Hallelujah, thank you, God! All I want is for Jake to be well.

Dr. Frampton explains that the surgical incision is larger than he had planned, and it looks like Jake is going to be spending the night in the hospital. Oops! There was never any mention of a hospital stay, so I do not have a plan for this contingency.

I am anxious and ask the doctor, "Hey Doc, think I can see Jake now?"

He smiles. "We usually wait a bit, but I'll take you back, you just won't be able to stay with him."

He is sleeping serenely, still under the influence of the anesthesia. I move close to his bedside and take comfort in his quiet, easy breathing. It calms my soul a bit to see him, know that he was okay. Nothing like it in the world, right, like knowing that your child is out of harm's way. Slowly, my sleepy one crawls out from his daze and looks for me. "How ya feeling?" He just smiles. It's all this Dad needs.

Valerie agrees to stay the night with Ryan and William. I stay with Jake in his hospital room, and it is a bit too familiar. With random thoughts and fears circling like vultures on the horizon, I fall into a fitful sleep, on a new version of torture, a couch/bed combo. Bright sunlight fills the room as I work to open my eyes, forced to face a new day. It certainly has to be better than the one we just closed out. Jake is still out of it, sleeping quietly in the hospital bed. The doctor checks Jake out mid-morning and tells us that he will need to be booted up for about a month and will need to continue using his crutches.

With a prescription for some pain meds in our hip pocket, we are free to go by early afternoon. Fully gauzed and booted, Jake grabs his crutches and quickly maneuvers his way to the exit. It seems as if nothing is going to slow him down, or maybe, he just wants to be as far away from a hospital as possible. I'm with him. Get me out of here!

The minute-to-minutes of my life become days, and days become weeks. Before I know it, school is staring us straight in the face. I cannot begin to face this part of my new reality. So, what do I do? I do what any other non-coping type person would do - I ignore it. Flat out pretend it is not going to happen. As a result, nothing gets done. That is, until Ryan says to me, "Dad, we need haircuts before school starts and we should check what supplies we'll need to have for school. This is not New Hampshire you know."

There is my responsible one, issuing a call to action. Not sure if he knows just how much I needed it. I have done nothing to get this family ready. Now the new school year is just a few days out, and panic hits me like a ton of bricks. I make plans with the boys to do haircuts and shopping tomorrow afternoon. I'll leave work early, and we will just knock it out.

I pick up the boys up as planned, and they are pretty excited about school. I am not so sure I am, but I thrive, for the moment, on their high energy levels. First stop, haircuts for all! I have been a bad Dad; it has been months since we have done this kind of thing. As I look at my young men, it is pretty obvious they needed a trim up long ago! Where have I been that I did not see this? We make an adventure out of clothes shopping, the boys trying on and showing off different clothing options. Too funny! I give them each a budget for when it comes time to select sneakers, and they like this. The good news is they all come in under budget.

I arrange to take Jake to school early so he can meet his teacher before the official start of school. I want him to have a chance getting around on his crutches and have a few minutes to meet with his teacher and let her know what is going on with the poor kid. Mrs. Connor is thoughtful and intentional, and I knew instantly that Jake was going to be in great hands.

I rise early before the sun, this first day of school, and stumble to the coffee machine, needing that jolt of caffeine to get my motor running. I get myself ready for the day, and then make the boys breakfast. Not just any breakfast, but bacon and eggs, the whole works kind of breakfast. It is nice to be together with them and to be celebrating the start of a new school year in a new land. I'm trying best I can to be the best Dad I can.

Jake is determined to walk to school, boot, crutches and all. It is a nice walk as we travel the open field that connects our subdivision to the school. It is beautiful, and I can feel the warm sun on our faces as we make our way across the field.

Maybe, just maybe, I can do this thing!

Inspiration

But those who hope in the Lord will renew their strength. They will soar on wings like eagles; they will run and not grow weary, they will walk and not be faint.

Isaiah 40:31

Reflection

Dark spirits, ever present, descend easily into my realm. In days gone by, they languished on my periphery, watching and waiting like birds of prey. These days, they circle closer and closer to my heart. When I least suspect it, they reach in and grab a part of me, stealthily claiming it as their own, a little piece of me dying along the way.

I am confused, confused of heart and mind, not sure what to think, what to do, how to feel. Days become my nights, and nights become my days. There is a relentless march of time; the drum beat of life forcing me forward, leaving me no choice but to muddle my way through. I am in a desperate place, a place that is unfamiliar to me. I am not sure how to navigate my way forward.

Nothing in my lifetime prepared me for this place! And this place sucks! It does, I don't like it. Natalie is gone. Here one minute, fighting for life and then gone. Gone, just like that! Picking out caskets, seriously? Planning a funeral, no way! This should not have happened to me. More importantly, it should not have happened to the boys. Jake is a wild unknown. What is going on with him? Just one more thing! Someone has confidence that I can carry this burden too, and live to tell the tale! I think this trust is misplaced. God, you surely think more of me than I think of myself!

People tell me I am courageous and undaunted, but I fail to see it. I am too conflicted to be strong, too conflicted to be courageous. Natalie was the courageous one. She was valiant throughout, never complaining. As the monster ravaged her body, her soul, she made each day matter. It became her goal. Her incredible strength allowed her to endure in spite of the pain, in spite of the fatigue! To fight the monster and hold him back so she could make sure the boys and I were all set. Calling the shots!

Why can't I be as courageous as her? To stare straight into the eyes of my storm-filled life and declare victory, no matter the circumstance? Is my struggle that I couldn't make for a different outcome? Am I angry with a God that would take a life, seemingly so carelessly? With a God that would keep throwing new challenges my way endlessly?

As sure as I am that Natalie is in heaven and that God is with her, I am not so sure He is with me. It seems as if God has packed up, moved on, and left me alone in my misery. His silence seems palpable. God seems to be absent when I need Him most! So many emotions flood my system, with little warning - a thought, a picture, a simple word. I need Him in these moments of crazy, and I reach out to Him, but He doesn't seem to be reaching back.

Why is it that I am so alone? Prayers not answered. Am I to learn something from all of this? Surely, all of this is not random chance. And this is not just about Natalie's death. This is about the fight against the monster, the move to a far away land, the untimely death of love and the unknowns about Jake. It is all of this. It just can't be randomness at play; it can't! So why no answers?

Am I at a place in my faith's journey where God is deliberately going to be silent? How can He be silent when I need Him so much? Why can't He simply come down, whisper in my ear, and tell me what I need to know and what I need to do? Give me the answers I seek. I just need to hear. God, don't leave me hanging in the balance.

Throughout the journey, there have been periods of silence, and here in my darkest hours, I am seemingly all alone. There is no Godly whisper in my ear. Is it that God expects me to figure things out on my own? That I am to learn from all of this and apply it to my world and my life? Is it that I want the easy way out, a shortcut? That there is no growth if it is easy? So is God intentionally making it tough? It sure would be easier if I did get that whisper in my ear!

I am then, left to figure it out on my own. How do I move from one minute to the next? Haven't a clue! How do I help the boys? Haven't a clue! How do I help Jake? Haven't a clue! No one seems to have a clue. What is going on with this kid's leg? How do I hold it all together? Haven't a clue! How do I mourn the loss of love? Haven't a clue! New land? Haven't a clue!

So then, is the big question for me 'how?' How do I live my life when half of me has already died? How do I put one foot in front of the other knowing that it takes more energy than I have? How do I thrive in a land so far away from family, friends and loved ones? Do I pick it all up and move back to New Hampshire; is that the how? The thought of leaving Natalie alone on the hillside is more than I can bear. How? I haven't a clue!

With no other option in sight, I decide to strike a deal with the man in the mirror. I will outwardly carry on; get dressed in matching socks and clean clothes. I promise myself that I will shower each day and be there for the boys to keep their lives as normal as possible. But I know, and only I will know, that inwardly, I will be struggling to survive, struggling to keep myself above water. I will pray for those answers that will guide me forward, bring calm to my troubled soul and heal a broken heart. Surely, answers are forthcoming.

As I work to outwardly carry on, I know others will try to make me think and be positive. I will play along. I will be alone in my heart, desiring most of all, to be left alone, in solitude, full of self-pity, self-reflection and deep, dark thoughts and feelings. These will be mine alone, my secrets. I will suffer alone in silence. No one has a right to take them away from me. I have given enough. The good news, they won't even know. I can do this. Yes, this will work. This is the how! And onward I will go.

I will wait for God's whisper in my ear. It has to come at some point, right? In the meantime, I will do whatever I can to deaden my pain, protect my heart and hope that I can survive the dark spirits. They gather strength, though, their hold tightening on my heart. It seems I will be alone in my battle against them. They own more and more of my heart, my soul, my life.

I am fearful that the dark spirits will one day gain control, get the upper hand, and I will fall victim to their prey, and that I will forfeit my being to them and lose my sense of self.

The dark spirits and their growing authority frighten me!

BOOK 9

Dark Spirits

Shadows Dance

Shadows dance
About a dispirit land
Wisps of gray
Create chaos
For the weak of heart
Struggling to escape
Shadows dance
With a ghostlike grip
On the spirits of the hurting
Building strength as they gather
Throwing sinister thoughts to the unsuspecting
Shadows dance
With shards of glass
Masterful puppeteers seize my heart
Using strings made with pain and fear
Controlling my spirit
Directing my mind
Shadows dance
While hurtful spirits gather
Knowingly they conspire
With the winds of time
Seizing my soul
While I dance to their command

By: Robert Mapes

Funny, I can feel Natalie around me this morning. It seems like she is walking to school with all of us. I remember her describing this walk when she envisioned our home and its proximity to the elementary school. I know it is as she pictured it, not at all how I pictured it though. This all seems to be wrong!

I decide it is time to get all three of my active young men back into swimming. I find a local swim team where the boys can all participate. Hurray for me. There is too much energy in these young lads, and I need to find something to burn it off. Sometimes it feels like three against one, not by what the boys do, just the law of numbers. Wow! Can I make it as a single Dad and come out the other end in one piece? Who knows, I might not make the week. I might not even make the day. I do the math again… ugh!

The first week of school is emotionally charged and full of chaos. It's so much for me to balance. I make it to the weekend, and feel like I've hit by a truck! The boys, early risers, get themselves to the family room bright and early Saturday morning. Luckily, they find themselves some cartoons. I can hear them but just lay in bed, trying to decide if I even want to get up and face another day. Eventually, I haul my tired, pathetic self out of bed, and head toward the family room.

As I pass Natalie's bureau, I stop dead in my tracks. I freeze, afraid to move. My senses whip into overdrive, especially my sense of smell. I slowly take a deep breath. There is a strong scent, one I know all too well. I shake my head; surely I imagining things. It's not possible, right? No way!

Yeah, that is it. My mind is playing a little ole' game with me this Saturday morning. I walk back to the master bath, throw some water on my face, questioningly look at the man in the mirror, shake my head side to side, clear my mind a bit, and head back into the master bedroom.

I stroll past Natalie's bureau again – bammo! There it is, as weighty as before. No doubt, I'm not imaging it! It's Natalie's perfume. I picture her dabbing it on. I want to reach out and touch her. I stand still, breathing in her essence. It seems as if I'm in an alternative universe. I can't explain it, but it brings me a moment of comfort. But duty calls, and I head out to greet the boys and the day.

The weekend melts away. Single parenthood is tough stuff! I find myself primary on everybody's everything. And after the debacle of our last grocery store outing, I try a new plan. Run to the grocery store while the boys are in Sunday school, make a mad dash home, get stuff in the house, hustle to church, pick them up after Sunday school and head all together to church. It works. No one suspects a thing.

It is a struggle to accept my current status. I am a widower! There is no doubt about it. I have this fear that somehow, someway, in some setting, marital status is going to come up, and I'll have to use the "w" word. I dread it. I try to say that awful "w" word in front of the mirror! A tired, sad man I don't recognize looks back at me. It unsettles me a bit. I try again… but it is too much. Maybe I'm not ready to accept that the "w" for what it means to my life. No matter, I decide I will just avoid the issue completely. I'll simply tell people I am a single parent, end of conversation. No need to disclose more.

Life is a whirlwind, and I am running to and fro trying to get our lives back to normal best I can. I often pray, and continue to ask God to PLEASE, PLEASE tell me Natalie is okay. I just need a bit of confirmation from the heavens. I have to know; it's that simple! But there is silence on that front, which I cannot wrap my spirit around. Why the silence? Am I asking too much, I wonder?

Finally, it is time for Jake's post-surgery doctor's appointment. I pick him up from school, and he is all smiles. I am in a funk of sorts, but his little boy smile lifts my spirits. I think he likes the notion of being with his Dad for a bit, no matter the circumstance.

The nurse takes us right back, and Jake is unbooted and ungauzed, and his wound is checked out. Everything is healing well, and Dr. Frampton gives him the all clear to swim. Hallelujah! He recommends Jake stay on crutches for another three weeks, giving everything time to heal fully and settle down. Dr. Frampton goes on to explain that the path report showed fluid of an *undefined origin*, and is most likely the result of arthritis.

What? Arthritis? I am confused; I am not sure what this disease of the aged has to do with Jake. Dr. Frampton goes on to explain that children can develop arthritis. Seriously? I had no clue. There are a variety of arthritic conditions that affect only children. It seems that I will need to find a rheumatoid pediatrician to identify Jake's specific kind of arthritis and treat him. Luckily, Dr. Frampton gives me the names of a couple of doctors we can check out.

Before we leave, he shakes my hand, and Jake's hand, and says, "Good luck, I know you've all been through a lot and it would seem as if you are not quite through it all, not just yet anyway!" You have no idea Doc. I am barely hanging on. He then asks, "How is everyone doing?" You don't have enough time to hear it all Doctor. But my better sense kicks in, and I say, "We're doing the best we can with what we got." He nods his head easily. "I understand; it must be difficult. If there is anything I can do at any point, please feel free to reach out."

Jake grabs my hand on the way to the car and holds on tightly. As we get to the car, he says, "Daddy, am I going to die too?" I get down on my knees and look my little guy straight in the eye. "No Jake no, you're not going to die, not even close." I work to keep my voice even, under control. "You are going to be fine; you'll see. We'll find the best docs, we will and we'll get you better!" And with that, he falls into my arms.

It is a pretty Sunday, and the boys and I are off to early Church. It is Communion Sunday, and I am looking forward to it. I am thinking a good reminder of what is important, and getting me focused on what really should matter, might be just what I need.

After Church, we head off to the cemetery to spend a few minutes graveside. This is part of our new normal. Intellectually and spiritually, I know Natalie is released from her earthly form, and most certainly, is nowhere near her final resting spot. Emotionally, it is nice to be at her grave. It is odd, and it is nothing I can explain, but I have a greater sense of tranquility here and feel a bit closer to her. Craziness at its best I figure, but it works.

The boys and I pray for Natalie. My prayer - that God tells me Natalie is okay. I am not letting go of this one, and just have to know, I have to. There will be no peace for me until I do and with certainty, which will require some kind of word from the heavens. A quiet whisper will do. Now the boys, they are good for a prayer but quickly become restless. Luckily, the cemetery is right next to a practice golf driving range. After prayers and reflection, they're off to see who can collect the most golf balls. Ah, a quiet moment for me, which is a novel concept these days.

Scouting night brings me a chance to be with all of the boys. Ryan and Jake return to the scouting program tonight, and William is prepared to enter Tiger Cubs. I am not sure how to cover three bases, but since this is William's first time around, I focus on him. As I had feared, I find myself in a meeting with Tiger Cub parents, and the dreaded introductions. I stick with the plan, introducing myself as Bob, a single parent and leave it at that. It works.

Today is Wednesday, Hump Day and school meeting day! Time to see what is going on with Jake and his slipping academics. At the school, the school secretary graciously greets me. She is a kind soul, and knows of our current state. She is sweet and offers to do anything to help the boys and me out. It is a reassuring feeling knowing others care. I have an independent source keeping an eye on the boys, if they only knew!

There is a room full of professionals waiting to meet me. Now, I'm overwhelmed. The teachers, principal, and the Resource Planning Team are all on hand. They are a kind, caring group focused on one thing - Jake. The bottom line, he is below grade level in his ability to read, and the gap is widening, and intervention is needed. They want to do a battery of tests so they can build a plan specific to Jake's needs. I take this opportunity to let everyone know about Jake and the whole arthritis thingy, so that they can be aware. Any wonder the kid has sliding academics?

Coffee, coffee, coffee! Getting up early is taking its toll. I reach for my glasses and watch. My glasses are right where I left them. My watch... what? Not next to my glasses. Interesting! Okay, so what did I do with it? Nothing is registering. I take a second and quickly run through last night. I remember putting the watch with the glasses, on the breakfast bar. Hmm, the boys? Could the boys have been up to no good? No... can't be, they aren't up yet, unless they did some sleep walking, or snuck around in the wee hours of the night. Guess it will be a no watch kind of day.

I make breakfast, throw lunches together, and get the savages out of bed for the beginning of their day. During breakfast, I ask, "Hey guys, you happen to see my watch around?" All three pipe in. "Isn't it right where you usually leave it?" Ryan, the quick and witty one adds, "Maybe you should tie a string to it!" I smile. "Very funny young son."

The watch, this thing is bugging me. Since the watch is a no show at the house, the office is the next best suspect. I look everywhere - desks, files, common areas, restrooms, any place I think of. I come up empty-handed. I even ask a few co-workers if they have seen it. Nobody has anything to report. Now I am perplexed. Am I this out of control? One would wonder!

The case of the missing watch continues through the week. I am not sure where I could have put it. It wasn't in the car. It wasn't in the garage. I check the house again, all the drawers, nothing! I question my sanity. I have to push the watch to the back burner for now. I have another focus today, Jake's first appointment with Dr. Yuccan, the rheumatoid pediatrician in Dallas.

Dr. Yuccan is much like my Mom, and with a gentle smile, she puts both Jake and me at ease. Not an easy task! I am on edge, nervous even. I am not sure what all of this arthritis stuff means, and what the journey might entail. Dr. Yuccan asks for a history, and how we came to be in this place. She should be careful what she asks for. I give her a history alright, more than she probably needs, but feel she should know everything that is happening in my little guy's life. The hardest part,

Dr. Yuccan wants to know how long Jake's symptoms have been present. Truth be told, I'm not sure. There have been a few things happening in our lives!

Dr. Yuccan tells us how sorry she is about our loss, and asks how we were all doing. I give my tagline. "We're doing the best we can with what we got." Not really, but it is the plan, the plan I made with the man in the mirror. Besides, does anyone want to listen to the real deal, the painful truth about where I am in all of this? I don't think that would be a good idea.

Dr. Yuccan has Jake walk, unaided, best he can across the exam room. It pains me to watch, his limp, ever so evident. After the observation, Jake jumps up on the exam table, and the doctor does a physical exam. She examines every single joint and tests everything, from his ten toes to his neck. I sit quietly, observing, wondering what she is seeing, what she is sensing, as she makes copious notes in Jake's file.

After her exam, Dr. Yuccan gets both Jake and me in her line of sight, and says, "It is evident on physical exam, that Jake has Juvenile Rheumatoid Arthritis or JRA."

Ugh, I think to myself! What now? I say to the doctor, "I didn't even know children could get arthritis, so I am just a little bit blown away. What is this JRA really, and what does it mean for Jake?"

Dr. Yuccan goes on to explain all about JRA. That it is inflammation of the joints and that it does occur in children. The inflammation creates joint pain, swelling, and stiffness, with many joints filling with fluid, often becoming warm to the touch. She has me touch Jake's ankle. It is warm. No, no, no! Not one more thing! My stomach starts flipping and flopping. I push forward. "What does all of this mean for Jake? How do you treat this thing?"

"Well, let me tell you what I found first, so we know where we are. I observed, touched, and moved Jake's joints, all of them. I also observed muscle strength and flexibility. My examination shows quite a few joints with active inflammation, and there is already some loss of joint function."

I quickly try to assess all I am hearing, working to understand what is happening. "So this is all about Jake's ankle, right?"

"No, this is about all of Jake's joints, and there are signs of inflammation in many of them."

Well, just club me with a 4 X 4! I did not see this coming our way. How could I have been so clueless? I had no idea there was swelling in any of Jake's joints other than his ankle. Am feeling like a really, really bad parent!

Dr. Yuccan has Jake lay down and asks me to join her at the exam table. She patiently shows me all the joints that are currently affected. With her guidance, I can see how swollen Jake's right thumb is and how his range of motion is impacted. It hurts him, and hurts my heart, as she moves his thumb around, and on it went, joint after joint. Wow, my poor little man. Where have I been?

Something in the far recesses of my little ole brain, speaks up, loudly. I cannot watch another loved one suffer at the hands of an invisible monster. We need to get this thing under control before it gets out of control. I look to the good doctor. "What do we do from here, and is this something we can get under control?"

Dr. Yuccan explains that we will have one main goal, which is, to help Jake live a normal life. JRA can get aggressive, and the focus will be slowing down the progression of the disease, to try to relieve Jake's symptoms and pain, and prevent joint damage. She goes on to say treatment may include physical therapy, academic assistance, and possibly counseling, all of it depending on the extent of the disease over time.

Ah man, one more thing. One more then I think I can handle. This is bigger than I thought, even bigger than life itself! I think I want to opt out. This feeling is way too familiar to me, haven't I been here before? Someone blow the ref's whistle in this game of life. But this is not about me, and it can't be. So I bravely ask, "Okay doctor, so where to from here?"

"Well, the first tool in our toolbox will be a nonsteroidal anti-inflammatory drug, a NSAID. It should help reduce Jake's inflammation, swelling, and pain. It will take about four weeks to determine if the medicine is going to work for Jake." Oh boy, here we go again with new terms and new meds. When is enough, enough?

I get Jake to the car and get down on my knees. "You are going to be okay, Buddy. You know that, right?" He nods his head up and down. "We're going to get through this thing, you and me together, I promise." Hope I can keep my promise. Speaking of promises, I have a few to keep.

Poor kid. Why can't he just have a chance to be a little boy? Maybe now is the time to work on that and turn this day around. Make it an adventure. So, I head to Sonic. Jake is a happy guy! Good thing I took the entire day off. I am fortunate to work for such a great guy and a great company. They really do get it. Jake is pretty quiet during lunch; I am sure his thoughts are spinning just like mine.

Swimming, apparently, is good for arthritis. Good thing, this kid needs to keep a normal life and stay active. He still has the energy to burn, and I think swimming will do just that! Woo Hoo. I cannot imagine a world where boys cannot burn off energy. Not sure I would make it. Jake limps a bit on his way to the pool for practice, but once in the pool, you would never know he had anything going on; he is just a little fish!

My watch is still MIA, and it is both intriguing and puzzling, all at the same time. I am ever vigilant, keeping an eye out for it. I am thinking it's going to show up in some obvious place, me unknowingly having placed it out of sight, but not actually believing that. How else can I explain it?

It is early evening, and it is quiet on the home front. All the fun of dinner, homework, showers and story time is behind me. I don't like this time of day, especially today. I am missing Natalie in so many ways! Today is a bit different. We had always had each other to talk things through, especially things happening with the boys. I have no one to turn to tonight, no one talk to tonight. I miss not being able to talk to her, especially about Jake.

Tonight, dark spirits start to circle and prepare for their descent much earlier than usual. I am sad, overwhelmed, and alone. It feels lousy! There is no one to turn to. I turn to the Lord and pray for insight and a calming of spirit. But once again, all seems quiet on that front. I just need Natalie; I need to talk to her. "God, can you please tell me that she is okay?" I wait for His answer… silence! Just a whisper, just a little whisper? I wonder, am I asking too much?

The night drags on, the minute hand on the clock is moving painfully slow. I am unsettled, and start walking around the house aimlessly. I am overwhelmed by it all. I am in a sorry, self-pity kind of state and not sure how to get myself out of this self-induced funk! Part of me doesn't even want to try. Maybe I need to be in this place; maybe it is part of life. I feel the weight of the world on my shoulders, though, and on my soul! Sigh!

It is a restless night! Tossing and turning, never quite asleep, but not really awake. I spend the night in that in-between state, and as the alarm sounds the start of a new day, I feel as if I have never left the prior one. All of that JRA stuff is a jumbled up mess, bouncing around in my brain. Wow, it's gonna be a rough one I think.

I'm not even out of bed yet and I am already overwhelmed. I think of the deal I have with the man in the mirror.

I walk the boys to school, the sun is bright and warm, and the sky is a beautiful blue. This seems to be the case many a day, and although there is just a slight hint of fall, I am, surprisingly, looking forward to something, a warm and snowless winter! Suddenly, out of nowhere, a thought hits me. Find your own joy. Get involved. I kind of shake my head, not sure where that bit of randomness came from, but it somehow, resonates with me. Find joy and get involved. Could work? Better than feeling sorry for myself night after night, so I tell myself anyway.

I remember the scouting meeting from a couple of weeks ago, and the plea from the podium for Den Leaders. Maybe I can be a Den Leader for Jake? That would get me involved, maybe find a bit of joy, and allow me to keep an eye on Jake. Yeah, that's exactly what I'll do; I'll try to find my own joy… try! I'll make a call when I get to work. I'll do it. A step forward, maybe.

I hate to admit it, but I am living for the weekends. As crazy as they are, they bring a bit of a respite, compared to the rest of the week. I get up early Saturday morning, not early enough to beat the boys, but early enough to greet a bright and sunny Saturday morning. I change into some junky yard work clothes and head out of the bedroom to start my day, and to greet the boys. As I walk past Natalie's bureau, a glint of light catches my attention, something bright and shiny perhaps? It is odd, makes me stop in my tracks. I scan the bureau, curiosity kicking in.

It is unexpected. I look closely at Natalie's bureau for the first time in many weeks, and I can't help but notice all of the dust that has collected. Since her death, I haven't touched, gone near, or attempted to clean any of her things. I'm just not ready. The bureau, left the same as it was on move-in day.

So many of the things I see, I had given her. I wonder if she had arranged all of these things, as a kind of message to me? And then I see it… that glimmer. At first, I deny what I see. I shake my head in an attempt to clear my thoughts. Do I imagine things now? Nothing changes, things are still the same. There, in front of me, in the corner of the bureau, sitting amongst the dust, is my watch. My watch!

It smiles at me from the corner of the bureau, the dust not disturbed. Is this even possible? It makes no sense. How? Who? Could I have done it in my sleep, somehow? Anything is possible, I guess. But, I distinctly remember putting the watch in the kitchen by the sink. Guess the how doesn't matter. I am just happy

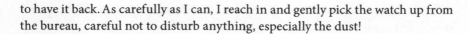

to have it back. As carefully as I can, I reach in and gently pick the watch up from the bureau, careful not to disturb anything, especially the dust!

The boys and I head out into the warm sun and tackle a bit of yard work. New house and all, there is lots of mowing and planting! The boys are great, and I am thankful they like being outside with me doing guy kind of things. They make a mess right alongside me. They help and work without complaint. As the day warms up, they jump into the pool. Wow, maybe a minute or two to be by myself while they have some kid fun.

Natalie's birthday is this coming Friday. I know it will be a tough one. On the dreaded day, I leave work early and grab the boys at the house. I want to try and make the celebration a special one. We make Natalie birthday cards, and the plan is to read them out loud at the cemetery. Kally, from hospice, thought this would be a great way to honor Natalie, and maybe a way for us to begin the process of closure. Yeah, good luck with that Bob!

The boys with cards in hand, race to the gravesite, Jake bringing up the rear, leaving me in the dust. As they close in on the gravesite, they stop in their tracks, lock step even. Odd I think! They freeze in place, heads facing down, no one moving! Then they turn and look my way. What now I wonder?

As I get closer, I see it. Unexpected! No wonder they stopped in their tracks. It surprises me too. The shiny surface proclaiming a life well lived, and one that was well loved. The sunshine dances gingerly in the reflections of the polished stone. I can see oceans and smiles, and the beauty of life. Tragedy overtakes the moment, and descends quietly upon us, bringing an eerie silence to the cemetery hilltop.

Ryan, Jake, and William all look at me with sad eyes, tears rolling down their cheeks. When all else fails, call for a group hug! I keep it together as we hang onto each other. "Hey guys, isn't Mom's headstone beautiful?" I stand up from our group hug, and move the boys around a bit until we form a circle around Natalie's headstone.

"Your Mom was so very special to me, and I miss her terribly. Not a minute goes by that I don't think of her." I am not sure where these words are coming from, but it feels like they are coming from some place deep in my heart. "I loved her… her courage, her love of you. You guys were the light of her life and, I know she misses you as much as you miss her." All I got, I can feel myself relinquishing control, I get down on my knees, and another group hug just happens, naturally. This time, though, the tears find me. Through my tears, I say, "Hey guys, how about we read those great cards you made?"

The reading of the cards is a great moment. No tears, just loving thoughts for someone well loved. After we all have our moment, I say to the boys, "I'll race you to the car, on the count of three." I take off immediately, running as I yell, "1, 2, 3!" And they are off, screaming how unfair I am. Jake brings up the rear, best he can! I tackle Ryan and William to the ground, giving Jake the time he needs to hobble his way to the car first. He is smiling as he claims victory and the brothers laugh yelling, "Not fair!"

As I step into the house, the phone rings. It is my brother Thomas, my witty, sarcastic, playing-you-for-a-fool brother. Without much fanfare, he says, "Bob, Christina had the baby."

I am silent for a second or two. "Get out of here. Christina's not due for almost a month."

"Bob, I'm telling you, Christina had the baby, and it's a girl."

"You better not be playing around with me here, you know what day this is?"

"I know exactly what day this is and that is why the baby's name is Natalie Alyce."

What are the chances, I think? Natalie Alyce, both born on the same day, September 1st. It is mindboggling. A birth, a new life, a new beginning. It takes the prospect of a rather glum night, and whips it into a rather special day. I hope I can maintain this sense of joy.

I continue to watch Jake closely, monitoring his JRA. As I watch him come down the stairs for breakfast this morning, it is evident that improvement in mobility is not in the stars. He struggles, hanging onto the banister for support. He smiles down at me just the same. It is reminiscence of Natalie, who always smiled. I am bummed though, I want things to get better. As he nears the end of the stairway, he hops from stair to stair using his right leg.

The walk to school has become a bit of an ordeal for Jake, so today I suggest that we drive. Jake quickly lets me know he is not in favor. "I can do it, Dad." Off we go, crutches and all, as we head across the field on the way to school. Jake is all smiles. What a trooper, never complains, or says he can't, like walking to school.

The notion of courage pops into my brain, and I think about how brave he is being. Just like his Mom. I am proud of my little man!

I have been burying myself in all kinds of activities. As busy as I am, life is still about going through the motions, and the deal with the man in the mirror seems to be standing the test of time. I play a good game for the outside world, l hide all of my hurt. I appear to be a man in control and moving forward. But the reality is that I am stuck in a place and time, and cannot move forward. It is too tough. It hurts too much. Plus, I don't have the foggiest idea what moving forward might look like.

It is time to meet with school officials again and get the results of Jake's testing. I knew of course that they would find something new to throw into the mix that has become my life. Tests identified a problem with Jake's processing abilities, and his reading skills are well below grade-level. The Resource Planning Staff walks me through the plan to help get Jake on track. The good news, I think things are salvageable! One more thing, just the same!

I leave the school in a funky state. Not sure why, but I am feeling unsettled today. I somehow manage to get through the rest of the day and the night. After all is said and done, and the boys are in bed, the demons of the night snuggle in close. I am overwhelmed. My insides are jumpy. It seems as if the dark spirits are gaining strength, and that I am powerless against them.

The spirits pull me into their sad, dismal, and threatening sphere - a sphere where the unthinkable can happen. Here in this place, I see harm coming my way. Harm and an escape from all of the madness. Yes, an escape! As I fall further into the dark spirits' realm, I sense a gentle essence brush up against my heart, sadness quickly dissipating. What an odd sensation. Was it the brush of angel wings? I am not sure what it was, but my funk disappears, bringing me an odd moment of serenity.

The Monday morning alarm sounds and beckons me from my restlessness. It is getting harder and harder to get any kind of sleep. Tossing and turning, dreams playing games with me. The dreams are troubling, and leave me unsettled in the morning. My bed sheets are always a mess, evidence of my nightly wrestling match.

The appointment with Dr. Yuccan today does little to lift my spirits. If anything, it encourages the dark spirits to get closer to me, to my heart, maybe a bit too close. She does an exam and tells us what she is seeing is typical for JRA. It is unrelenting and progressing. Not what I want to hear. She is concerned about Jake's right hand.

She fits him with a brace, hoping to reduce the pain and improve function. Of course, the kid is right-handed.

Life marches forward, slowly it seems. I know it is going to keep on moving, with or without me along for the ride. Being busy with Scouts has been a blessing of sorts. It keeps me from myself! I know I have to find my joy, but it is a struggle. It is too much like work. Seems easier these days just to succumb to the dark spirits. The three-month mark is headed straight for me, and it feels like a train wreck is just around the corner. It... is... pulling... heavy... on... my... soul! Like a gathering Texas storm, darkness seems more my norm, especially at night.

Life becomes a matter of routine. I wake in the morning, try to be everyone's everything, sticking a smile on my face. To an unknowing public, I appear to be fine. This has always been part of the game. Keep the dark place a secret. The gathering darkness promises the possibility of freedom and a way out. At times, it scares me. The dark spirits take me on a magic carpet ride to a place where the unthinkable happens. When I try to push them away, they fight back just a bit harder. God seems to be silent, leaving prayers unanswered and leaving me to wonder.

The alarm sounds the call to begin a new day! Though, I am reluctant to do so. I hit the snooze button three times, refusing to acknowledge the day. Instead of rising in the dark, which, itself is a call to the dark spirits, I wait until sunrise! I lay in bed with dark thoughts bouncing around, and as the sun peeks in through the window, I throw back the covers and force myself to confront the new day. This is not just any day; it is the three-month mark. Yes, I can do it! I can get through the day unharmed.

I hustle around, doing my best to get breakfast ready. But there is this darkness inside me, so I put on my outward face. You know what? I am pretty good at it. No one knows I have been entertaining such dark thoughts. This is good, the less others know, the better. I muddle through the day. The smile on my face hides the turmoil and pain. No one has a clue what day this is, do they? I am confident no one even cares.

I head to the cemetery on my way home. Dinner is just going to have to wait. I hope to get out of this dark place, thinking a visit to the cemetery will help. It doesn't! I find no spirit lift here. It gives the dark shadows greater authority over my thoughts, gaining strength, and there seems little I can do to hold them at bay.

Dinner is a quiet affair; I do little to engage the boys. I send them on their way after dinner, and completely skip the story time gig, saying I do not feel well. It isn't too far from the truth. I do not feel like myself, so maybe it isn't a lie? It doesn't matter. Something evil is lurking inside me, and the dark spirits seem to have gained the upper hand.

I end the day the same way I began it. I muddle through it. I try watching TV, but it is just noise. I feel like I am living a poltergeist moment. I decide to call it a day, a tough one at that. Sleep is not going to come easy this night, not that it has on any other. The dark spirits swirl, prompting me to do their beckoning. I willingly listen to them and consider the options they have laid down before me. It is oddly appealing tonight. I try to push their evil plot from my consciousness. I pray... to God for a way out... I wait... there is silence.

The pain of the world, and the spirits circle my heart for hours, and sleep is just a fading memory. Like a bolt of lightning, all of the dark spirits and their hurtful thoughts coalesce easily into a single call to action. I know exactly what I have to do. I have to end it! Simple as that. It is time to take my miserable, no good self out of the equation, and find harmony. I have to find peace. It is too much - the battle, the monster's victory, a new land, new job, and now Jake, the wild card. The spirits promise to lead the way.

I crawl out of bed and head to the kitchen. I have a clear plan, and it will be a quick and easy one. I move without thinking, as there is no sense of fear. The dark spirits clear the path. They quietly whisper, guiding me. I am in a trace, spellbound by their powers, swallowed whole. A part of me tries to gain the upper hand, but they will not relinquish control. I am no longer an innocent soul!

I am propelled to the kitchen drawer and I feel like I am floating. I quietly open the drawer; a sharp knife seems to wink at me, the reflection from the hall light dances on its shiny surface. I know this one will do the trick, and the dark spirits sing their praise! The water in the sink comes to life. I guess it is me that has turned it on. Maybe the spirits did it for me? I am not sure, but it doesn't matter. The dark spirits issue a call to action, their melodies proclaiming my release from the pain, freedom from the burdens of this world.

Their voices strengthen and unify, giving me the all clear. I knowingly place my wrists over the sink. The world around me has disappeared. It is absent love, the spirits do not care, as they thrive on my pain, prompting me to move the knife. The thought of scarlet droplets beckons to me. Seemingly, I know which way to cut. The spirits are guiding me. I move the cold blade across my skin, it tingles, and I see the bridge to another world. It beckons to me.

As I draw the knife back preparing to act, there is sudden and intense pressure on my shoulders. It's heavy, in an unworldly way. The dark spirits seem to be scattering, the pressure growing. Their voices silenced by the presence of a growing light. My thoughts are a jumbled mess, spinning wildly. There is no clear path, only uncertainty. My heart feels different, lighter. I look down and see the glimmer of the knife in my hand, and it startles me. How did that get there?

The pressure on my shoulders intensifies, becoming stronger. As the dark spirits continue their retreat, I see that I am in the kitchen. It confuses me. I am having a hard time standing up. The pressure intensifies; it is almost fierce. My spirit begins to settle; thoughts of self-harm lessen as the pressure on my shoulders becomes forcible. I hear the water running; I look down and shake my head. I am perplexed, why am I at the sink? The pressure on my shoulders is now unbearable. It is too much to bear. It pushes me down... down... down... until I find myself on my knees.

The house is eerily silent. I can hear the water running in the sink above me. I don't move, I am still, frozen. The knife slips from my hand, it clinks as it hits the tile floor, echoing loudly. I shake my head from side to side, pushing away any remaining dark spirits, freeing myself. Oddly, my spirit feels a bit lighter.

An image of me lying on the kitchen floor covered in my blood jumps into view. It is vivid. Its presence startles me. I hear the water still running wildly in the sink above. I see the knife just to my right. My head falls forward, my chin hitting my chest and my forehead hitting the cabinet at the same time. Tears spring to my eyes. "What have I done? What have I done? What... have... I done?"

I stay on my knees. It seems the right place to be. "Lord, is that you? Was that you? What was I going to do? Oh, no! Oh, no! Not that, noooooooo, not that!" A quiet sob escapes from the pit of my stomach. "Are you there, Lord? Dear God... please... help... me. Please! I don't want any of this Lord, I don't! I don't know what to do, how to do it ... how to move forward... the battle! ... the death! ... the move! ... the pain! ... Jake! ... single parenthood! It is all too much! I need you by my side Lord, I do... will you join me in this?"

I spin on my knees and sit down, my back against the cabinet. The running water, it seems to calm my soul. The glistening knife reminds me of what I was preparing to do. I shudder at the mere thought. My thoughts are clear now. The notion of self-harm is on the retreat, taking the dark spirits with it. My heart seems lighter, and for the first time, I feel lightness in my soul; things don't appear gray and dark. Have the spirits lost their stronghold? I take a deep breath, and let it out slowly. It feels good, different in a way. Yes, I have clarity of mind for the moment anyway.

I lose track of time. The sound of the running water eventually becomes a call to action. As I stand up to turn the water off, I see the knife. I pick it up, and without much thought, I find my way to the garage, and drop it there. I return to the sink, turning the water off. I find my way to bed, and in the remaining hours of night, I toss and tumble. Neither asleep nor awake, I am in that in-between world, where dreams meet my saddened reality, and create a kind of confused state.

It is the alarm again. Why can't it just go away? I don't want a new day. I am still recovering from the last one. I am exhausted! No, I am worn way down! The minute I put my tired feet on the floor, I realize, I will be of no value to anyone this day. I have missed little work since our return from Maine, and think I need to get my act together if I am going to be of any value in the world I find myself. I call the office, and leave a message, I am not feeling well, and I won't be making it in.

I motor on through the morning, doing my best to keep a smile on my face, knowing that deep down inside I am in shambles. I almost did the dark spirits beckoning. Scary! I get the boys ready for school, and walk with them across the field. Jake is struggling today, so many things swollen and inflamed, especially the leg. It is a crutch kind of day for him, probably should be for me as well! I think to myself as I walk; William's hand in mine, what is going to come of me? Will I make it? Will the Lord let me know Natalie is okay?"

Back at the house, the quiet is deafening! Odd concept, I think, but true! I know it will be a mistake to stay in the house alone. I grab a book and my Bible and head off to the lake. It is a beautiful fall day, bright sunshine, warm blue skies, maybe all I need is a few minutes to collect myself.

I spend the entire day alone with my thoughts, and try to figure out where I am and who I am. I'm not in a good place, but I am not sure what to do about it, or how to move forward through the rest of the storm. My journey through adversity has been marked by a number of missteps and misfires. I'm not sure how to navigate through these tumultuous seas. I think the eye of the storm is still ahead of me and that healing me will require complete acceptance about everything that has happened. I am not sure I am ready for acceptance; it seems so final.

I don't bother eating. I am not hungry. I am just numb. Maybe it all is catching up with me? Who knows? Time melts away all too quickly, and before I know it, the hands on my watch declare it is 2:00! I could stay at the lake, pretending I have no responsibilities or burdens, ignoring it all. Or I could head home and walk to the school and surprise the boys! I smile as I grab my stuff. This could be fun. Make your own joy, Bob! Where did that come from?

Once home, I make a quick jaunt out to the mailbox to grab the mail. There is a large manila envelope in the box along with the usual junk. It is a thin envelope and has a return address from our local New Hampshire Newspaper. What is this? What could this possibly be?

I go into the master bedroom and sit in the rocking chair. I carefully inspect the envelope, looking for clues of sorts. There is nothing evident, so I carefully peel away the envelope flap so I can pull out the contents. I slowly pull out a couple of pieces of cardboard. I carefully lift the top piece and see the most beautiful sight I have seen in months.

The black and white images are soothing, and tell me of our happy times! I am drawn immediately to Natalie's image, her features crystal clear. She is radiant, although she was in the middle of those horrific treatments in Boston. The boys are smiling joyfully, happy to have their Mom with them. We are just hanging out on the picnic table. It is especially meaningful as it is the last picture taken of us as a family. It is the photo that ran in the newspaper detailing Natalie's brave fight

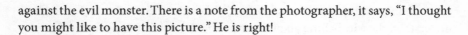

against the evil monster. There is a note from the photographer, it says, "I thought you might like to have this picture." He is right!

Given my state of mind, and the recent work of the dark spirits, I surprise myself by staying in the moment, celebrating what I have, and not what I lost! Wow, is that me trying to move forward? I am surprised by the change up in my perspective. It is great seeing us all together, smiling and happy! Yes, we were once happy, and we can once again be happy, right? I can't wait to show the boys!

I feel alive as I walk through the fields with the boys after school. There are no dark spirits here today. Have the spirits scattered for good? Jake keeps right up along with us, crutches and all! Too funny, he moves like a graceful dancer, the crutch an extension of his body! How is he doing that? Everything hurts him, poor kid. Good thing, we have a doctor's appointment coming up.

Sleep is elusive again; my conscious mixes with my unconscious in a swirling world of what is and what was! I toss and turn fitfully. I am deeply troubled by the events of the night before, unsettled even. And it is playing out in a big way in my sleep- deprived state. I am so worried about Jake, and this sense of helplessness. Been here before, and I didn't like those outcomes.

At Jake's appointment, Dr. Yuccan does the usual exam, checking every joint in the poor kid's body, recording flexibility and agility. It seems to take forever. After the exam, she tells us she is not pleased with the change in Jake's condition, which is not a news flash. It seems that the arthritis is continuing its progression. She then explains that she is ready to move Jake from NSAIDs to DMARDs. Great, I think, another acronym, lucky me. The plan is to put Jake on Methotrexate. It should reduce his pain, and help gain control over the disease. I'm all about it. Time to get this thing on the track!

It is a beautiful afternoon, and I am enjoying the warm southern fall. This fall will be one for the ages! The Northeast is already moving into the cold zone, and I am not missing that one little bit. The sun and skies help me consider the possibility of joy. I finish with work for the day, and I know Jake loves the lake. So, I make an unexpected turn on the way home, and head to the lake. He knows where we are headed immediately. The smile on his face tells me everything I need to know, priceless.

It is just another Sunday night, and I think a Sunday night church service might be good for all of us. Especially me, after the week I had. After all, I had thought about calling it quits in the game of life. I can't believe I let the dark spirits own my soul. I am trying to stay close to God, although I feel so distant. I struggle to understand the why behind all of the mess that is my life. It is a tough service for me; it tells me that I am in a sorry state. I am in a sad place, so distant from the world around me.

It is a quiet ride home. It is an especially crisp night with clear skies, lots of stars, and dew on the lawns, all a sure sign that fall is here. I pull into the driveway, deep in thought, in my own little world. Before I have a chance to turn the car off, William opens his door, and he is gone. I mean gone, flew the coup! He is running down the street like a mad man!

I turn to Ryan and Jake and angrily say, "What did you guys do now?"

They look at me with confusion in their eyes. "We didn't do anything Dad."

With a terse tone, I answer back. "Of course you did!"

Meanwhile, William is running and quickly. I jump out of the car and yell for him to return, to come back, but to no avail. Great, this is just great! What is going on here? I don't need this. As I watch, my little guy turns the corner and heads down the cross street, moving out of my sight. It is obvious he is not going to return. So, I take off in hot pursuit. He has a good lead; it takes me a few minutes to catch up to him. I am winded when I get close to him, breathing heavily I say, "William, please stop running. Tell me what is going on?"

No response! He is now just moving about, jumping, trying to avoid me. "Please stop William." He continues dancing about me; at least he is not running. Again, no response. I guess I am just going to have to tackle this kid.

We are both dancing about on a neighbor's front lawn that is two streets over. I have no clue what the trigger was and what is bouncing around in his little boy mind. I have a suspicion, but don't want to admit it to myself, at least not here on the front lawn, in the bright moonlight while the stars do their own dance in the sky.

What's a guy to do? A guy thing, of course. I leap into the air and throw myself at him. I grab him and tackle him to the ground. The grass provides for a soft landing. I feel the moon dew, chilly on my skin, cold even. I pull William toward me in a tight embrace, but he wants nothing to do with it. His little hands beating on me and yelling at me to let go. I grab him tightly, I don't move, all the while

trying to comfort him. Eventually, he gives up the fight and slumps against my chest. I can feel the tension begin to slip away from his little body.

With a calm voice I say, "Hey, William, can you tell me what is going on here?"

Silence meets me. I whisper, "There is something going on here, William. Please tell me what it is. Let me help."

More silence! It is awful. I let it ride for a bit. I hold him tight, the dampness of the grass beginning to seep through my clothes, chilling me.

"Hey, William, I can help. Please tell me."

A sob catches in his throat. "I want to die!"

Sidekick to the ribs! This nearly knocks the breath out of me. Did I hear right? My little guy wants to die. Oh no, this can't be, not this! My heart begins to beat wildly in my chest. How can this be?

"William, how can you say that? Why would you want to die?"

"You know, Dad… you know."

I do? I have no clue. I am trying to put some pieces together but come up empty. I have no earthly idea what is going on, so I say, "William, I am not so sure that I know!"

"Yes you do, Dad, yes… you do!"

"William, I don't. Really, I don't! Please… tell me please?"

"Because you do too, Dad!"

Bam! Double bam! Right upside the head! Nearly takes my breath away. How can this be? Why does he think this? What have I done to make him think I want to die? What, hadn't I done a great job at keeping that little secret all to myself? I take a long breath and try my best to gather my thoughts. "William, how can you say this?"

He sternly replies, "Just face it, Dad. You want to die!"

And there it is! Intuitive! Wowser! Proverbial or what? Out of the mouth of babes, they say. And in this instant, I know he is right. After all, I did try to end it all. It saddens me to hear him verbalize the intent of my heart. And to think he has been carrying this burden around in his little boy heart, all because of me! Guilt is quickly rising in my throat.

Before I know it, lying there in the grass, the cool moon dew against my face, William is quietly weeping in my arms. It quickly escalates into soulful sobs. I hold him as close as I can while big ole tears roll down his cheeks and fall onto the grass. I can't help but sob quietly with him. We lay there, in the moon dew for a good bit, each of us being a lifeline for the other.

How can this 6-year old wonder see so easily into my heart? It is evident that I am failing miserably. I guess I knew that already, but needed a little something to knock me upside the head. It seems the man in the mirror was leading me down the wrong path. The 'stick-a-smile-on-my-face' game is not fooling anyone, except me. What do I do from here? I know something has to change, and it has to begin with me. I am not sure what that means, or what it might look like, but I want it!

I pick myself up, damp and cold. I grab William, and pick him up in my arms, and he easily falls into my embrace. I have nothing to say and am unsure what to say. No one prepares you for this stuff. You have to wing it! It's not a good feeling. Death and dying, ugh! Will it ever leave my world?

As I carry him home, I quietly whisper, "It is going to be okay! You know how I know William? Cause we have one another, and we love one another, and because we both want to live to tell our story one day. I promise one day we will tell our story. It will be the story of a courageous Mom and her brave fight. And it will be about her brave children who were there with her every step of the way. It will be a wonderful story, one that will paint a beautiful rainbow. You'll see."

When the craziness of the day is over, prayers said, and all three boys are tucked in for the night, I can collect myself. It has been an evening of epic proportions! I am not sure about anything, but know I have to do something. Given my current trajectory, I am destined for big trouble in the new world I find myself. I am well beyond my means, and I need to get some help, maybe lots of it. The only way through this mess is to journey through it.

Time to change my trajectory!

Inspiration..

How long, Lord? Will you forget me forever? How long will you hide your face from me? How long must I wrestle with my thoughts and every day have sorrow in my heart? How long will my enemy triumph over me?

Psalm 13:1-2

Reflection ....

Can't someone make it all go away? Can't we go back and make the outcome different? Is that asking too much? God, is that you? Are you out there? Any chance you made a mistake here? Can you go back and make for better outcomes? I am not sure I can do this thing, Lord. My heart is heavy. So very heavy that it hurts sometimes!

There are no words that can describe how this feels. There are not enough tears to reflect the immensity of my loss. Everything is changed, in an instant. An unseen foe has robbed me of my future. The place where Natalie should be is now a void, a place where her laughter and light should live, no longer thrives. So many questions, unanswered, and physical love is absent.

I am overwhelmed and have no reason to endure. Dark are my mornings, dark are my days, dark are my nights. I feel numb on the inside. It seems as if each part of my body weighs a ton. I can't seem to do anything right, but I'm not sure what right looks like. I ache in ways I do not understand, and struggle to find a little bit of happiness or even a glimmer of hope. I find myself in a deep, dark hole, and I can't climb out. And don't know how to climb out. Maybe I just don't want to!

I can see a light far off in the distance, but it seems beyond my grasp. Besides, I have no earthly idea how to get to it. I look in the mirror each morning and see a man, a shell of what he once was. I might be able to put my happy face on for others, but the man in the mirror, he knows the real deal. I question the man, when does the pain subside? There is no response; he has no answer. The lack of response hangs in the air, swallowing me whole. I wonder when it will end?

The lack of light gives the dark spirits free rein, and they seem to own me outright. I have given them that authority. I invite all of them in. They become welcome members of my world. They circle the periphery of my life, twisting, squeezing, and hurting my very heart. They deliver crushing, visceral blows that wreak havoc on my body. I am torn between lands and carry a heavy burden.

The burden... the battle ... the move... the job... the death... the pain... the loneliness... Jake... single parenthood! Collectively it is all too much! Seriously Lord, have You completely lost Your mind? Wasn't the battle against an unseen foe enough? Apparently not! You feel the need to challenge me even more? What do you exactly expect from me, Lord?

I know the Lord will only give me as much as He thinks I can handle! Well, I think He just might have gone too far. I've told Him before that I am not His man. He clearly thinks more of me than I do of myself. Look at me Lord, just look at me. Is there no rest for me? Honestly, I can't do this Lord! I don't want to do this, I am not your man!

My plan was to muddle my way forward and do the best I can with what I've got. Go through the motions and put the smile on the face and just try to get through the day, minute by minute. The man in the mirror approves my plan and works alongside me to pull it off. It was a good plan on the surface, but it does not work out exactly as planned. It all comes to a crushing blow on a moonlit night, damp dew against my face, and the tears of a child. The pain I have caused my son, my children, hurts me as much as Natalie's death! William's words bounce against my heart, "Because you do too, Dad!"

Did I mean to get so wrapped up in myself? Wallowing along in my world filled with self-pity. Did it just happen? I don't remember making a conscious decision in advance of the march of the dark spirits. I cannot believe I let the man in the mirror convince me that only he and I would know of the pain. That only he and I would understand the role of the dark spirits. That only he and I would know the game plan. Which wasn't much of a plan!

I admit it; I allowed the dark spirits to own me. I existed with them in the blackest parts of the human soul! I lived by their standards. I let them in, gave them full authority, and paid the price. To think I could have ended it all. I could have harmed myself. I think about the pain that I would have inflicted on Ryan, Jake, and William. I try and picture them in a world without me.

I didn't mind playing the 'point-and-blame' game either, especially when it came to pointing to the heavens. Maybe it was easier that way. I get that I can't change what happens in life and life's outcomes. I get that there is no 'redo' option in the game of life. It would be nice, but there is not one, just the same. How I feel about what has happened and is happening, is something I can change.

The bottom line is that I don't like this dark place. I wonder if this is where the devil resides? Now that is a scary thought. Maybe so, but it is my call to action. How do

I get out of this horrible funk? I have got to get beyond this somehow. I don't know how. Maybe someone who is practiced in the ways of a mournful soul can help me?

A good thought, but not one for the ages quite yet. I need to visit with the man in the mirror first and look him straight in the eye and tell him it is over! The dark spirits need to leave, now! They can no longer control my world! There is too much at risk.

As I toss the dark spirits from my life, I begin to see the world more clearly. I couldn't see a world without them before. Maybe I didn't want to? Maybe the dark spirits are just part of the process, part of the journey. But I was overwhelmed, and the dark spirits took advantage of me, feeding on the pain, the confusion, and the negativity. It was a bona fide feeding frenzy.

I realize that I can let the dark spirits stay, or I can ask them to leave. So I am going to have that chat with the man in the mirror, right now. And I am going to put myself on track for healing, eliminating pain, sending the dark spirits to the dark hole of despair where forth they came. See ya later dark ones! It is time for you to pack up and leave, you have worn out your welcome.

I can do this. No, I will do this! It is time to push through the eye of the storm, time to see what might be waiting for me on the other side. There is only one way forward, only one. Yes, there is, and I think that time is now.

BOOK 10

Angels

<u>Angel Wings</u>

On angel wings I long to soar
Escaping the bounds of my life
To be closer to you now
In the heavens and the skies
The beauty of your spirit
Is possible to behold
By looking to the stars
Spreading the luminance of your wisdom
Life is not fair
Apart we are, never again as one
But your Godly mission fulfilled
The promises of a life well lived
Your love for your life still exists
In the souls that remain behind
Carrying on your passions
Your dreams yet to be granted
On angel wings I will one day soar
To be with you again
Where the spirits greet the universe
Where new life begins

By: Robert Mapes

The Story ....

The alarm jumps to life, pulling me into the now, willingly or not. My reality was blown wide open by the events of last night. I have a choice to make; I know that now. I feel different this morning, somehow. The dark spirits seem to be doing their own thing off in the distance, leaving me alone. Their grasp is weakening;

I can feel it. They aren't welcome in my realm, and I think they know that now. Sleep continues to be elusive, just the same.

The day wears me down! I am spent. I head to bed as soon as the boys are squared away. I fall into a fitful slumber and hang there until something begins tugging at my subconscious, trying to take me from the land of dreams into the present. I am caught between lands, choosing to ignore whatever it is that is tugging at me. As I wrestle between the conscious and unconscious, I feel the tug again. Something is determined to pull me into the present. I break free of slumber's tight grip and step into the twilight of my consciousness. And then I hear it, a soft voice, it says a name very lightly, almost a whisper. I can't make sense of it in my twilight state. Am I dreaming?

My twilight state holds on tight, not willing to release me into the present. Again, I hear a soft whisper, this time, I think I hear my name. But that can't be! I fight my way through the fogginess of the twilight and into the present. My eyes fly open; I quickly prop myself up in bed. My vision takes a moment or two to adjust. The sight before me is surreal! I close my eyes, shake my head about, trying to knock the cobwebs out, thinking they are playing with me.

I open my eyes. The sight is the same. The image is Natalie, in all her glory, standing by the side of my bed, looking as great as she ever did, yet different at the same time. She is angelic, covered in a flowing teal gown, her skin glowing, a soft luminance surrounding her. I am speechless.

I try to make sense of the sight before me, but I can't. I wonder if it is it my overactive imagination, a wish come true, or her? Of course, it is Natalie, but it can't be, can it? And she looks good, all signs of trauma gone, glowing in an unworldly way. I must be losing my mind. I lightly shake my head. It is just a dream; that's what it is. But it isn't, because I am awake - wide awake!

She speaks softly, her voice almost musical. "It's okay. It really is me. You're not dreaming."

I open my mouth to speak, but before I can utter a single word, Natalie says, "Just listen, you need to listen." Not always one of my better attributes, but listen I will.

I nod slowly, still questioning. It makes no sense! Thoughts are racing, I am unsure. Natalie reads this knowingly. "You need to know I am okay now. Look, my hair."

At that, she shakes her head, which is full of luxurious, brown curls, outlining her delicate features, exactly as I remember. Her hair different than the short crop she wore when she left this world.

"I don't have pain. You need to know that I am okay. You need to let go. It is time for me to move on. I'm okay now."

She smiles knowingly. Ah, that smile! It seems to light up the room. It comforts me, just as it always has. "You need to let go. It is time to let go."

And at that, she is gone. Poof! Here, then gone. I jump out of bed, turn on the light, look around the room, glance up at the ceiling, and try to make sense out of what just happened! Did I just have an angel moment? Naw, it can't be! This kind of stuff doesn't happen in real life. It might happen to godly people, but not me. This is the kind of stuff that happens in movies. It doesn't actually happen, does it? An angel?

My thoughts tumble, pieces of realities hanging on the cusp of the surreal. I get back in bed, unsure. Time seems to stand still. I want to reach back just a few minutes and lock it in, maybe relive it! Questions bounce around my brain. I am confused and oddly at peace.

I put my head down, try to find my way to the land of slumber and dreams, but it is not meant to be. I toss and turn, the sheets a tangled mess by the time the alarm beckons. Tired as I am, I start another day. Today, though, I am encouraged.

The man in the mirror looks back at me this morning; he is shaking his head in disbelief. It isn't possible, is it? There is no way, right. An angel? Maybe I imagined it. I was wide-awake, and I know what I saw. There is no question. It was real. Me? An angel? Who would have thought? Am I to learn something from this?

I can't focus. I debate with myself most of the day. Meetings on the work front are just noise around me. I wonder if I should talk to someone about this. I talk myself out of that, quickly. People would listen to my story, be kind, but think I crossed the line. Too risky! No one would ever believe my story.

The events of the last couple of weeks weigh heavily on me. Man, I got dangerously close to my end game. William called me out and revealed the true state of my heart. And then, a visit from an angel. I am not sure how to process all of this, what does it all tell me? Better yet, what am I to do with all that has happened? I am in over my head and am going to need help if I want to claim final victory over the dark spirits and push them into another universe.

I try to put all the pieces of the puzzle together and to make some sense out of them: the scent in the bedroom, the watch, the birth of Natalie Alyce, something preventing me from self-harm, and the visit by an angel. I question the significance to my life. My gut tells me that these things didn't happen, because I can't explain them. Why is that? Is this a faith thing for me? A topic for the ages, I suspect.

Life motors on, and Thanksgiving heads my way. As it approaches, I find myself with mixed emotions. I am happy that my parents, Todd and Alice, and my sister Grace and her husband Rick, will be spending time with us. The tough part is this will be the first Thanksgiving without Natalie, her favorite holiday. Just the thought makes my emotions bubble and boil.

Thanksgiving week arrives with lots of visitors, and a bit of a chill. Not at all like the Texas I am expecting. The fall had been delightfully warm, until now. Go figure. I welcome my visitors and relish the extra hands I'll have on deck to help out. I like it. The numbers are now in my favor and I'm feeling good about that! Watch out my young sons, game rules just got changed up. It is a new day!

The holiday itself arrives with the promise of all things, snow, and ice! What is this? We're in Texas now! Did this stuff follow me from New Hampshire? I am hoping that the weatherman has it all wrong. I set my alarm so I can get up early before anyone wakes up! I want to go to the cemetery; I just need to do it.

It is cold on the hilltop. I stand by Natalie's headstone, the wind cutting through to the bone. Old man winter is making some noise this Thanksgiving. I shiver a bit, not sure if it is the cold, or the darkness that followed me here. I feel alone today. Being the 'one left behind' is tough stuff. But someone has to go first, just the way it is. I always thought it would be me. But, that is not the way life has played out. It was not supposed to happen like this! A tear breaks free, just kind of happens. I stay there, graveside, till the tears stop.

As we sit down for our grand Thanksgiving feast, I try to focus on the gifts of life and not the losses, giving thanks to the Lord for all of His mighty blessings. Old Man Winter finally grabs hold of the day, throwing pellets of freezing rain and snow, reminding us who is in control. Grace and I spend the afternoon and a good part of the night getting a Christmas shopping list together for Ryan, Jake, and William. The goal - to knock out Christmas shopping while the family is in town - and tomorrow is that day. Crazy notion, but I like it. Close it down!

A beautiful blue morning sky and crisp temperatures greet us. I look out the window and see a New Hampshire kind of landscape. It seems I can't escape it! It is a winter wonderland; a layer of frozen precipitation covers the land. The Yankee in me won't be deterred. A little ole' bit of white stuff is not going to stop Grace and me from pulling Christmas together. Off we go into the bright, sunlit day.

Time with family flies on by, and before I know it, goodbyes are said, and everyone is on their way home. The house is eerily quiet after everyone leaves, especially at dinnertime! There is an empty seat at the table again tonight, a reminder of what we lost.

The boys make their way to bed, and the house becomes so quiet I can hear a pin drop. The silence is the all clear for my hurting heart to invite the dark spirits in. I try to push them away, to no avail. The silence becomes palpable. I do not hear Ryan come down the stairs. "Dad?"

Ryan tries again, this time, a bit louder. "Dad." This time it sticks.

I shake my head, bringing myself back to the present. "Hey Ryan, what's up?"

"I miss Mom."

Ugh! Out of the blue. Unexpected. A call to reality! Okay, got to own this one. "Hey kiddo, I miss Mom too. Come on over, sit on the couch with me. We can talk a little bit. So, what have you missed the most?"

"I miss Mom's pie. I didn't get a pie for my birthday."

Man, he is on spot! Natalie loved to bake pies, the lemon meringue was a specialty. We had pies, not cakes, for birthdays.

"I miss those pies too, Ryan. They were pretty special. Not everybody gets a pie for his birthday. You know what else I miss? I miss all of the craft stuff and how we all helped her with her craft fairs. What else do you miss?"

"I miss her hugs and her reading to me. She always read to me, to all of us."

"She did love to read, didn't she? You know who else she got to be a great reader?"

Ryan looks my way, thinking maybe he should know the answer, but doesn't.

"It was me. I know, can you believe it? Mom always loved to read, and I was never a great reader. She got me a book when we were dating in college, and she encouraged me for weeks to read, read, read. I did so, painfully at first. But over time, the book drew me in, the characters coming alive for me in exciting ways. Before I knew it, I had read the entire book, cover-to-cover. I love to read, and I have her to thank for it. We all have so many things to be thankful for, don't we?"

"I still miss the pies!" There is my humorous son.

"I know you do! Hey, how about I read some to you tonight, just you and me?"

The smile I get is all I need. It's a 'finding joy' moment. I grab a book and start reading to my son, who very much needs his Dad and a Dad who very much needs his son. I am glad I am here, really here for him. Maybe a key lesson in the game of life tonight. I need to get better at being there for my children. Maybe it's a bit of progress or at least a beginning.

The alarm clock rings. Time to rejoin the never-ending rat race and let the games begin. I pull myself out of my slumber and crawl out of my bed in the predawn hour. Time to wake Jake, run his bath, carry him downstairs, and get him soaking. I'll do anything to try and ease his pain. His condition continues to deteriorate, and my once active son is anything but active. It is evident JRA is rocking his world. The bath, a new tool we are experimenting with, seems to help, lessening his symptoms a bit. I'll take it for now.

My world gets rocked a bit at work. There is a big announcement about a change in our health care plan. No big deal, I hope. Dr. Yuccan has to be in the new network. A quick phone call tells me that life is not going to be that kind to us. Of course, Dr. Yuccan is not in the network! Seriously, why is life so tough? No big deal, I can handle this one. No, I will handle this one.

I reach out to Vicky, a friend of mine who I know has a contact working at our new provider network. Vicky agrees to help me out, and bamo, I have the name of a new physician, one that specializes in the treatment of JRA. Welcome, Dr. Donnington! Wow, simple and done. I can do this, can't I? Yes, I will do this.

I want to get ahead of things before Christmas starts, so I make an appointment with Dr. Donnington for early January. I don't want to lose any momentum we have made. Based on how Jake is hobbling about, we cannot afford to lose our footing against this monster! Hard to believe the sands of time are moving so quickly, I am almost at the 6-month anniversary.

Christmas was always a special time. Natalie was a gifted quilter and craftswomen, so we have many special handmade quilts, table runners, ornaments, you name it. I would call them meaningful keepsakes, mementos; things that connect the past to the present. As beautiful as they are, they threaten my future with their chains of sorrow. Christmas is hovering just beyond the horizon, carrying with it a quilt of dark despair and Christmases past. That, with the thought of Christmas present, makes my heart heavy. I feel the dark spirits beckon; I silence their call with joyful thoughts of Christmases yet to come.

One of our great traditions had been to go to a Christmas tree farm and pick out a tree together. It was always a family affair and lots of fun. I decide that I should keep the tradition alive, hoping a familiar tradition might help all of us through the Christmas Holiday.

Texas is not New Hampshire! Finding a Christmas tree farm is a challenge. There are not many choices actually, which should have been my first clue. But, what do I know? My goal - keep the tradition alive! I am not sure if it is more important for the boys, or for me. No matter, I talk it up all week with the boys, working to build excitement, and to move my own spirit in the right direction. I know I need to focus on the real reason for the season. Great concept, sure hope I can deliver!

I am pretty pumped about a family-type outing, and I am excited when Saturday finally rolls around. Time for a Christmas tree adventure! It is a 45-minute jaunt to the outskirts of Fort Worth. I keep a watchful eye on the landscape as we travel the byways and highways. I am certain we are going to encounter some kind of forest, a sure indication that a Christmas tree farm is nearby. In my conscious, I thought New Hampshire and Texas were equal when it came to Christmas trees.

As we journey along, I keep expecting that forest to be just over the horizon. Interestingly, though, the horizon never delivers a forest. It is always the same; a flat, arid-looking landscape; nothing close to a forest with lots of wide-open fields and plains, cattle, but nothing really forest-like. As we draw closer to the Christmas tree farm, bells and whistles start sounding. What is going on here? I thought for sure we would be seeing a gathering of trees of some type by now?

Jake sees it first, the official welcome sign to the Christmas tree farm. As I pull into the nearly empty parking lot, I look about and am surprised when I see a few low hills. The boys eagerly jump out of the car, with William shouting, "Where are the trees Daddy, where are the trees?" To tell the truth, I'm not sure. I am still expecting to see a forest of sorts, and there is certainly no forest where we now gather. "Hey boys, maybe the trees are on the other side of that knoll?"

And they are off! Running all out for the top of the knoll, and the Christmas trees that must lie just beyond. Jake is doing his best to keep up, dragging his left leg behind him. As Ryan and William near the top of the knoll, they come to a complete and abrupt stop, frozen in place. Slowly, they turn my way, not moving an inch. Now this is odd! Usually, there is pushing and shoving going on amongst loving brothers. What now I think?

As I reach the top of the knoll with Jake, I realize, with great dismay that I am not in New Hampshire! There is no forest. There isn't even a small gathering of trees! For that matter, it seems that there isn't even a Christmas tree farm. From my purview, atop the grassy knoll, I see a smattering of trees, sad in a Charlie Brown kind of way. All of the trees, every last one, appear to be leaning to the left, crooked as can be. The effects of the Texas wind hollowing across the plains I reckon, forcing them to bow down to their will.

Not what I expect and clearly not what the boys expected. What to do now? I can give in to the moment, and let life take control. Or I can seize the opportunity, and make it something other than what it is. I can make it a part of a bigger adventure. Quickly assessing the landscape, I find the ugliest, and by far, the scraggliest tree, and shout, "I see the one I want!"

Their faces, priceless! All eyes are on me, disbelieving. They think I have stepped completely over the edge. While not too far from the truth, here in this moment, I know exactly what to do. While the boys are thinking Dad has flipped out, I take off in the direction of my sad kind of tree. The boys are not moving. I turn, run backward shouting, "Got ya!" I continue in my dash. They know immediately they have been pranked, and they join in the dash along with me.

We make it a fun outing, each of us selecting the saddest tree we can find, each trying to sell the other on the merits of their selection. This is so much fun and no, we will not be going home with anything from this tree farm. We do, however, make a stop at Lowe's on the way home, and find ourselves a beautiful blue spruce, Natalie's favorite. We all agree that Mom would approve!

We waste no time when we get home and get right to putting up the tree. The good spirits are with us it seems, I take advantage of the positive vibe from our jaunt to the tree farm. The boys go into the garage, and play a game called 'Find the Stuff!' Not an easy task, the garage is still filled with stuff I have yet to unpack from our move. Just not enough hours in the day! Luckily, their determination pays off, and they haul out all of the Christmas paraphernalia without fanfare, or a fight. Wow.

The good spirits are with us indeed. I get to firing up some Christmas music. It is sure to be a bit of fun, so I hope.

We get the lights on the tree, and then turn to the decorations. This will be a family tree this year, no matter what gets put where. There are many of Natalie's handmade Christmas items in the mix, her absence clearly obvious, all of us a bit on edge. No matter how hard I try to stay positive, I can sense just how much the boys are missing their Mom. I can see it in their eyes, the roadway to their young hearts. I can just imagine how tough it is for them. And then it hit me like a ton of bricks. Every Christmas will be like this for them, now until the end of time!

I make some popcorn and promise the boys we will go out to dinner once we finish decorating the tree. I am still working to keep my spirit, and theirs, positive. As we continue to unwrap Christmas type items, the boys get quieter and quieter. I can see the joy easily slipping away, and I can suddenly feel the pain of loss in the family room. I want to fix it, make it better.

It is sudden and happens without warning. I know what it is the minute Ryan takes it out of the storage container. I can tell by the shape and the wrapping. I had forgotten all about it, I want to yell 'put it down' to Ryan, but I am too late. I watch, mesmerized, as he continues to free it gently from its delicate wrapping. Jake and William, they are locked in place, neither moving. All eyes are now on Ryan, and the precious cargo in his hands.

After what seems an eternity, I catch a glimpse of an off-white gown. With loving care, Ryan frees the delicate wing. The object seems bathed in light, glowing of its own accord. It is as precious as ever, and I am surprised it made the trip to Texas in one piece. It is our Christmas Tree Angel, special because it is the Christmas Angel that Natalie made.

That is all I need to see, and I am done! Tears spring from the open hole in my heart. I don't want to be the one to ruin the day. Things had been going along so well! I look to my wonderful children, and can see that I am not alone. We fall into each other. There is no sobbing, just a comfortable group hug, each trying to be there for the other. We embrace each other for a few minutes, I dig deep and say, "Let's make Mom proud, finish decorating this tree, and place the Angel on top of the tree, in honor and love."

I grab the stepladder and a couple of bar stools, so we can all place the Angel on top of the tree. It feels like Natalie is making the spirit of Christmas come alive from beyond the grave. We gather the stools and ladders. I grab William in my arms, and we all stretch, placing the angel atop the tree. We step back and take in its beauty. I sense Natalie smiling down at us. Not because the tree is beautiful, but because we are trying to remember the spirit of the season. Just the same, memories of Christmases past dance about me, dark spirits rush to the scene, trying to steal my heart. Not today. The spirit of the season holds the menace at bay!

After Church on Sunday, I take an unannounced detour. Noise quickly greets me from all quadrants of the car. Almost in unison, I hear, "Dad, what are you doing? Dad, where are you going? Dad, aren't we going to Mom's?" Their desire is encouraging; it surprises me. I say to the boys, "Yes guys, relax. Don't worry. We are going to Mom's. I have a special stop I want to make first. You'll see."

They quiet down, all eyes peering out car windows, taking in the scenes, as they try to figure out what is up, and where I am going. They have no clue, though. They'll never figure this one out. I smile to myself. I pull the car into the parking lot of a local craft store.

This rallies the troops. "Dad, what are we doing at a craft store? What are we doing here?"

I try to soothe them. "Relax boys; it is all good... promise."

The store, Christmas on steroids! It is grand... Christmas is scattered to the winds of retail design. I gather the troops up close. "Okay guys, we are going to do something special for Mom. I want you each to pick out flowers, or other Christmas type items, you would like to put at Mom's gravesite. We'll go to the cemetery, and we'll decorate Mom's grave. No one says we can't celebrate Christmas together."

I am not sure if this crazy idea is going to float! My heart tells me we need a way to express our love of Christ, our love of a Mom, and the love of a best friend. I think a positive spin on this holiday will help us all get through it and come out the other side in one piece. I think Christmas will set the tone for the coming New Year. I want to fill it with promises of joy for all of us. No, I need to fill it with joy!

The boys are cute as I watch them inspect and select items that are meaningful to them, ones that they think will be meaningful to Natalie. They are so serious and intentional. The store clerk observes this activity with great interest. "You guys are on a mission; you must be up to something special."

Oh, wow! How will they respond? Ryan jumps right in. "We're buying some special stuff for our Mom."

The store clerk smiles, "She must be a pretty special Mom."

Three uneasy sets of eyes dart my way. The moment I was hoping for feels melancholy! I hear my own voice. "She is indeed a special Mom, and she will feel really special today." The boys smiled. "Okay guys, let's finish picking out stuff... we have a job to do."

Ryan and Jake strike out on their own to finish up, leaving William and me to work together. I need to get in on the fun, so while helping him, I plot my own decorating strategy. I certainly don't want to be outdone by the boys!

The car barely stops at the cemetery, and three doors fly open. With their packages tightly in hand, Ryan, Jake, and William make a mad dash for a very special grave. For Jake, it is more of a mad hobble than a dash, but he does it without a crutch! A good sign, or is it a moment driven by a competitive spirit? No matter, he is in the middle of the mix and playing right along.

There is no fighting or complaining as Ryan, Jake, and William each do their own thing, respecting the others right to do the same. As it evolves, they all end up with a bit of real estate near Natalie's headstone. I find a place to set up my own decorations. The boys are obviously determined to make it perfect and put thought into what they place where. William is too cute; his smile brings a glow to my heart. When it is all said and done, we stand quietly at the top of the headstone. William grabs my hand, and the warmth of his hand is reassuring.

"Ryan," I say almost in a whisper, "What will you miss most about your Mom this Christmas?" Not missing a beat he says, "Her pies."

I say, "No doubt. Jake, how about you?" He thinks for a second or two. "Christmas morning breakfast." I say, "How about I make breakfast this Christmas?" I get a few head bobs!

"William, what will you miss most about Mom this Christmas?" He squeezes my hand and says, "I'll just miss her!"

I get down low, making eye contact with William. "I'll miss her too." He falls into my arms. I give him a good hug, and say, "I'll miss Christmas morning stockings most."

I stand back up, and notice that all eyes are on me, and I know exactly what that means. Time for action, lots of boy energy to burn off, and there is no time like the present. "Okay guys; let's see who can find the most golf balls. Ready... Set... Go!" And they are gone!

It is a good thing; I have one more ornament I want to add to my decorations. I gently pull it out of the bag, and carefully unwrap it. It is beautiful, and it seemingly glistens in the bright sunlight. It sends prisms of color all about me, making a rainbow of sorts. I know it is going to get destroyed by the weather. That doesn't matter a bit. I take the crystal angel, and carefully place it on Natalie's headstone. I stand back and take it all in.

I think about our journey and cannot believe I find myself in this place. Living in a strange land, single Dad and all, and a widower! I think of Natalie's love for life, and her passion for Christmas. It saddens me that I am alone. As great as this moment has been with the boys, it does little to change my lot in the game of life.

In a soft voice, with the wind gently harkening me, I say, "I miss you, Natalie, I cannot imagine this Christmas without you. You were the glue baby, and without that glue, I feel like I am... unglued... all of the time. Was that you that came to visit?"

There is no answer, not that I expected one. I am filled with a whirlpool of conflicting thoughts; is it even possible an angel came to visit? I know what I saw, no question. Why the deniability? Am I somewhat hardened? Do I believe that something like that cannot happen to a regular guy like me?

Nighttime descends, and with the routine of bedtime complete, comes the dreaded quiet of the day. The silence tonight is louder than a war amongst the brothers three! I feel as if I am in a kind of twilight zone. The pain of loss, an open wound on my heart, works to hold me tightly in the past, while I work to survive in the present. The past seemingly reaches into my present, holding me hostage, while the prospect of a future is a concept I won't allow myself to consider.

Each passing day brings less and less sunlight, and nighttime darkness controls more and more of my world, and the dark spirits are working to regain control. I work hard to keep them at bay and find myself barely existing as Christmas gets closer.

Julie calls me at work as she has done regularly to check in with me. I try to be positive during our conversation and paint a picture of a man who is in control of his life and almost wish I could believe it. But it is obvious Julie isn't buying any of this, she interrupts me and says, "Bob, I think you need to find someone to help you through the storm; someone with grief therapy experience. Someone who can help you move forward from the past and help you figure out how to let go."

And there it is, letting go! Isn't that what the angel told me? Maybe I don't want to let go. It will hurt too much, and I don't want to go there! Deep down, I know she is right. I cannot continue to do this to myself. I am no good to anyone, least of all myself. I guess I should have already done something. Funny thing about the past, it can tightly encircle you, maybe even hold you hostage, and that is exactly where I am. I made sure the boys got some help, so why didn't I get some for myself? Maybe I just wasn't ready? No maybe about it, I wasn't.

After our call, I place the phone down slowly, quietly. I decide to act in the now, so I grab the phone book and go to the Yellow Pages, and start calling therapists, randomly. I want to find someone who specializes in grief, someone with a spiritual approach. After just a few calls, I have myself an appointment after the first of the New Year. A New Year! Hard to believe! A New Year is heading my way, so why not a new start? I can do this… I will do this.

Time waits for no one; neither does Christmas. It is coming my way, like it or not! It is on the horizon, and the closer it gets, the more on edge I become. Christmas music is now on every radio station, and it haunts me, each song bringing the past into the present, memories ever ready to hunt me down. I work to listen to the true meaning of these songs, and kind of muddle my way through them, but there is one in particular I cannot bring myself to hear, fearful I will have an unannounced meltdown. I just cannot go there! No way, no how, not yet!

Adam, Becky and my brother Brad arrive for the Christmas Holiday. I am excited to have them with us. I celebrate the extra hands; watch out boys, a new sheriff is in town! I hope their presence will get us through the dark days just around the corner. Christmas Eve jumps into the present without notice. My spiritual side yearns to celebrate the birth of my Savior, Jesus Christ. But my past haunts me, a tight rein on my present.

The Christmas Eve Church Service is uplifting, and I hold my own, keeping my past bottled up best I can. Try as I might, I am not prepared for it, although I knew it would come at some point. It always does. The ushers begin by lighting the candles at the end of the pews; the choir joins in, lifting their joyous voices heavenward. It is a beautiful hymn, but the solemn sound tugs at my heart.

I am no longer in Texas, but in a land far away. In a time and place where there is joy and happiness. Where Natalie is at my side along with three young boys, all lifting our voices to God, celebrating His greatest gift to us. The past melds with my present, as Natalie's favorite Christmas Hymn, Silent Night, fills the Church. The pain of my loss bubbles to the surface. Jake reaches to light my candle. Tears fall carelessly. I smile at Jake best I can, only to see I am not alone in my tears. I put my arm around him and pull him close.

The service comes to an end, with Pastor Jacob blessing us all. Everyone leaves the service in silence. I am thankful; I know I would lose it if I had to talk to someone. The boys gather closely, Jake and William grabbing my hands. It is a lifeline for me. I know they are struggling, I can feel it in the air about me. I just need to get home in one piece.

Thanks to Grace, Santa is ready for the big day, and the boys are pretty excited that Santa found his way to Texas. The day brings an unexpected gift. Bright blue skies that are cloudless, and a warm breeze that calls out for shorts. I picture Christmases past, where cold and snow dampened my spirits. How great it is to be here, where warmth seemingly calls our names and beckons us to the outside world. The boys celebrate this great gift by trying out their new rollerblades, all decked in shorts. What a great sight!

Adam, Becky, Brad and I sit on the porch, watching the boys hone their rollerblading skills. Interestingly, Jake is pretty mobile on those blades. You'd hardly know he was struggling with mobility these days. It looks like the boot portion of the blades helps support his leg. Although he gimps a bit, you can hardly tell there is anything wrong with him. Watching him be normal lifts my spirits. What a great Christmas present! I realize how much Jake's monster consumed me, and how much it contributed to the presence of the dark spirits.

It is an early and quiet retreat to bed. The blades tired the brothers three, an unexpected gift to me! It has been an emotional day, the past working to blend in with the present, both of them tugging on my future. As I put my head down on the pillow for the night, I realize I have confronted one of my greatest fears - being alone on Christmas. I have made it through this, and many other firsts, and I am still in the land of the living. Maybe, the New Year will bring the possibility of new beginnings, even Peace.

Inspiration ....

For He will command His angels concerning you to guard you in all your ways.

Psalm 91:11

Reflection ....

The whirlpools of self-pity and despair have owned me outright. They have been given exclusive rights to my very being. The interesting part, I gave them those rights. Just handed them on over, no questions asked. I did not let it happen in a moment of time, but rather relinquished control over time. I see this now. It happened all too easily. A slippery slope, as they say. And slip slide I do. I find myself in the hands of the dark spirits. After a painful reality check and some hard talk with the man in the mirror, I know I have to make a change.

I frequently prayed to the Lord, asking for insight into Natalie's well-being, and her new life amongst the angels. All I seem to get in response is silence! After months of praying, it seems as if God has no intention of answering my simple prayer. I struggle with this. Surely, He sees me in my funk, trying to find my way forward. I know He has got to see that I am lost and that there is this huge roadblock in my way. It seems serenity will only come to me if I can get the insight I need, my prayer answered… is it too much to ask?

Hearing Natalie whisper my name, beckoning me from a deep slumber was very unsettling. If Natalie died, how is possible that she stood by my bedside? That she could now have a presence in my world… the physical world? That she could speak my name? And share words that could give me comfort. Was this an answer to a prayer?

I cannot make practical sense of it. I question if I saw an angel or if I saw anything at all. I wonder if this is about me wanting an answer so badly that I create an answer of my own. Did I envision this angel to get the answer I needed? I can't come up with an earthly explanation. Is my struggle here an intellectual one? The real world tells me it is not possible. There is no way Natalie could have been with me, or spoken to me. Natalie is gone from this world. I watched her die.

Here is my rub. Intellectually, I know it can't happen; I get that. But, it did happen. I was completely awake. It was Natalie as I once knew her, beautiful, with a special radiance. All signs of the battle were gone, completely! She spoke words I needed to hear, and then she disappeared into the quieting of my heavy heart. So if it did happen, and I saw it, why do I doubt it occurred?

Is there a bigger question in play for me? Is there a faith question in the mix? If faith is the substance of things hoped for, the evidence of things not seen, and my angel was the substance of my hope and was evidence certainly seen, it would then seem I should not question myself.

Is my struggle, the struggle of mankind? To explain the things that are unexplainable by rational thought, or by knowledge of the universe? Our intellectual prowess? But science tells me that discovery is based on facts and evidence. What facts do I have, what evidence? My word that I saw something? So, my inner conflict remains, and the question still weighs heavily on me. Did I see an angel? Did Natalie come to me with the promise of peace? I wonder if the spiritual world and angels are above science?

Maybe it doesn't matter what science might say. It might not matter what anyone has to say. Maybe what matters most is what is in my heart, and in my mind. No denying my angel visitation. Be gone science, you have no right to meddle in my world! There is the unexplainable, and it is possible something unexplainable came into my world, and it is just possible that the unexplained, an angel, came into my world as an answer to a prayer, and the promise of a path toward peace.

What seals the deal for me are the words she spoke. They were specific to me, and no one else. "You need to let go, it is time for me to move on. I'm okay now." Was God using this angel to minister to my hurtful soul, to silence the dark spirits, and to answer my prayer? Only He knew these words, and only He could arrange for an angel to speak them back to me. I am thankful for the answer to my prayer and am blessed it was delivered in such a special way.

While mankind will certainly struggle with the notion of angels, I am letting go of my struggle, this conflict of faith and intellect. I know unequivocally that angels do exist. How can I be so certain? I think we both know the answer to that!

BOOK 11

Peace

<u>A Mother's Love</u>

A mother's love
Is like the oceans of the earth
Their melodious rhythm of life
Brings calm and tranquility
To the challenges of the day
A mother's love
Is like the stars twinkling at night
Their special sparkle spans the miles
Creating a path for those
Lost along the way
A mother's love
Is like the flowers of the field
Their majestic blossoms
Follow the cold nights of winter
With the promise of a new day
A mother's love
Is like an early morning dawn
The first rays of light
Burn bright on the horizon
Giving encouragement to the dark days of our lives
A mother's love
Is forever in our hearts
A love that will always protect and nurture
It guides us through difficult times
And brings a special kind of happiness
A mother's love
Does not die
It soars with the heaven and earth
A love that will last an eternity
Like the sea, sun and stars

By: Robert Mapes

The Story ....

The New Year comes on like a storm. Aside from the return to normal craziness, the week is slated to position Jake and me to confront our monsters. Jake has an appointment with a new doc this week, and I have my first appointment with a therapist. I am tired of hauling all of this baggage along with me. It is like a heavy noose of chains. I know I need to do something with it before I die under the weight of it all. I am a bit nervous, though, but figure it can't be any worse than the road already traveled.

Jake's appointment is on a crisp, clear day, and I pick him up early from school for our commute into Dallas. At Dr. Donnington's office, I spend a good bit of time filling out the usual heath history stuff as well as a questionnaire. Why can't these docs share this stuff with one another? It's crazy to be filling the same stuff out all over again. Once the paperwork is done, the nurse brings us back to an exam room.

Dr. Donnington smiles warmly as he introduces himself. After a review of Jake's history, he has Jake walk, unaided, best he can. It pains me to watch. Jake then jumps up on the exam table and gets a physical exam. The doctor examines everything, even looking into Jake's eyes, carefully assessing Jake for signs of arthritis, but in his eyes?

Dr. Donnington explains children with JRA can develop something called uveitis, an inflammation of the inner parts of the eye. If the inflammation is not detected and treated early, scarring and vision problems can occur. Wow, I am blessed to be here with the right doctor!

At the end of the exam, Dr. Donnington recommends that we stay the course with the current treatment plan. Then he says something magical. "Did you know that the Texas Specialty Hospital for Children, just outside of Dallas, provides care for children with conditions affecting joints and bones, such as Jake's JRA? I think Jake is the perfect candidate. Who knew? Suddenly, I don't feel so alone, and maybe, there's hope for Jake.

After our appointment, Jake and I make a field trip to the Texas Specialty Hospital for Children. I am blown away by what I see. Spectacular! I park the car, and we walk into the facility. The main lobby is alive with color, it is amazingly kid-friendly, and I feel like we are arriving at a carnival. I look to Jake, he is grinning from ear to ear! I don't hesitate; I head to the appointment desk and make arrangements for Jake's first visit.

I think it would be fun to celebrate the day! We head to the Pioneer Plaza, which honors the Dallas' cowboy past. We easily find it and enjoy the recreation of a real cattle drive, made with bronze statues of longhorns and cowboys. Jake is amazed at the size of the cattle. A stream and waterfall adds to the reality. What a great way to make this a special day for Jake.

I slam the snooze button this morning, silencing the alarm. It can't be time already. Ugh! Is it time to get the bath ready for my little man? Guess so, and an early start it is. Coffee. Let me get a cup of brew before we jump into this one. It is going to be wide open. Today is my first appointment with a therapist, and I'm a tad bit nervous. My heart thumps in my chest just thinking about it.

I patiently sit in the waiting room, my palms going clammy. I'll admit it, I am a bit nervous about the monsters that I might have to slay as I journey through the rest of the storm. I am fearful of the unknown. But I have come to realize that the only way forward is forward, directly through whatever it is or whatever it becomes.

Mary Gregory quietly enters the small waiting area and invites me into her office. The office is soft, very soothing. Warm colors create a tranquil sense for me. I immediately begin to panic as Mary invites me to take a seat. Choices! Does the choice where I sit mean something? Oh heck, I go with the comfort choice.

Mary immediately creates a welcoming and caring atmosphere. We visit like old friends, initially staying away from topics that would create angst for me. Any trepidation I had about journeying forward melts away quickly. It is clear that my overall well-being will be Mary's primary concern. I have to say I don't feel so all alone. Mary will help me reduce the baggage I have been hauling around with me.

I knew it would come; I am a realist at heart. Mary begins to explore my current state. I learn that to move forward, I am going to have to verbalize that state. Our goal today is for me to say the word that has been terrorizing me, a word that has haunted me. A word I have yet to verbalize! Oh no, not that, not ready! Mary queues me up.

I take a slow and deliberate breath, hold it in for a couple of seconds, and exhale. Here goes nothing! With a slight quiver in my voice, I say, "I am... a... a..." That's all I can get out!

I am not as ready as I thought I might be. I know I have to confront it. Mary is ever so patient, and she sits quietly as the tears escape from my tormented soul. Dang tears! I don't want to be some crazy crying fool, but I can't control it, and

can't be the powerhouse I want to be. Isn't that what men are supposed to do, power through?

Mary quietly says, "The greater the love... the greater the pain. You have lost a great love so you will feel a great pain."

These words resound with me, and it seems as if someone finally gets where I am, and how deeply I hurt. Mary lets the silence hang over the room, then with great kindness she says, "You ready to try one more time?"

I sense her encouragement and try one more time. "I am a... a... a... wid..." I can't finish, and an awkward silence fills the room. Mary says nothing, not a word. I can feel the pressure building, and know what I have to do, what I will do. "Okay, here goes. I am a... a... widow... widower. I am a widower... a widower... a widower. I am a widower!"

Mary gently smiles, as she passes the Kleenex box my way. I think she has done this before. As tears continue seeping from my eyes, I can't help think I just took my first brave step. I am not sure what the rest of the journey looks like, but I do know I have finally taken a step in the right direction. I think it might get messy along the way, but it is the only way straight through the storm.

Mary gives me time to recover. "You are a widower... You've lost a great love... You are alone... You are a single Dad... You are in a new place with a new job... You have a son with JRA... He will be okay... You will be okay."

For the first time in a very long time, I think I just might be ok! It doesn't last long. Mary gives me an assignment. How dare her. In preparation for our next session, I am to buy Natalie a Valentines' Day card. And, I am to write I how I feel about her leaving. It gets better. I have to go to the cemetery and read it out loud. Oh, joy! Maybe I am wrong about this therapy thing. Forget a God moment; I think this might be a Godzilla moment!

I have the morning off, so I ride my post-therapy session high right to the local Hallmark store. No time like the present to knock out part of my assignment, the easy part. There are displays loaded with cards, and I notice I am not alone in the selection process. I can't help but wonder if anyone else is struggling like I am, with some kind of pain, some kind of loss. I want to reach out to each and everyone and offer kind words of encouragement. Wow, thinking beyond myself.

This arthritis thing is taking on a life of its' own. It seems as if things are swelling up all over the place. Fingers, toes, ankles, elbows, knees, you name it. The right hand, swollen in a big way! It makes it hard for Jake to write, making school work a big challenge.

I don't sense the dark spirits as much these days. They don't seem to circle my realm as often. Is it possible I have learned how best to manage their presence? Is it that I have a glimmer of hope, and hope gives me the strength to push them back to the far recesses of my soul? Is it that I have found my balance? I am not sure what has shifted, but it sure feels good to have someone sharing the heavy weight life seems to have placed on me.

The bright sunrise greets me this morning and helps lift my spirits, which are already high. Today is Jake's appointment with Texas Specialty Hospital for Children, and I am hopeful that I will learn new things, perhaps have a better understanding of JRA, and Jake's prospects for a cure. A chance for Jake, I can certainly hope!

Texas Specialty Hospital for Children greets Jake and me with its joyful environment, bright and cheery, so welcoming. The doctors and nurses are exceptional. We meet many wonderful practitioners, so many I can't keep their names and roles straight. The leading practitioner is Dr. Perry. She is caring, and it is evident she has had experience managing the monster now plaguing Jake.

Dr. Perry explains that Jake's kind of arthritis is most likely genetic. They will do a number of blood tests, and will take a look at Jake's chromosomes using a genetic tool. This assessment will help determine the best treatment option. Makes me wonder about the powerful role the gene pool plays in our lives? An ophthalmologist and a dentist check Jake. All these professionals in one spot… awesome!

Jake walks away with a plan. Dr. Perry has him on the same meds, just a higher dosage. Jake then visits the orthotics team and leaves with a supporting device for his hand and his leg. Both should stabilize and support, reducing pain and improving mobility. I leave with a doctor's note detailing Jake's physical limitations. Dr. Perry thinks Jake might need some academic and physical support at school as well. Good news, I am already on top of the school thing.

Nighttime has a well-established routine. With the boys in bed, I am all alone, again! Instead of risking a visit by the dark spirits tonight, I decide to parlay the positive outcomes of the day into writing a meaningful message for Natalie. I

know this is going to be a tough one. I think it is going to be tough to capture my thoughts, as jumbled as they are at the moment.

I set up in the breakfast nook. I diddle and dawdle for close to 30 minutes, and come up with nothing but scribbles. Seriously, I think to myself. I know I am stalling because I just don't want to do it. I admit it. It will hurt too much. Who wants to do something like this anyway? Okay Bob, focus… focus! You can do this! You have to do this! Here goes nothing. I continue in my struggle and land on my opening line, "My Dearest Natalie." That is it, that's all I got. So I close up shop for the night.

Days are getting longer, and the sunrise is always a gift from the heavens. The blues and grays blend magnificently with the pink and crimson hues to create a beautiful painting in the sky. God's gift to me most days, at least when I take the time to notice. Why do I take these for granted? I don't remember wintry sunrises being as spectacular in New Hampshire. All I remember are lots of gray skies and dirty white stuff covering the landscape, creating for me, a sense of hopelessness. This Texas thing seems to be working well for my spirits.

It is just another day of crazy, and crazy comes to a close once the boys are in bed. Whew! I have a burden weighing heavily on me, as I am running out of time to get my card done. No time like the present to tackle it and be done with it. Take that brave step. I start and stop multiple times. Everything I write feels clunky and disjointed. It shouldn't be this tough, but it is. I start and stop… so… many… times. I crumple up each and every attempt, tossing paper balls all around me. In a fit of frustration, my arm makes a wide, rapid sweep across the table, sending everything flying in all directions.

I get up from the chair; I still feel the burden. I know what I need to do. I just don't want to, but I have to do this! I have to move forward. This baggage I am hauling around is going to completely consume me. I pace a bit and look at my mess. Like all things in life, I realize I have choices. I can choose to clean up the mess that has become my life, or I can continue to live with the mess that is my life.

I reluctantly pick up the scattered pieces of paper that represent my life and decide I will make a fire, and burn all of the crumpled paper scattered about me. It will be a symbolic rite of passage. I'll make it my official re-entry into the world of the living. The air is chilly and damp as I step outside, and head to the top of the driveway. The glowing stars above encourage me. I put down enough paper balls to get things started, and then each crumbled ball goes into the fire, generating a quick burst of light. With each burst of light, I say out loud, "I can do this!" The fire sputters for a few minutes before dying off. I know what I need to do; I know what I have to do… and I will do it… and I do!

I leave work early, heading to the cemetery; I need to do this before the three wild men get home from school, wreaking havoc on the world. I stand at Natalie's grave, sealed card in hand. I hold the card in front of me. I try to find the strength to open the envelope, knowing what it is going to take to read the card. I gently open the envelope; my stomach doing a few flips flops. I look at the words I struggled so hard to find. After reading the opening three words, I pause. I find I am still breathing and amongst the living. It seems so far that I am okay… so I press forward.

> My Dearest Natalie,
>
> It seems like years since I saw you last. I remember your easy smile and your caring heart. I remember the fun and the sacrifice. I see your courage all about me. I still cannot believe you are gone.
>
> You need to know that a part of me died along with you on that fateful day. I cannot believe I am now standing at your grave. I cannot believe I am all alone. On that special day, we pledged our love, I always thought "till death do us part" applied to me, not you.
>
> But here I stand, your headstone a stark reminder of all that has been lost. I seem to be stuck Natalie and cannot find my way forward. I guess I am afraid to move forward, it will mean I have to accept that you are gone. Just the thought of that hurts my heart.
>
> In all things, know how much I love you, and how much of you I carry with me. I am the man I am because of you. I will be courageous because you taught how to be courageous. I will be strong because you taught me to be strong. I will care for others because you taught me how to care for others. I will keep your spirit alive, always and for forever. Keep an open eye for me at Heaven's Gate. I'll see you there!
>
> I love you!
> Bob

My words come out haltingly, nervous energy forcing them from my lips. The heartfelt words I composed sting as I say them. I work my way through it, reaching the final sentence, saying, "Keep an open eye for me at Heaven's Gate. I'll see you there!" And with that, I fall to my knees, head down, and whisper through my tears, "It should have been me… it should have been me."

And there it is. Guilt! I wonder if that has been my underlying struggle? That I feel guilty that it wasn't me! That I should have been the one to suffer? That I should have been the one to die? Is this all about guilt then? Guilt that I am left and she is gone? Guilt that I could not protect her from the fall of the mighty hammer of fate?

I can see Natalie's image. She is grabbing my shoulders, and looking me square in the eyes. I can feel her easy touch. I can hear her voice. It is as if she is with me. I hear her words too. "It had to be me." She knew, long before I did that she wasn't going to make it. She had already confronted her own mortality. Did she somehow know I would find myself feeling guilty? Did she lovingly try to remove the guilt she knew I would feel one day? Was it her plan to give me peace from beyond the grave?

I stay on my knees for awhile, thankful that I was able to read my loving words. But I owe Natalie more, something better. I have to do a strong, heartfelt reading. I pick myself up, gather my emotions, and read the card like it deserved to be read. I do it with strength and conviction; there is not a tear. I did it right. A huge, first step!

I lay in wait, dreading this appointment. Mary gathers me up from the waiting area, and we head to her office. As she closes her door, she smiles. "How did it feel to read your card at the cemetery?"

I don't answer immediately, hesitating a bit. "It was some hard stuff."

She smiles knowingly. "But how did you feel?"

I think for a minute or two, try to collect my thoughts. "I felt guilty."

I just had to put it out there. It is exactly how I feel. I learn from Mary that I am not alone in this feeling of guilt. Guilt is common after a loved one is lost, or after a traumatic experience. I think I have had some of both! And guilt is the culprit encircling my heart, preventing me from moving forward. I am a hostage. My guilt lay hidden and unresolved. My roadblock! I know my monster now, and I will manage his presence in my world.

After exploring this notion of guilt, Mary asks, "How did it feel to write the card to Natalie?" I gather my random thoughts. "It sucked... I didn't like it one bit... it was hard."

Mary smiles encouragingly. "Could you do it again?"

"I think it is just one more pressure I don't need. It was tough, not something I found easy. Not that I expect any of this to be easy."

"You know, Bob, there is significant work ahead of us, and finding an outlet that works for you is an important part of your healing. If writing is burdensome, how would you feel about poetry?"

Me? Poetry? Are you kidding? I flash back to my high school English Lit days, where poetry was a requirement. As I remember it, poetry was not something that was in my wheelhouse. It was a struggle for me at best. At this point in my life, I do not see poetry as a means to an end, no way, no how!

Mary encourages me to at least try it, to explore the possibility, to be open to something new and different. If writing is not going to work, I guess I have to be open to something else. I don't want to do either, honestly. I leave the appointment thinking about poetry, and decide I'll give it a go! Nothing ventured, nothing gained.

The silence of the night creeps up on me. It seems to call to my dark spirits, the last thing I need. The boys are in bed, so I get out pen and paper, and give poetry a shot. At first, I just stare at the paper trying to figure out how to begin a poem. But I am clueless. I decide to check Shel Silverstein's book of poems. Why not? The boys love his poems. I'll check it out and see how poems work, maybe something will jumpstart me on my way.

The poems are all fun, and there is no observable rationale to how they start or were shaped. Maybe I am making this harder than it needs to be. I write my first line, and I kind of like it. It resonates with me. I hate to say it, but wow, it came easily! So I try the next line, and it just falls into place. Words and thoughts coalesce, and easily make their way to paper. In no time, I have a poem in front of me. With just a little bit of tweaking, I have something I like. I wrote a poem, and I am alive to tell the tale.

It is March before I know it. Where is the year going? It will be Spring Break for the boys soon. I want to do something really special with them, so I make arrangements to visit our friends John and Sally in California, and spend some time at Disneyland! The boys are all kinds of excited. I am too, for the most part. But I am worried about Jake's mobility, especially in a big place like Disneyland. Poor kid can't even walk to school these days without his crutches.

During our appointment at the Texas Specialty Hospital for Children, I talk with the medical team about our visit to California, and my concerns for Jake. They recommend a wheelchair. That hits me like a ton of bricks. I had never contemplated a wheelchair. Their idea is to get one at the park and that makes sense. It will be a good way for Jake to enjoy the park. All I need is a note from a doctor. I leave Jake's appointment with one in hand.

Time waits for no one, and the promise of time in California, especially Disneyland, propels me forward. Just the mention of our excursion brings a quick, easy smile to the boy's faces. And their smiles lighten my heart, and make me feel like the family we were before catastrophe struck! Packing and getting three boys ready for a week's excursion… wowser! Chaotic would be an understatement.

John and Sally greet us at the Los Angeles Airport, and it is so awesome to see them. Being together with them immediately feels like old times. But I can't help feeling like something is missing. Something is missing! But I know Natalie is smiling down from the heavens and is hopeful we will have a grand time. I plan to deliver!

Disneyland is every kid's dream come true, and so it is for the boys! Their excitement is palpable; they are nearly jumping out of their skin when we first arrive. I take the doctor's note and get the wheelchair, no problem. Jake is so ready. He jumps right on in and is ready to go. He is relieved knowing he won't have to struggle today. JRA, you have no place in our world this day!

We are first timers at Disneyland, so where does a young family with three boys head first? Space Mountain of course! And we are off. We are in line for quite a while, when a Disney team member approaches and mentions to me that we are in the wrong line. I nearly fall over. Wrong line? How can that be? Clearly, we are in the line for Space Mountain, or so the sign proclaims.

The Disney team member goes on to tell us that we are in the line for regular patrons. Yeah, okay, that would be us, right? I think she senses my confusion, she explains that there is a separate line for the handicapped. She offers to take us there if we all would just follow her. I think seriously, so we have to get out of a line we had been waiting in and get into another line? Hardly seems fair.

Off we go. It doesn't take me too long to figure out that Disney created a special handicapped point of entry for all of their rides. And, the best part for us? There is no one in that line, just us! Right to the front we go. Those running the ride are so kind to Jake, they even help him out of the wheelchair and into the ride. The look on his face - priceless! The boys are all giddy with excitement. I look out at the long line we left behind and feel a pang of guilt. Then I think, "When life gives you lemons, let someone else make you lemonade!" This is our lemonade moment. We ride Space Mountain three times in a row!

One day we dedicate as a Bob and boys day. John and Sally had to work, and I like the idea of us being alone and out of their hair! The four of us descending upon their lives, in mass, had to be a bit overwhelming. So the boys and I decide we would spend the day at the beach, along the shore of the great and mighty Pacific Ocean.

It is a glorious, bright, sunny California day. It is a weekday, so the beach is relatively quiet. There is plenty of space for running and horseplay, just perfect for three young boys. The waves are huge, the boys run to and fro, dodging the waves, but not always successfully. The waves knock them around a bit, but they quickly pick themselves up and head back in for more! Of course, I have to get into the mix; can't let the boys have all the fun. We run around like crazed madmen, the laughing, and taunting, it is like old times. It helps me believe we can have fun again! Maybe now is the perfect time. I grab Ryan and throw him up against a monster wave. He is all smiles. Welcome back, Dad!

Eventually, I find my way to a beach chair, a bit away from the boys and the beaten path. I need a few minutes just for myself. I have been making decent progress in therapy with Mary, and writing poems is easier than I would've imagined. Reading my poems out loud is an entirely different matter. I brought my poems along, and thought I would take the time, here on the beach, close to the boys, and close to God, to read them out loud. Yes, right on the beach!

It is a crazy notion! The good news, the roar of the ocean covers my voice, and my tears. It is time to do this important 'me' thing. I am going to move forward through the rest of the storm. I am! So I read, and I even write. The tears flow easily, but they feel different today somehow. They are not borne of pain but are born of joyful reflection. It brings me a sense of relief. Wow, that is a first. Tears not tied to pain.

Our return to Texas is also a return to the craziness of everyday life. We jump right on the arthritis track with an appointment at Texas Specialty Hospital for

Children. After sharing all about our California excursion with Dr. Perry, she performs a thorough exam of Jake and then turns to the results of the blood test. Wow, I had completely forgotten about the blood tests. The doctor explains that the blood work showed Jake was positive for HLA-B27 arthritis. Dr. Perry goes on to explain that Jake's 27th chromosome shows a predisposition for JRA. As I understood her explanation, there was an on switch on Jake's chromosome, and something had flipped the switch on. Poor kid!

Dr. Perry goes on to say that HLA-B27 Arthritis in boys can go into remission. Hurray, I think! Although it doesn't seem like it, she feels that we are making progress with Jake. This is a good thing. If we are able to beat this thing back into remission, it typically, for whatever reason, will stay in remission. In most boys, though, it comes back at age 25. No one seems to know why that is yet. It is just something that has been tracked over time.

As for Jake's treatment, it is going to be status quo. Stay the course with the meds, and do as much as I can to keep Jake as active as possible. Thankfully, Jake likes to be active, and this makes it a bit easier for me. The good news, swimming is still a great option for him. On a high note, Dr. Perry shares that Texas Specialty Hospital for Children sponsors a camp every year for children with arthritis and that Jake is eligible for that camp. It is called The Grand Joint Excursion. A camp designed to encourage healthy lifestyles and independence for children that have arthritis.

Jake is stoked about the camp! I never slowed down long enough to think how all alone he must feel in his fight with JRA. Now, he will have a chance to be with other children who are having the same struggle, and they will be gathered together, at the same time, exploring life in a meaningful and well-managed way. Hats off Texas Specialty Hospital for Children, and great big thanks to Dr. Donnington for having the foresight to send us here!

I make great strides in therapy. I am in a place where I can write a poem, and get through reading it, either at the cemetery or in Mary's office, without coming unhinged. Who would have thought this possible? Not me! Never in my wildest dreams. Is it possible I am on the other side of the storm?

William is particularly quiet during dinner tonight, almost withdrawn, which is not at all like him. I try to draw him into our dinner conversation, but to no avail. Just a bad day of sorts I figure. We go through our usual nighttime routine, and when I go to his room to say prayers and tuck him in, I notice he is crying. I knew something was wrong.

I sit on his bed, and ask, "William, what's going on there, buddy?"

He reaches under his pillow and produces a crumpled piece of paper, which he thrusts at me. "Here!" His teary-eyed face falls into his pillow.

Oh boy. Here it comes. Must be some kind of failing grade he hasn't yet shared, or some kind of disciplinary note. I am wrong on both fronts. The sad piece of paper, all crumpled and worn, is an invitation to the upcoming Mother's Day Tea sponsored by his kindergarten class. Ahhh man! Poor kid. I can feel his pain. Mother's Day and no mother!

I dig deep, and say ever so softly, "William, I am so, so sorry."

He leaps into my arms and holds on with a fierce grip. I hug him tight in return, and whisper softly, "It will be all right, it will... I promise."

I hang with him as long as he needs me. Eventually, he relaxes and slips down into his bed. "It will be okay, buddy! You'll see."

He smiles and says, "I love you, Dad".

"I love you, William. You're my favorite youngest son!"

I take a break at work and make a phone call to William's teacher. I know this is a big deal for him, and I am not sure the right way forward. Do I force him to confront his loss, and go to a Tea knowing his Mom can only be with him in spirit? Do I let him stay home, and avoid the turmoil it would create for him, an escape? I know we all have to deal with this stuff at times, but I don't feel like a Mother's Day Tea is the right time for my little boy.

I explain the situation to Mrs. Gellens, and she completely and totally understands. Without missing a beat, she suggests that we have a Parents Day Tea. What a great idea! It is neutral, and will not cause William too much pain. I like it! With that, Mrs. Gellens invites me to the Tea. Too funny! Looks like William is going to be stuck with his Dad for a long time. I do some quick math... hope we can make it in one piece.

During my next therapy session with Mary, we talk about the Mother's Day Tea. She tells me how pleased she is with how I had handled it, and that the collective solution is a great one. I tell her I wish I could take the credit, but I can't. I am just happy we have a viable solution that works for everyone, especially my little guy.

As we talk, I notice Mary glance at my left hand, and I know immediately what is coming next. The thought, it frightens me. I am still wearing my wedding band. And on that horrible, no good, awful June 30th, I slid Natalie's wedding band on the pinky finger of my left hand. It has been there ever since. Those bands of gold, they bring me great comfort! Wearing her ring helps me feel close to her, that there is some kind of connection between our worlds. It works.

Mary asks, "Are you ready to take one, or both rings off?"

I stare at my left hand for a bit, trying to picture my ring hand, ringless. I pull on my wedding band for a little bit, moving it about, but make no motion to take the ring off. I smile and say, "I'm not quite ready, not yet."

Mary smiles in return. "You'll know when you are."

I leave the session feeling pretty good. The blue sky graces the horizon, the warmth of spring, makes me feel lucky to be alive. I knew I would need to do something with the rings, but I wasn't sure what that something was. I couldn't see hiding the rings away in a box, never to be seen again. Then I had a thought, what if I take the gold and make something special out of it? What could that something be? Like a lightning strike, I knew what I had to do.

I have a bit of time left before the boys get home from school, so I drive myself down to the jewelers, the one close to the house. I think they can help me work some magic. The jeweler is most gracious. I explain that I want to take my wedding band, melt it down, and make a cross. A cross I could wear. Then with Natalie's ring, I would have three crosses made, one for each of the boys. One I could give them on the day they graduate from high school. I like it. I look at my left hand for a few moments, working up the courage to do the task at hand. And then slowly, ever so slowly, I slide the bands of gold off of my hand, placing them on the counter.

The jeweler senses my pain. "I am so sorry for your loss, and your children's suffering."

I get quiet and say softly to him, "Thank you… she was a wonderful woman… so courageous… she was my college sweetheart and the mother of my children… it has been a tough road!"

As I leave the jewelers, I am feeling something, but I am not sure what it is. Is it pain? Is it freedom? Is it hope? Is it relief? I am a bit twisted up. As I walk to the car, I decide it is relief I feel. Like I have just freed myself from a prison, my own prison. Have I been holding myself a prisoner of war? I wonder?

Becky and Christina will be heading to Texas to visit with the boys and me. I am so excited. Christina is a great cook and makes the best of everything Italian. The boys and I are her biggest fans! We so appreciate her gift, especially her meatballs! Truth be told, though, I am just so dang happy that there will be another set of hands or two.

I love having family with me, and a chance to share my burden. It helps lift my spirits to share stories and to talk about the journey. But my spirits are dashed just a bit when Christina and Becky ask me to join them in the master bedroom. They sit me on the bed and say, "We think it is time to begin going through some of Natalie's stuff." Ugh, right to the gut! My mind screams no, not ready! Emotions begin to bubble up. My heart starts thumping away in my chest. I'm not ready! Can't they see this? Can't they know this?

I look at Natalie's bureau, which sits exactly as it did almost a year ago, dust and all. Has it really been that long? Seems like days sometimes, and other times it seems as if it has been years. The reality is that nothing has been changed. Nothing? Yeowser! And after that much time, her bureau is just a gnarly, dirty, dusty mess. Why? Guess it was a way for me to hold on. Lingering in the past, perhaps?

As I look at the mess, Mary's words echo about me, about me knowing when I would be ready. So, why haven't I touched anything, or dusted anything? Does it mean that I am afraid of letting go, not knowing what comes next? I guess the reason really doesn't matter. There are two people here that love me and are willing to help me with the task at hand. After my spirit settles just a bit, I say to them, "What did you have in mind?"

Christina and Becky describe the concept of a memory box to me, and that they thought we should go through Natalie's things, together. Drink a glass of wine, stroll down memory lane, have a laugh or two, and maybe shed a few tears. As we journey, we will look for the things that are most meaningful to me, and put them in a special box, a memory box. Not everything, just a few things. Am I really ready for this big step? No time like the present, right? Here goes!

I never thought parting with clothes would be so difficult, but it is! I can still get a whiff of Natalie's scent when I am close to them. As I step into our closet, I take a deep breath. It oddly comforts me and encourages me forward. I wonder if she is close at hand? So together, Christina, Becky and I, tackle the monster, and handle the daunting task!

I hold it together. Must have been the wine! I keep my head glued on and my emotions under control. We then tackle the bureau and Natalie's jewelry. This is a bit tougher. So many special moments and memories are linked to her jewelry, who would have thought? It is fun to talk about all those memories, but the pearls push me over the edge. The pearls. The pearls I gave Natalie on our 5th wedding anniversary, when we had nothing between us but love. I kinda start falling apart. Christina and Becky are in the same place, and swoop in for a group hug, which is just what I need. We end up having a good ole group cry. Guess we all needed it.

I am spent, and tell my partners in crime. "I think I am done for now." And with that, I close up the memory box. Christina and Becky get right to the dusting! I have to admit, it ends up looking a whole lot better.

Parent's Day Tea comes up right after Christina and Becky's visit. They were a welcome addition to my life for a brief time and helped restore me more than they realize. The memory box, what a great idea! The house is now spotless. The freezer, filled with all kinds of great Italian treats. I know now that I can press forward, working to keep the puzzle that has become my life put and kept together.

William is all smiles this morning. Must be the Parent's Day Tea. It is nice to see him smiling. Makes me smile too! I walk into William's classroom for the Tea, and all eyes are on me. Like..... ON ME! A quick scan of the room shows me that this is still a Mother's Day Tea. I do not see another Dad, doesn't matter! That isn't why I am here. I scan the room and see a little tow-headed boy with bright blue eyes, grinning from ear to ear. That's all any parent really needs, and all this Dad needs to see! I go to him, stoop down, and he falls into my embrace.

Saturday is another beautiful day, and I think it would be nice to do something fun with the boys, and make ready for our first Mother's Day without a Mom. I remember this exact time a year ago and marvel at how much time had passed. I realize too, in this moment, just how sick Natalie was, and how hard she was fighting to stay with us, especially through her last Mother's Day. The boys enjoyed the lake and cooking out and playing around in the water. It seems only natural that we would return to the lake and have some fun.

But first, we are going to have a family outing of sorts. Time to decorate in honor of a very special mother and wife. And decorate we will. We make a run to the craft store, and the boys select flowers and such that they can use to decorate at Natalie's headstone. They are cute as they each go about the task, their unique personalities evident in the things they select. The headstone and all the decorations look great! Flowers of all kinds are stuck in the ground. No rhyme or reason, the end product the result of the boys just being boys. It is the kind of beauty only a parent can appreciate. We stand back and have a good laugh at what we created!

"Hey, guys, what was your favorite part of last year's Mother's Day?"

Ryan jumps right in. "Having Mom with us."

"Things sure have changed, haven't they Ryan? You know what? Mom loves you as much today as she did a year ago." He looks up at me, a big smile on his face.

"So Jake, how about you? What was your favorite part of last year's Mother's Day?"

"Taking care of Mom."

"I remember that Jake, she loved you for that. You know that, right?" A small nod of his head, with a Cheshire cat kind of smile.

"And you William, what was your favorite part of last year's Mother's Day?"

He looks up at me, with his big blue eyes, and it breaks my heart. I bend over, grab him up, and as he falls into my embrace. "I miss everything, Dad. I miss everything."

"You know what my favorite part was, all of us being together, being a family. I miss that, I miss that a lot! I miss your Mom! Lots! How about a group hug, and then you guys can go hunt for golf balls?" And with that, they are gone.

The lake is pristine. The Texas winds generate all kinds of waves along the shore, making the water fun to play in. The boys are slathered in sun block. The sun is so intense today; shade is my best option. We grill burgers and sausages, and it is mighty tasty.

While we are dining, I pose a big question to my young lads. "How about we plan a special memorial service for Mom? Do something really special in her honor. We can plan it together, make it ours. What do you think?"

They all look at me like I am crazy. Maybe I am! But a year ago, I was not in a good place. No surprise there. I was not ready for what life had just dealt me... dealt us.

So many demands at that time, so much pressure, everything happening so fast, and decisions having to be made so quickly. I was so distraught that I didn't have a chance to have my voice heard. I want a bit of a redo, a chance to think it all through and do something really meaningful, a special memorial service. I think Natalie deserves that!

Natalie Mapes
MEMORIAL SERVICE
June 30th

Greeting:	Jacob	
Open Hymn:	Hymn Of Promise	All
Opening Prayer:	Jacob	
Old Testament Lesson:	Isaiah 43: 1-3, 5l 18-19	Jacob
Poetry:		
Rainbows		Bob
Courage Has New Meaning		Ryan
Scripture Reading:	Psalm: 23	Bob
Music:	Memory	Dedra
New Testament Lesson:	1 Peter 1: 3-9, 13, 21-25	Jacob
Poetry:		
Bands Of Gold		Bob
Angels Wings		Jake
A Word Of Thankfulness:		Jacob
Poetry:		
A Mother's Love		William
Moving On		Bob
Prayer Of Thanksgiving:		Jacob
Closing Hymn:	This Is A Day Of New Beginnings	All
Benediction:		Jacob

June 30th is upon me before I know it, and I am ready this time! The boys are ready, too. Natalie's Memorial is a special affair at the Church. The boys, all decked out in white shorts and red shirts, are on their best behavior. They are gracious and well mannered. Natalie would be proud. No, she is proud!

The Memorial is filled with song and my poetry. Ryan, Jake and William, each read a poem during the ceremony, William needing an assist from his Dad. The English teacher, Mom, sure is proud this day as she gazes at her most precious treasures from heaven's window! There is beautiful music, and some special words coming from Jacob. At the end of the memorial service, everyone heads to the cemetery to close out our special memorial.

Dozens of colored balloons greet us at the cemetery, along with labels and writing instruments. Everyone gets to write and attach a special message to Natalie on each of the brilliantly colored balloons. The boys' eyes light up when they see the balloons and are really excited to know that they will get to send their messages to their Mom up in the heavens. Everyone quickly gets down to business and works to craft their message. There are a couple of boys who need a helping hand, so I jump in and help best I can.

I miss you, Mom! I love you! Sweet. Simple. Captures it all. As William works to attach his message to his balloon, I gaze around, watching friends and family writing and attaching their own message to the balloons. There are smiles on faces; a sense of joy seems to come from each and every one. I feel, for the first time, a sense of peace, a kind of calm that I have not felt in a very long time, not since that dreadful New Year's Day. Now just a shadow in my rearview mirror.

For a second, I try to deny myself that sense of joy, that sense of soulful harmony. I try to tell myself it is wrong to feel that way, especially today. How can I feel joy? And in this moment, I remember that we have to make our own joy. We are all designed to feel joy, and we need to give ourselves the freedom to do so. Today, I choose joy. I know Natalie chooses it as well.

Jacob coordinates the release of the balloons, and on his command, all the balloons begin their ascent toward the heavens, hopefully reaching Natalie. That is my hope anyway. As I stare toward the heavens, the balloons seemingly collect in some kind of fashion, creating a rainbow of sorts along the distant horizon. It is incredible to see. But wait, how can that be? Maybe it is just some wishful thinking on my part. A rainbow! Natalie, is that you?

The boys find their way to me once the balloons are released. They all gather close, close to one another and to me. It is reassuring! They are smiling, yes, smiling, as they watch the balloons continue their climb toward the heavens with their messages to their Mom. As I look around, I find everyone frozen in place, watching the skies. As the balloons float closer and closer to the heavens, I feel an amazing sense of tranquility. It overwhelms me. I think that I just might make it. "I can do this," I say to myself! I think I've made my way through the eye of the storm.

Suddenly, out of the blue, an excited voice rings out. It is William. "Daddy, look! Mom got my message, Mom got my message!"

I can't help but smile. "How do you know that William?"

He smiles back and excitedly says, "Because my balloon is gone Dad, because it's gone... she got it, she got it!"

I get down to my little man's level. "She sure did William, she sure did."

And at that, my little man falls into my arms. It feels good... it feels right! Peace... at last!

Inspiration...

I sought the LORD, and he answered me; He delivered me from all my fears. Those who look to him are radiant; their faces are never covered with shame.

Psalm 34:4-5

Reflection ....

Free will... a burden? Free will... a blessing? It can be a tough call sometimes. To have faith... or have something else. To believe in God... or believe in something else. To be happy and at peace... or be something else. So is free will about choices... the choices we make? I admit it; I don't mind making choices about the things I want to make choices about. Or making choices about the simple and easy things in life. Making choices that affect life, or cause me to reflect and evaluate who I am, not so much so. Having to make the hard choices I did, is not easy. Sometimes it was hard, and sometimes it hurt.

To be happy and at peace... or to be something else. That choice was mine. Maybe I didn't realize I had that choice. Maybe I was afraid to make that choice. Was the anguish so great that I couldn't see my choice? Is it that I was purely focused on survival? On getting through the day... minute by minute? Balancing it all? Cancer! Death! Move! New land! New job! The boys! Jake! JRA! Just a few things to balance. Maybe... I didn't want to see the choice. Maybe I was afraid... afraid that making a choice to have happiness and peace, would hurt somehow?

Life gave me no breaks, and it wore me down. Emptiness wore me down. Swirling emotions wore me down. Dark days wore me down. Everything was a painful everything. I was living in an agonizing world. Would anyone purposely make such a choice? To live such a torturous life? Is it something that we just let happen? Something I let happen? Existing... that is all I was doing. And after time, this approach to life started to hurt as much as the storm itself. I was suffocating under the weight of it, the weight of my choice to be something other than happy and at peace. I had that choice, I guess I always had.

The contemplation about choice is my first brave step forward through the rest of the storm. I just wasn't sure what to do with it. I was stuck in the quagmires of my own head, so clueless about the how... how to move forward. Was it possible I was in over my head and my ability to cope? You know it. There was no way I was going to figure it out on my own. I think it would have happened long ago if I understood what the fix looked like. I explore the possibility of an intervention of some kind. If I use an expert, a mechanic, to fix my car, maybe I needed an expert to help fix my heart and soul? This becomes my second brave step forward. Help! Go figure. What took me so long to get here? Was I afraid of the stigma attached to getting the kind of help I needed? Why is it that mankind is reluctant to seek help to heal the heart and the mind?

I make that courageous move. I reach out for help... I ask for help... I accept help. It is crazy, though, I learned earlier in my journey that courage was about asking for and accepting help. Learned it... but did nothing with it. Why is that? Shouldn't we all try to learn from life, and apply it to our life? Great theory, too bad I didn't apply it to my own world. Might have kept me from spending so much time with the dark spirits.

It is awkward at first... a stranger and the exploration of the heart. Disclosure and the exploration of feelings were not easy for me. But I needed a guide to help me blend my past, my present, and my future, they are after all, what makes me... me! The only way to make me whole again. Mary puts me on track for peace, bolstering me as I traverse new lands. But deep reflection of self calls out to the fears of my unknowns. As I delve deeper, the dark spirits circle my periphery, just waiting to strike. Overtime, understanding brings clarity of mind and hope. I become stronger and refuse to give the dark spirits the power they seek. I am able to prevail against them, and it felt great to gain the upper hand!

A card becomes my key; who would have thought? My guide takes me to places of the heart that I had closed off. I journey until I reach the intersection of raw and vulnerable, where I find complete emotional disclosure. Along the way, I confront my own mortality and a host of feelings I did not realize I had. After just a few false starts coming off the block, and a fire of confirmation, I am able to craft a meaningful message to put on my card. This becomes my third brave step. Journeying through that intersection is harder than I imagine, for right smack in the middle of the intersection is a roadblock... and it is clearly marked... guilt. Guilt that it was not me that suffered and died!

How could I have not seen it? Was the guilt so well hidden, tucked away, that I was not able to see it for what it was? Were there so many dark spirits circling that I could not see it, the dark spirits blocking it from my view? Mary helps me find my roadblock, helps me understand this feeling of guilt. Guilt, it can immobilize, and it did. Guilt, it can hinder well-being, and it did. Guilt, it can impede recovery, and it did. It is easy to see it now. I could still be stuck in that guilt-ridden state had I not taken that first brave step.

Pain, whether it is emotional or physical, is a condition of human existence. Death too is part of this same human existence. No one gets to escape these circumstances of life and the pain they bring, as much as we would like to. Dealing with the pain is the only way forward. Finding an outlet is just part of the journey. It is important to find the right release and the right way to explore emotions, and find healing. I experiment and find something that works for me. Finding my outlet is freeing!

So where is God in all of this? Is the struggle, by His design, part of the grieving process? Is the journey toward peace intentionally difficult? Was it difficult because God intended for me to grow, to become a better, stronger Christian and member of humankind? I believe my healing was brought about by a God that loves me and understands my pain, and that He walked with me through it, step by painful step. Does the difficulty help me grow? Absolutely, more than I imagine, and more than words can ever express. But God watches as I struggle, and allows me to hit rock bottom first. He waits patiently for me to make the first move. He was always there, as he has always been. But I had to want it... it was up to me. God was not going to do it for me... as much as I would have preferred that! A huge life lesson for me... you have to want it.... and be willing to do something about it!

Peace is a journey, and I am well on my way. My journey has been filled with challenges and self-discovery. And the peace I do have is because I traveled through the storm of adversity. It took work, hard work! Natalie lost her life at the hands of an evil monster, and through it all, she was strong. Where did her strength come from? It came from a God she loved and trusted. She left this world with this love and trust in her heart, and she gifted it to me. Too bad I didn't see it for what it was.

Free will... a blessing. To be happy and at peace... my choice.

BOOK 12

Enlightenment

As I journeyed through the storms of life along the windy path to the rainbow promise, I often times found myself overwhelmed. Emotions were bouncing around that played games with my heart. Through it all, I was seeking answers to questions and prayers. The tough part as I journeyed, questions seemed to go unanswered while prayers seemed to be unheard. So I thought anyway.

The storms of life can overwhelm and overpower. Interestingly, as with so many things in life, time can bring clarity. As I reflect back and gaze in the rearview mirror of this stormy time in my life, I can see answers to many of the questions that plagued me as I journeyed. Now I don't have all the answers, and I don't think anyone does. While I may not understand all of what happened along the way, having a complete understanding was not a prerequisite for me to move forward. Now I can see where God was actively involved in my chaotic life, clearing debris from my path, even preventing me from self-harm.

Adversity had a lock on me, creating a tumultuous environment, pain and struggles prevented me from seeing how God was at work in my life. And that He did answer my prayers. If I know this now, you might be asking yourself why I didn't see God's hand in my life as I journeyed. Here's the deal. God answers prayers in His own way and in His own time. I had expected God to answer my prayers according to my timeline, and in my way. It doesn't work that way… lesson learned.

The journey through the storm and the promise of the rainbow is a complicated one, a jigsaw puzzle of sorts. Pieces and parts seemed to be unconnected as I journeyed. As I look back, I can see how things are connected, and I am able to put the pieces together and see the full picture that is my life. Where there once was noise, there is now wisdom. Where there was once chaos, there is understanding.

Let's face it; we will all deal with something sometime along the way. The question will always be… when? It just shows up unannounced with no warning. Unexpected circumstance and adversity will enter our lives, each and everyone when we least expect it. Yes, some of us will be dealt more horrific circumstances, but we all have to deal with them, whatever they are. Some will get a bum deal, and are dealt circumstances that are so overwhelming that there seems to be no way forward or through. The only way to get to the rainbow promise, though, is to journey straight through the adversity, the eye of the storm. There is no way over, under or around. Straight through is the only way.

There was always a rainbow promise out there for me. But, I never saw it as I fought my demons. Maybe I chose not to see it. Who knows? Sometimes, it is hard to see there is something out there for you when you are fighting to hang on, and everything is a struggle. It saddens me to think I did not see the possibility, and how much pain and suffering I could have spared myself.

I wonder if God deliberately put me into the storm? Did he have a greater purpose? I know He did, He wanted to help me learn as we faced the storm together. He expected me to grow from my circumstance and to do something with what I learned. I offer my insight to you and hope it will inspire you forward, wherever you find yourself in the game of life, no matter the circumstance staring you down. If you feel your back is up against the wall, and there seems no way out, I offer you these words of comfort. If you are struggling in your relationship with God, or you have yet to meet Him, I hope my words will bring you both together.

Was God Silent When I Needed Him?

Contemplation..

Forsaken

> *Oh Lord*
> *Why have you forsaken me?*
> *This is more than I can bear*
> *An innocent bystander*
> *Helpless against an evil monster*
> *Lurking behind the beauty*
> *Quietly on the attack*
> *Oh Lord*
> *Why have you forsaken me?*
> *Leaving me helpless to intervene*
> *I pray to You for guidance*
> *Yet your voice seems to be silent*
> *As life spins out of control*
> *Leaving a silent void*
> *Oh Lord*
> *Why have you forsaken me?*

I feel so all alone
As the monster grows strong
Destroying the life of many
Like the march of winter's first frost
Quietly reshaping the world
Oh Lord
Why have you forsaken me?

By: Robert Mapes

The Story ....

It is difficult to believe in God when it seems He is absent, silent even. It is difficult for me as it seems as if He was experimenting with me. I was in a place in my life where I needed God to be in the present with me, and yet he seemed forever distant. I needed to hear from Him. Tragedy was looming large on my horizon. Dark spirits circled my soul, life as I knew it was at risk. I was in the middle of a huge storm, and yet there was silence. I wanted it to end, the suffering and the pain, my suffering and pain. It had been too much. It was too much! As the silence continued, my ability to understand His intent became as great as the trial.

I just wanted God to swoop down and simply tell me what to do to get through the storm. A simple whisper was all I needed. Any answer would work, as long as it was His. I took His silence to mean He was indifferent to me while I struggled, in a losing situation where I saw no way out. When God was silent, the enemy played upon my fears. Dark spirits swarmed, circling my heavy heart. They seized my pathetic being and owned my soul. The enemy was formidable, testing my own flesh. They pushed me hard, so hard and tirelessly, that I almost ended it all. I almost did. It scares me just how close I came.

On that fateful night, there was no whisper in my ear! But, God was not absent. He was present in all His living glory. He was with me. He knew He had to be. A life hung in the balance, and it was mine. I cannot explain the physical presence I felt that night. A force of some kind jostled with me, jumped on my shoulders, and pushed me to my knees, which is exactly where I needed to be.

It makes me wonder, is part of the trial then, by design, that God will be silent, at least in part? Is it that we must find our own way forward? That we must confront our deepest, darkest secrets and enemies solo, before God will intervene? I have to say, God has never revealed Himself like this before. Did He plan to bring me to my knees? Was that always part of the plan?

Maybe my trail was really a trial of faith? Maybe it was never about Natalie, Jake, the move or any of that stuff. Maybe the trail was about Him? Is that possible? I guess it is. So then, maybe the trial itself intentionally included a silent God. Could that be? I always took the silence to mean that something was wrong. Did I miss the mark there? Was it a sign that everything was right? Was God proving my faith?

So it seems to me then, that God wasn't silent to me because He didn't want to tell me things, things about Himself, or what He was up to. Is it that God wanted to do more then tell me things? Was the whisper I longed for the easy way out, a shortcut? During my stormy, heartfelt trial, did God want to do more through me than for me? Interesting! Do more through me than for me. Was it intentional then? That through me there would be a story to tell? Was the plan then that I would be tested? That I would confront my adversity and grow in spirit and heart? That through me, I could make a more meaningful contribution to mankind?

So what is all of this stuff about a plan? Does God have a plan? I don't think God plans things like you and I plan things. I believe God has a purpose for us, you and me. As I journeyed through the storm, I came to appreciate that God was present and standing with me as I made my own choices, you know, the free will concept. His promise… to protect and guide, was evident throughout the storm-filled journey.

As I look into my experience and play it like a movie on the big screen, I can see how overwhelmed I was by it all. I wonder how anyone could journey through so much and come out the other side in one piece and at peace. But I did. I journeyed! I waivered! I lost faith in God, and myself! I was never alone, though, was I? God was not experimenting with me. When I needed God most, He was not silent! He was present in ways that transcend the physical.

Inspiration...

Be strong and courageous. Do not be afraid or terrified because of them, for the Lord your God goes with you; He will never leave you nor forsake you.

Deuteronomy 31:6

Reflection ....

Was God silent when I needed Him most? Not at all! He intervened, and just might have saved me from myself, and those that I loved most! Maybe it wasn't that God was silent, maybe it was that I had stopped listening? Maybe I had let the pain of .

my world plug my spiritual ears and I listened instead to the dark spirits? Maybe He just wasn't ready to speak to me, and I wasn't ready to listen?

Maybe, He wanted me to learn something first? Learn something? Learn something about myself, perhaps? Was He intentionally, teaching me to be patient? Not a strength of mine. I learn that patience is important and that God speaks in His own way and in His own time.

Sometimes, we don't get what we want, or what we ask for. But instead, we get what we need when we need it most. God was not silent when I needed Him. It was me, it was my expectation that got in the way, and my belief that He was silent! He had my back the entire time. I just couldn't hear His voice.

I now listen for God's voice around me and hear it often in ways I never would have considered before. Beware, He might be speaking to you right now! Maybe my words are His voice?

Is God working through you right now? Are you listening?

Did God Answer My Prayer?

Contemplation...

<u>Destiny</u>

Is the die cast and the fate known
Will it have a mournful end?
Like the songs of lives lived past
Lonely and desolate and comfortless
"Destiny, will thou have thy way?"
A strong hold it has on my mind
Wild feelings and broken hopes
Agonies my knowledge creates
"Destiny, will thou have thy way?"
Desolation pounds my saddened soul
Like the winds against a hilltop barn
Shadows disappear from moonlit skies
Sadness engulfs me
"Destiny, will thou have thy way?"
Destiny hides behind the hands of time
I wonder - to weep with me

Desolation penetrates my heavy heart
My perspective blocked by ugly realities
"Destiny, will thou have thy way?"
Shadows grow in future lands
Images and thoughts take frightening shape
Just beyond my reach
Where loves dreams dwell
"Destiny, will thou have thy way?"
Days turn to nights and nights to days
Melancholy is the spirit around me
Can summer breezes thaw my wintry heart
With an inward eye toward the soul
"Destiny, will thou have thy way?"

By: Robert Mapes

The Story

I admit it, I was caught in a whirlpool of chaos, so it might have been difficult for me to hear God's voice. Could it be possible that when I didn't get the whisper in the ear or the card in the mail that I wanted, that I did not recognize or hear His answers when He gave them? Could I have been so wrapped up in myself and the storm that I did not see that He was answering my prayers? I missed Him when He used the voice of my Mom. I missed Him when He used the voice of an innocent child. I missed Him when He used the voice of a pastor. I missed the mark, not ever considering that others could have been His voice, answering my prayers and providing the guidance I needed.

I did have one fervent and endless prayer that nearly consumed my waking hours. The prayer, a simple one... "Please God, tell me Natalie is okay, I just have to know." While I waited for the postcard or the email from God.com, He tries to answer my prayer... His way. God was so determined to answer me that he tried four times. Four different times! I was just that clueless!

God starts by using Natalie's scent one Saturday morning. I know I didn't imagine it. But what do I do? I deny! There is no earthly way to explain it, so what choice did I have? So I simply push the entire experience aside, and fail to see it as an answer to my prayer? That God was trying to reach me? Hello Bob, are you there?

I continue my simple prayer. "Please God, tell me Natalie is okay, I have to know." While I check the mailbox one more time, my watch goes MIA, and I see the boys as the most likely culprits, so I think. Until I find the watch, sitting on Natalie's bureau, all alone, in a dusty corner… untouched. I try to make sense of this, and I can't. I try to pin it on the boys, but I can't make that work either. There is no way I imagined this one either. Why am I compelled to believe I have to find a worldly way to explain things? Am I so locked in on this that I miss out? Is it possible this was an answer to my prayer? That God was trying… again… to get me a message?

My never ending prayer continues. "Please God, tell me Natalie is okay, I just have to know." I check email one more time to be sure I haven't missed something. Natalie's birthday arrives just the same, and along with it the birth of my niece, Natalie. Now both are born on the same day! What are the chances? Yeah, it happens all the time, right? That is exactly what I was thinking. There surely can't be a heavenly explanation. No way! An answer to a prayer, maybe?

As I wait for my overnight to arrive as an answer to my prayer, "Please God, tell me Natalie is okay, I just have to know," an angel appears by my bedside with a clear message! Yet, I deny! I deny my angel sighting. I struggle with the possibility and think that only godly men and women deserve such a visitor. What a conundrum. The world around me tells me it cannot be, but I know what I saw. So begins my internal debate, intellect versus spiritual.

An unexplained scent, a watch that goes MIA, a special birth and the arrival of an angel. The perfect storm brews, where my spirit fights against the sea of my intellect, and the intellect wins… telling me to deny all of these things! Why is that? Why do I deny? Is it normal for us to first doubt? To be reluctant to believe? Is it part of our hard wiring?

Maybe there are a number of things in play for me. Was it that I wanted to have control, and that I wanted to own the 'how and the when' my prayer would get answered? Was I somehow preconditioned to expect an answer in a certain way and time? Was I not open to the ways in which I might get an answer? Wow, there it is. I had locked myself in and had a set an expectation of my own, precluding me from a world of possibilities. Looks like I built a barrier for myself.

Inspiration...

Answer me when I call to you, O my righteous God. Give me relief from my distress; be merciful to me and hear my prayer.

Psalm 4: 1

Reflection ....

Did God answer my prayer? You know it! In ways I never thought possible. No cards or emails for Bob, just a simple angel, and a couple of things that cannot be explained in an earthly way. Well, maybe they can. Maybe that is the marvel in all of this.

In answering my prayer, God saved my life. No question about it. He threw me the lifeline I needed when I needed it most and pulled me from the storm… my storm. But it was all about His timing, not mine. It was all about His purpose, not mine. I had to appreciate that He was always present with me. I was just clueless… and I end up missing out on His presence.

Control, man do I like to be in control of the "plan". I wanted to be in control, and did not want to give it up. It was a struggle for me. I need to continually remind myself that it shall all be according to His timing and not mine and that the answer I get to my prayers might not be what I want, but it will be just what I need. Even if the answer is no!

I had to believe that I was worthy. That we are all worthy. I had to be open to God's purpose and presence in my life, and how and when He might answer my prayers. I had to believe in the possibility of unearthly things happening, things that the mind and intellect will always deny as being real.

I know God is actively present in my life and in the world around me. I know I am worthy; after all, He made me and loves me. A slight perspective adjustment allows me to be open to His voice and His answer, which may come in an unworldly way. He might even be answering you right now. Are you open?

Is it possible that God is sharing your life with you? Have you explored the possibility? Might just be possible, and you might want to visit with Him sometime soon.

Is The Power Of Hope Important When Facing Adversity?

Contemplation ....

<u>**Hoping**</u>

I weep when hope's light
Fails to reach my saddened soul
Into adversity's valley I go

Seeking to understand
Why the circumstance was sent
My burdens weigh heavily
As I begin my hazardous decent
I travel with the dark spirits
As I traverse the darkened land
I question the mighty hammer of fate
And the journey becomes perilous
Hardening my heart
So much to overcome
My energy, foolishly, soon spent
With each painful step
I begin to set aside
The tumultuous emotions not needed
For being alive
And I slowly come to realize
That hope matters most
Offering me a power
To strengthen my resolve
In my desolate land
Allowing me to believe
In the work of His Holy Hand
Giving me the might to see
The glory of a life lived by choice, vibrantly

By: Robert Mapes

The Story

Hope, when the world is falling apart? I think not! Hope, when the life of the one I love is hanging in the balance? I think not. Hope, when death comes knocking and throws the world into chaos? I think not. Hope, when circumstance takes me from friends and family? I think not. Hope, when my child is up against his own monster? I think not! It was too much, it was just too much… or was it?

Throughout the entire journey, I try to be valiant. To be that hopeful guy, I do! But sometimes, I find myself so overwhelmed that I cave, I do! Negativity easily creeps in, steals hope from my soul, and I give in to the moment. I give life total and complete control, and let chaos, catastrophe, confusion and circumstance reign supreme. But who wouldn't, right? How can you be valiant in the face of the storm? It isn't possible, is it? I was not equipped to deal with all of the emotions, and the questions of faith, that accompanied me as I traveled through the valley of adversity.

Yeah, I was on my A-game when it came to caring for Natalie. Yup, me, the guy who hates needles and wounds and blood and all that good stuff! The guy, who in spite of it all, did that stuff day after day, week after week, and month after month. I am not sure how it happened, but not once did Natalie develop an infection at the wound site or because of the wound. Not once. And while I was able to see my way through that tough, physical stuff, the emotional side of the journey takes me into the dark corners of despair.

Somehow, I am able to work myself out of despair after the initial terror of the cancer diagnosis. It is not easy, but I work my way forward. Early on in the journey, I had hope, and in spite of the mortality tables and overall odds, and in spite of Dr. Davidsen's grim prediction, I had hope. I had hope that we would overcome the evil monster within. Yes, my hope wavered in those early days, but I had to want to hang on to that glimmer, that little bit of hope.

Yes, it was easy to be overwhelmed. Sometimes it was the day, sometimes it was the hour, sometimes it was the minute! Without warning, the rules of engagement changed, and new challenges would enter the storm. There was the collective fight against a monster, the mastectomy and the move to a strange land. Then there was the death march and the mighty hammer of fate and then an unexplained foe that plagues a young soul. These things push me beyond my ability to cope. It is a heavy burden, and it weighs… me… down. It brings me so low I don't think I'll ever be able to hope again.

I am not sure when the dark spirits first show up. I kind of think they were always circling my world, just outside my periphery, waiting for a chance to throw spears of pain into my heart and put a lasso around my soul. This way they could hold me tight to their will. A will of deceit, confusion, and fear! Whatever they did, they did it well. Over time, they come to own my hopeless self.

I had to try and figure out a way to move my sad, sorry self forward. So I strike up a deal with the man in the mirror. For the sake of the boys and the world, I will put a smile on my face, hide the pain and pretend all is well in the world, and let the dark spirits control my heart! It seemed like a good plan… and the man in the mirror led me to believe I had this thing locked down.

I relinquish control to the spirits, and I can never seem to get it back. They strengthen their hold. So many emotions, their complexities, make it difficult for me to find a way forward. Life hands me a brutal reality check when William bolts from the car, "Just face it! You want to die too!" I thought I had seen the worst, but I was wrong. This is the absolute worst! How is it a six-year-old could see so easily into my heart? I realize that the only person I was fooling was the man in the mirror.

Losing hope was easy. Is that it; that I wanted easy? Did life consume me in a minute- to-minute kind of way, forcing my focus to turn to survival and away from hope? Well, an unintended consequence resulted; I lost hope and the power of the positive spirit. Hope, what power it holds over our spirit and our attitude.

Is this a question of faith for me? Isn't hope tied to faith? Is it possible that as my hope waned, so did my faith, allowing me to fall victim to forces I believed were outside of my control? So what changed? What happened that changed it up for me? How did I get back on track, and rejoin life of the hopeful and faithful?

God sends me a powerful wake-up call, and uses William to deliver it. In that single moment, I could see that I had lost hope, and was in the dark pits of despair. I had given control of my spirit to the dark ones. They owned me outright. I had crowned negativity as my new king.

I wanted to regain hope and control my dark spirits. It was not easy. But nothing about this journey had been easy. Try as I might, I just can't find my way forward. I find myself stuck in the quicksand of life, trying to get from one minute to the next in one piece. And then I have an epiphany, Julie plants a seed. Get help! I am beyond my means, and beyond my ability to figure things out. All the hope in the world was not going to help fix my brokenness; I needed to get my heart in the right place.

Getting help is freeing. I made a choice, and immediately I sense the dark spirits quiet retreat. The journey of self-discovery is intense and hurtful. It is through that exploration of self that I am able to free myself, and find a way to break the chains that held me hostage. The only way to find hope was to journey through the storm, the past, and the present… setting up for a hopeful future… my future.

Inspiration...

And we rejoice in the hope of the glory of God. Not only so, but we also rejoice in our sufferings, because we know that suffering produces perseverance; perseverance, character; and character, hope.

Romans 5: 2-5

Reflection ....

I had to believe in hope. Yes, my life sucked, and I had been handed a lot more than what I thought was my fair share. Angry at God? No question about it! Why did He pick on me so? What did I ever do to deserve such strife? Was I a bad person? Somehow, I had made it all about me. Maybe I was missing the point in all of this?

As the storm grew in intensity so did my disappointment in God. At times, I felt completely abandoned, all alone in the word, a spirit lost in the seas of life. So begins my descent into the darkest of days. It does not happen overnight, or over a number of days. It is a slippery slope. It seems to feed on itself, tearing me apart from the inside out. It almost consumes me whole. Was it the devil's hand?

Without hope, my life just hung in the balance. I began a downward spiral that pushed hope aside, taking me deeper and deeper into a world filled with negative and hurtful thoughts. Hope had no value for me, a place where my faith was questioned. It felt natural to cave into my pain and to let my own despair rule my life. It was a matter of my choice. Why not take the easy way out?

I liked playing the blame game too. So I blame life, and God, for what happened to me, all of it, and for where I found myself. Farewell hope, see ya later! The scary part is that I had no idea how much I was hurting those that I loved most. Well, God sends me a wake-up call using the voice of my young son.

This becomes my wake-up call, putting me on a path toward hope. I realized that if I was going to make it for the long haul, I was going to have to man up. It was going to be entirely up to me to admit I was not in control, and that I would have to reach out and take God's hopeful hand. It was hope that pushed the dark spirits away. Hope was what would help fix my brokenness.

Hope... the victor over adversity! It is our choice, and we can choose to play the victim card, or we can own it, whatever it is, and all that it is, and fight our way forward, and bravely walk out of the darkness into the grace of God's light. I am blessed to have seen hope in such visible ways in my lifetime.

I choose hope and the power of the light. No matter what anguish you may be facing, or what might lie just around the corner, grab hold of hope and hold on for dear life. Never let go!

Are you like me? Have you misplaced it? Or have you completely lost hope? It doesn't matter. Hope is out there for you just the same, no matter your circumstance. Do you know who to turn to for hope? The answer might surprise you!

What Is The Rainbow Promise?

Contemplation...

Hand In Hand

A victim of adverse circumstance
Well outside my control
Questioning my ability to understand
The realities of my once simple life
I look to the road of the rainbow
Recognizing it is not easy for the forlorn
There is a great task before me
Filled with grief and hurt and fear
Determined I am to control
My soul, my mind
And not fall victim
To adversity's perilous command
Weakened is my love of life
In spite of dark spirits hold
I sense I can prevail
By lifting my soul on high
Walking into my forlorn circumstance
Through night's mournful storm
Toward daylights bright rainbow morn
Where courage resides
Allowing me to stand strong
Learning about life as I go
Reaching for God's glorious hand
Fulfilling my destiny
While holding God's magnificent hand

By: Robert Mapes

The Story ....

The battles were all consuming, so I thought anyway. I struggled to maintain while monsters lurked stealthily on the periphery of my life. The idea that there was a promise of any kind out there for me was unimaginable. Promise, yeah right! As I journeyed through the storm, it seemed as if God had completely lost His sense of well-being. Why would He pick a family up in the middle of a crisis, a battle raging against an unseen foe, and drop them in a land far away? Made no sense! None!

It seemed that my life was completely out of control. And then the unimaginable happens. A new foe enters the scene, and begins to wreak havoc on a young soul, unannounced - JRA! There was just too much stuff on my mountain top. Piece of cake? Not a chance. It seemed God thought more of me than I thought of myself!

Well, what if all of this was about me, but not in a way I thought? What if the move to Texas had absolutely nothing to do with Natalie? What if it was about me? Wow, where did that come from? Seriously, what if it was all about me? What if I didn't see it? Is that possible? God works with each and everyone one of us in the way we need Him to. We may not know what we need, but He does!

As I journeyed through the tunnels of darkness, I realized I might not have made it in one piece, had I stayed in Plymouth. No, I'll be honest here, no might about it. I wouldn't have made it. No way. It is not a matter of convenient thinking. I know that the memories of life, and love lost, would have suffocated me completely in New Hampshire. There I would have been a tormented soul with no hope in sight, and I would have found myself suffering endlessly in the eye of the storm. No hope of escape for me. Hard to imagine living like that.

So, it begs the question, what if God knew me better than I knew myself? Interesting notion! What if He knew I would not have made it in New Hampshire? What if he knew it would be in my best interest to move to a new land, given that He knew Natalie was destined for His Pearly Gates. What if the move to Texas had nothing to do with Natalie and had everything to do with me? What if the move was a way to protect me… from me?

What if the move to Texas was about Jake then? Amidst an already turbulent world, Jake is diagnosed with something called JRA! Well, consider this - what if God knew this was heading our way. What if He wanted Jake to be in the best place in this great country to get the help he would need? To fight his own evil monster, and to come out the victor? What if God knew Jake could be healed with the right treatments? What if?

Why is it we need immediacy in our world? Is it part of our own human condition, this need? Is it something we are taught, or is it just part of our natural wiring? And why do we doubt so, and question everything? The journey through the storm nearly consumed me, and I thought I was at the mercy of random forces, and that there was no God in control of anything.

Is it possible that things were in motion, and I just couldn't see them? Is it that I would not get everything I wanted? I would get what I needed when I needed it most? Isn't that just like a parent, to know what their children need most, and what is in their best interest? Is it possible then, that my Heavenly Father knew what I needed most, and worked to provide it for me, when I needed it, all the while I am ungrateful and thoughtless, just like a child can be?

But God watches over me just the same, and I falter, and I fall some times, for any of a number of reasons. But He is there, patiently watching over me, helping me up each time, propping me up time and time again, walking me forward. He is always there, He never waivers, no matter my state, no matter my spirit! His love undying! He delivers the promise… the rainbow promise!

Inspiration..

Whenever the rainbow appears in the clouds, I will see it and remember the everlasting covenant between God and all living creatures of every kind on the earth.

Genesis 9:16

Reflection ....

The rainbow, a symbol of promise after the storm! The rainbow, a symbol of God's promise to Noah, a promise I like to think of as the "rainbow promise." And like Noah, God makes a promise to all of us, that a rainbow will follow the storm. That He will provide, no matter the flood of circumstance that overwhelms us.

I am not like Noah, unfortunately. Noah was a steady eddy, forever faithful, a true servant of the Lord. He followed God's lead, even when he questioned the direction. I questioned every step of the way, became easily frustrated, and all too easily caved to the call of the dark spirits. I even wondered, at times, if God was even around.

While Noah seemed to trust, I did everything but trust. Why was trust such a struggle for me? It seemed to me, that God had abandoned me, and left me to suffer at the hands of fate, maybe left me at the mercy of my will. It seems I was my own worst enemy. My faith wavered… and I found myself wandering the deserts of despair. At times, I failed to see any purpose to my life. Was it because I couldn't

see what God saw, the bigger picture? Maybe God didn't want me to see the bigger picture. Maybe He knew I couldn't handle it.

Why is it that we turn from Him when we can't see the picture, or when we don't like what we see? Was I resentful when things did not play out my way? Did I let my hurt simmer, creating bitterness in my own heart? Did these things lead me to believe that I had to motor along on my own, that I had no other choice?

There was always a choice, a way forward for me. But to do that, I had to trust, and I had to surrender, totally and completely. I had to give up my earthly desire to control. That was not easy, and it took me a long time... many months. There was a promise there for me; I just had to look to the skies if I wanted to see it. After all, you do have to look up to see a rainbow!

I have come to realize that the God that created the heavens and hung the stars is the same God that will watch out over me. Is the same God that would stand by His promise. Is the same God that loved me when I didn't love Him back. Is the same God that would carry me when I was too weak to carry myself. Is the same God that was at my side, in spite of the 'me' that I had become.

I questioned God, like many of His children, and saw my pain and suffering as punishment of some kind. All of us, you and me, will be subject to pain. It is a way of life, our life. It is just a matter of our human existence. It has nothing to do with how good or bad we are. Life isn't always fair. But there is a purpose in the pain. It will bring us to the promise of the rainbow.

What matters, is what we do with what we learn as we journey through the storm to the rainbow. My journey has defined the 'me' that I am. I could have turned from my journey, or caved during the journey, but I didn't. God wants to do more through me than for me, and I see my journey as a way to help others, to teach others in ways I never thought possible... God working through me.

I know I made mistakes as I journeyed through the storm. I know I couldn't see the bigger picture. I know the choice to find the tranquility that comes after the storm, was mine, as it is yours. And harmony in life comes from the what - the what we do with what we learn - as we journey through life together, through the darkest of times, and the most joyous of times.

Adversity and the mighty storms of life can consume you, or they can help define you. It is laid purposely before you. If you let it, it will devour you and leave just the shell of a soul behind. Or you can become stronger in character and faith, with a closer relationship to God. I almost let adversity consume me, but with interventions from the Lord, I was saved from the saddened me that I had become. It is never too late to change a trajectory, even for you.

As you consider the events unfolding before you, or the ones that are already behind you, will you seek the promise of peace that comes after the storm, and let God guide you forward? What dark times are staring you straight in the face? Is your storm brewing, just beyond the horizon, waiting to strike? When the storm hits your life, how will you respond?

Adversity and dark times, these are part of the circle of life. Your life and my life! No one is exempt. The question; to whom will you reach to when you need help or feel lost and overwhelmed? Not sure how to take the next step? Believe you can't do it all on your own?

It is your choice... so choose wisely. If you are not sure who to reach to, I'd like to make a recommendation!

BOOK 13

Promises Made Promise Kept

It was on a rather dark and dreadful day that Natalie made me promise to do certain things over the course of my lifetime. Things she felt were in the best interest of those she loved most. I have kept those promises alive in my heart and have fulfilled almost every single one of them. Proud? You know it! Life without her, raising three boys all on my own, was not what I signed up for. But it was what I got, and I was determined to do the best with the gift of life I was given.

About those promises:

"Promise me that you'll make sure the boys all graduate from high school. That they will get some kind of advanced education after graduation!"

Success! We did it together, Ryan, Jake, William and I! Was it tough at times? You know it, but I was determined to make it happen! Ryan is a Network Engineer for a large credit card processing company, Jake is a paramedic with the fire department, and William, who is still working toward that degree, is a Network Analyst and provides all the technical support for a large franchisee in Georgia.

"Promise me that you will let the boys explore all the sports that inspire them."

Did I ever! And I have the battle scars to prove it. I was blessed that all the boys gravitated toward the same sports, and at the same times, which made it a tad bit easier to meet this promise. The boys all did swimming, soccer, and even wrestling. They really got into that one! I worked every committee I could to be involved with them. And when I could, I helped with scoring and officiating - fun stuff!

"Promise me that you'll expose the boys to culture and that they'll have a chance to explore cultural kinds of things, whether music or art, whatever floats their boat."

We explored all kinds of things, and Ryan created art for a while, but the world of technology was a greater call. Jake played the trombone and William the drums. They both participated in the High School band and all of that craziness. I was right there with them, involved as much as I could be!

"Promise me that there will be no drugs, alcohol, smoking or promiscuity while the boys live under your roof."

Not on my watch! I was involved in all aspects of their young lives and watched everything. I knew life's temptations were out there, but did my best to talk about all this good stuff and was always on guard. It sometimes felt like me against the world. But I knew where they were each and every night, and there were always other kids around spending the night. I must have been doing something right! My favorites, I had to meet any girl before they could go out on dates, and I called every parent when there was a sleepover, to make sure things were all above board. Do what ya got to do when you make a promise!

"Promise me that you will continue your spiritual journey no matter how angry you are or become and that you will help the boys in their own spiritual journeys."

I did continue in my spiritual journey, as angry as a person could be. The boys continued in their spiritual journeys, and were active in church and church youth groups, and I was active right there beside them.

It is through my journey (the storm, the suffering, the pain) that I can fully appreciate how precious life is and how fortunate we are to have the families that we do have. I celebrate mine!

"Promise me that you'll move on one day and that you will share your love with another!"

This was a tough one! As part of His plan, God sent me to Georgia to work for a great company, Aflac, whose promise is to be there in a time of need for a consumer. It was important for me to be aligned with a company who was passionate about caring for others. I also wanted to work for a company that would bring important resources to the table when "adversity" came a-calling. It was a great feeling working for a company that could step in and help when the chips were down and cancer came a- knocking.

As for the love of another, wow! Did not think it was possible! But God put several women in my life who helped me see that it was possible to love again. I have been happily married for over 11 years now to a wonderful woman named Judy, who has been a big supporter of our children, my story, my book, and celebrates my past. It is what makes me "me"! Can't wait for Judy and Natalie to meet. No rush, though!

AUTHOR'S NOTE

"When life gives you lemons, make a good cabernet."

The journey to, and through the many storms that became my life, to the promise of the rainbow, was all consuming! I slipped and fell many a time, and somehow managed to pick myself up, no matter the sorry state my spirit was in.

I could not have journeyed through the storms without the love and support of so many. Family and friends, too many to name, stood by my side, the side of the boys, as times became challenging and the days dark. When the light of life seemed to darken, they offered their light of hope!

The world of science and medicine was overwhelming, and to all of those health care professionals involved in the holistic care of a family in crisis, I offer my heartfelt thanks for your love and care, and your commitment to the battle. This journey was so much more than the battle against the many physical and emotional monsters, although it was a big part of the journey. Bringing Jake into remission, and the healing of mind and spirit was also part of the journey.

The preservation and healing of the soul could not have happened, without spiritual guidance and love. To those who ministered to our spirits, throughout the journey, and the heinous aftermath, know your encouragement and inspiration, made a difference. It helped bring us through some very dark times.

We all go through something at some point, and I know others have carried burdens much larger than mine. I thank you for your strength and insight, at times it was all I had to hang on to. Just knowing you made it propelled me forward.

If you find yourself in a dark place against dark days, I offer you the promise of a rainbow, and a life beyond the storm, no matter how tough it may be right now. So pick yourself up, dust yourself off, and make your way the best you can through the day you have. It is a gift, so treasure it and treat it like one!

Look for me at my website, Beyond The Rainbow Promise, for my personal blog and words of insight and wisdom coming from my personal journey through adversity. The hope we all carry, that life will get better, I offer to you!